Praise for *The Undefeated Mind*

"Alex Lickerman mines life's greatest challenges with an artist's eye, a scientist's rigor, and a Buddhist's wise hand. The result is a book that I could not stop reading. Dr. Lickerman's unique gifts as a writer, doctor, and scientific thinker make for an epiphany-studded quest to tame his own mind and to enter and commune with the minds of others. The result is a book like no other: profound, compassionate, and inspiring."

—**Kaja Perina**, editor-in-chief of *Psychology Today*

"Buddhism and Western medicine would seem an incongruous mixture, but in the hands of Alex Lickerman they meld seamlessly into a recipe for overcoming life's hardships—indeed, for turning them into advantages. An accomplished physician, Lickerman has no truck for the supernatural, but recognizes that the tenets of Nichiren Buddhism have been honed over centuries to help alleviate life's inevitable sufferings. *The Undefeated Mind* is a deeply engaging story of how Lickerman has fused modern medicine with ancient wisdom to heal his patients both physically and psychologically—lessons that apply to all of us."

—**Jerry Coyne**, professor of ecology and evolution at University of Chicago and author of *Why Evolution is True*

"Eastern religious practices such as chanting are often brushed aside as 'mysticism' by Western science. In this highly original book based on extensive case studies, Lickerman effectively bridges these two great traditions, providing novel insights along the way regarding how we can all triumph over the psychological impact of adversity and live joyfully, even in this 'vale of tears.'"

—**V. S. Ramachandran**, director of the Center for Brain and Cognition at University of California San Diego and author of the *New York Times* bestseller *The Tell-Tale Brain*

D0042971

"Dr. Lickerman's wisdom and compassion are evident on every page of this outstanding book. Inspired by his many years of practice in the Nichiren Buddhist tradition, Dr. Lickerman, a practicing physician, sets forth nine principles for developing an 'undefeated mind.' By sharing personal stories of how he and his patients have benefited from these nine principles, Dr. Lickerman turns them into easy-to-apply tools that everyone can put to use immediately. Incorporating the nine principles of *The Undefeated Mind* into your everyday life will open the door to limitless compassion for others and to unshakeable happiness for yourself. This profound book has the power to change your life."

—**Toni Bernhard**, author of *How to Be Sick: A Buddhist-Inspired Guide for the Chronically Ill and Their Caregivers*

"A terrific read that was hard to put down. Dr. Lickerman provides valuable insights into common problems facing patients, such as obesity, nicotine addiction, chronic pain, and significant illness. He eloquently illuminates the path to employing our mental powers to live a fulfilled life using the teachings of Nichiren Buddhism, which provide guideposts for living a healthy, productive, and moral life. Most importantly, he shows how to do more good than harm."

—**Emil F. Coccaro, MD**, E. C. Manning professor and chairman of Psychiatry & Behavioral Neuroscience, University of Chicago

"Dr. Lickerman beautifully weaves Eastern and Western wisdom, rigorous research, and poetic storytelling in *The Undefeated Mind*. This is a book that can help you become stronger and happier."

—**Tal Ben-Shahar, PhD.**, bestselling author of *Choose the Life You Want*

The Undefeated Mind

On the Science of Constructing an Indestructible Self

Alex Lickerman, MD

Health Communications, Inc.
Deerfield Beach, Florida

www.hcibooks.com

The names, identifying details, and histories of the patients whose stories appear in this book have been altered and condensed to preserve their privacy and protect their confidentiality.

A portion of the text in Chapter 5 appeared originally in the April 2010 edition of *Psychology Today* and is reprinted with permission. Additionally, material in some chapters has appeared previously on the author's blog at www.happinessinthisworld.com.

Library of Congress Cataloging-in-Publication Data

Lickerman, Alex.
  The undefeated mind : on the science of constructing an indestructible self /
Alex Lickerman.
      p. cm.
  Includes bibliographical references and index.
  ISBN 978-0-7573-1642-5 (trade paper)
  ISBN 0-7573-1642-5 (trade paper)
  ISBN 978-0-7573-1643-2 (e-book)
  ISBN 0-7573-1643-3 (e-book)
  1. Self-realization.   2. Self-actualization (Psychology)   3. Resilience (Personality trait)
4. Autonomy (Psychology)   I. Title.
  BF637.S4L496   2012
  158.1—dc23
                                                                2012029179

Publisher: Health Communications, Inc.
          3201 S.W. 15th Street
          Deerfield Beach, FL 33442–8190

Cover design by Dane Wesolko
Interior design and formatting by Lawna Patterson Oldfield

for my parents

Contents

Acknowledgments

Thanks goes first to my agent, Stephany Evans, who agreed to represent *The Undefeated Mind* within two days of reading the book proposal and then proceeded not only to get it into the hands of a terrific publisher, but also to teach me how the world of publishing works in general. Thanks also to my editor at HCI, Candace Johnson, whose editorial expertise, positive spirit, and willingness to indulge my controlling nature made the process of turning the manuscript into a book a genuine pleasure.

Thanks to Jerry Coyne, Ash ElDifrawi, John Kolligian, Janet Lickerman, Michael Nix, and Scott Stern, all of whom read early drafts of the manuscript and provided invaluable feedback. Thanks to Lori Corbett for helping to create both my website and blog, and to Paul Woodard for fixing them when they break.

I owe a great debt of gratitude as well to all the patients for whom I've cared over the years whose stories—albeit in a disguised form—appear in the pages that follow. It's been a privilege both to care for and learn from them.

To my wife, Rhea Campbell, though, I owe the greatest debt of gratitude of all. Few writers are given the luxury of wide swaths of time to write, which means they have to carve out such swaths from their lives at home. So thank you, Rhea, for taking our son, Cruise, on so many weekends while I stayed home writing. Thank you for your emotional support and unflagging optimism, for pushing me to take on what remains for me the hardest part of publishing a book, marketing and promotion, and for your belief in the value of my ideas. Thank you, in short, for making my dreams as important to you as your own. I couldn't have done this without you.

Introduction

Six months into my second year of medical school, the first woman I ever loved brought our year-and-a-half-long relationship to an end, causing me to fall immediately into a paralyzing depression. As a result, my ability to study declined dramatically—and as a result of *that,* six months later I failed Part I of the National Board Exam.

It was a devastating blow, not just to my ego, but also to my potential future: if I couldn't pass Part I, I wouldn't be allowed to graduate from medical school. My dean told me I could retake the test, but the next opportunity to do so was at the end of my *third* year of medical school. This was—to put it mildly—problematic: at the start of the third year, students leave the classroom and begin caring for patients in the hospital, an activity renowned for swallowing entire days of time at one stretch and causing all personal dimensions of a student's life to atrophy. I'd have little opportunity to study the material I was expected to learn on the wards, much less the basic science I was already supposed to have learned during my previous two years of classroom work.

I had no idea what to do. My thinking spiraled in useless circles as I hunted for a solution, my depression intensifying as none appeared, and soon I found myself crouching at the edge of despair.

Personality Hardiness

Are you feeling discouraged about something, too? Do you need to find a job in an overcrowded field? Pay a mortgage you can't afford? Overcome an illness with a grim prognosis? Prepare yourself for the death of a loved one? Or has the omnipresent cacophony of misery, injustice, and cruelty in the world just become too much for you to bear?

You're not alone. Even before the U.S. economy nearly collapsed in 2008, data from the National Comorbidity Survey told us that an astonishing 50 percent of Americans report having suffered at some point in their lives from a psychiatric disorder, most commonly depression, alcohol dependence, social phobia, or simple phobia.[1] Even more startling, research shows that Americans have only a 35 percent chance of rating themselves "very happy" by the time they reach their late eighties.[2] Given that the same research showed happiness tends to *increase* with age, it would seem that most of us are destined to live the majority of our lives without much joy.

But things aren't as bleak as they seem. Or rather, things arc *only* as bleak as they seem, for the way events impact us depends far more on the lens through which we view them—our inner life state—than on the events themselves.[3] Not that mustering up courage, hope, and confidence in the face of adversity is easy. Viktor Frankl was only half right when he argued in his book *Man's Search for Meaning* that we have control over how we respond to what happens to us.[4] In fact, often we don't. At least, not how we respond *emotionally* to what happens to us. And as emotion usually wins the tug-of-war with intellect in determining behavior, unless we happen to be gifted with a mighty will, controlling how we respond to what happens to us can be almost as difficult as controlling what actually happens to us.

But Frankl wasn't entirely wrong, either. Though absolute control over our response to adversity may elude us, *influence* over it need not. If we can't change our emotional reactions by force of will, we can at least increase the likelihood that our reactions are constructive by cultivating something psychologists call *personality hardiness*: the capacity to survive and even thrive under difficult conditions—what in Buddhist terms would be considered a strong life force.

This book is about how we can develop that force. For hardiness, contrary to popular belief, isn't something with which only a fortunate few of us have been born, but rather is something we can all create. Hardiness of a kind I've come to call an undefeated mind.

Nichiren Buddhism

The kind of Buddhism I practice isn't Zen or Tibetan, the two most popular forms in the United States, but rather Nichiren Buddhism, named after its founder, Nichiren Daishonin. Currently, 12 million people in 192 countries and territories practice Nichiren Buddhism; most of them, like me, are members of the Soka Gakkai, a lay organization of Nichiren Buddhists whose name means "value creation society." The practice of Nichiren Buddhism doesn't involve meditation, mindfulness, centering oneself, or learning to live in the moment as do most other forms of Buddhism, but rather something even more foreign and discomforting to those of us raised in the traditions of the West: chanting. Every morning and every night I chant the phrase *Nam-myoho-renge-kyo* with a focused determination to challenge my negativity in an effort to bring forth wisdom.

And over twenty-three years of Buddhist practice, wisdom has indeed emerged for me—and often in the most surprising of ways. After spending many months of such chanting to free myself from the anguish that the loss of my girlfriend had caused me, I realized one morning that my suffering wasn't coming at all from what I'd thought (the loss of my girlfriend), but rather from the misguided belief that I needed her to love me to be happy. I'd always known intellectually this wasn't true—had even pointed it out to friends struggling with the debris of their own failed relationships—but not until that moment in front of my Gohonzon (the scroll to which Nichiren Buddhists chant) did that knowledge become wisdom—that is, become how I *felt*. Insight, that most mysterious of experiences in which knowledge takes root in a person's psyche and alters what he believes and therefore how he behaves (expressed, for example, in the moment an alcoholic understands he needs to stop drinking and does) had at last found me. What I achieved in my moment of insight wasn't a greater intellectual understanding that I didn't need my girlfriend to love me to be happy, but rather an emotional belief: a belief based on an acceptance of evidence that seemed abruptly so convincing I became incapable of refuting it. No longer did I have to work to remind myself I didn't need a woman's love to be happy; now, I couldn't forget it. And in the act of coming to know it in this way—the same way I knew that if I stared at the sun too long it would blind me—my suffering ceased.

I was flabbergasted. How had this happened? *What* had happened? Strong emotional reactions to traumatic events rarely end abruptly but usually taper off gradually, so only after some time had passed did I come to accept that I had indeed freed myself from suffering, and further that it had happened because insight had transformed intellectual knowledge into wisdom. But as to how that insight had occurred—as to the possibility that chanting a phrase over and over could have taken an idea that I'd neither been pursuing as a remedy nor even been wondering about and turned it into a belief imbued with the power to end my suffering—well, frankly, it was preposterous. (Not that a newly minted belief could have ended my suffering, but rather that chanting could have been responsible for my coming to believe it.) And yet the possibility that this answer, this transformation, had taken place serendipitously or as a result of a general focus on my problem seemed equally unlikely to me. But because I couldn't split myself into one person who continued to chant and one who didn't to see which became happier, I resolved to continue chanting to see if other insights would follow.

To my surprise, they did, several times in as many months. A skeptic to my core, I nevertheless began to find myself viewing what now amounted to a series of life-changing revelations less and less as coincidences and more and more as evidence that chanting *Nam-myoho-renge-kyo* did have the power to catalyze aversive life experience into an engine for growth, to shatter delusions of which I remained unconscious but that nevertheless limited the degree of happiness I was capable of experiencing. Whether by a general meditative effect (something supported by a growing body of research) or through the activation of some as-yet uncharacterized force inherent within my life, I didn't—and still don't—know.

So I continued, reminding myself that subjective experiences *can* be scientifically investigated even when the investigator is investigating himself. When patients tell me, for example, that eating pizza predictably causes them abdominal pain, the fact that only they can observe the dependent variable, abdominal pain, in no way invalidates the conclusion that the independent variable, pizza, is the cause.

On the other hand, I've had to recognize that the insights I've attributed to my practice of Nichiren Buddhism have never come with the same regularity that abdominal pain has come to my pizza-eating patients. Sometimes breakthroughs have occurred after chanting for years about a particular problem; at other times after only a few minutes, a fact that's prompted many of my non-Buddhist friends and family to ask just how confident I can be that chanting *Nam-myoho-renge-kyo* has in fact *caused* all the life-changing revelations that have come my way since I started practicing Buddhism. To which I've continued to answer since experiencing that first insight over twenty years ago that I'm just confident enough to continue looking for more definitive proof.

So my experiment goes on: The scientist in me continuing to argue with the Buddhist, demanding not just more convincing evidence that chanting generates wisdom but trying to understand the mechanism by which it does so, a mechanism couched in terms of established physical, chemical, and biological laws—one that provides a natural rather than supernatural explanation. The Buddhist, in turn, reminds the scientist that I don't entirely understand how my car works either, but I still get into it every morning and drive it to work.

Building Strength from Adversity

That which doesn't kill us *can* make us stronger, as Nietzsche tells us, but few sources offer any insight into just *how* one springboards from adversity into strength. Most presume, like Nietzsche did himself, that it occurs automatically as part and parcel of being human. But it doesn't.[5] As anyone working in health care today can attest, lives filled with misfortune frequently add up only to lives filled with suffering. To build strength out of adversity, we need a catalyst.

That catalyst, according to Nichiren Buddhism, is wisdom. Inner strength, Nichiren Buddhism teaches, doesn't come from the experience of adversity itself but from the wisdom that the experience of adversity has the potential to impart. Nichiren Buddhism considers the development of strength through the acquisition of wisdom—a process it terms *human revolution*—the sole means by which we can establish a state of indestructible happiness. This, Nichiren Buddhism argues, is the purpose for which we were all born.

Drawing then on the tenets of both Nichiren Buddhism and new scientific research, this book attempts to distill that wisdom into nine principles—principles anyone can incorporate into their thinking and behavior, whether they have any interest in chanting or not. In the opening chapter, I lay the groundwork for this exploration of resilience by defining the concept of the undefeated mind itself. In subsequent chapters, then, I describe the nine principles in detail by telling the stories of nine patients, each of whom used one of the principles to overcome suffering caused variously by unemployment, unwanted weight gain, addiction, rejection, chronic pain, retirement, illness, loss, and even death.

Offering a set of guidelines not for solving problems but for establishing a life state that makes all problems solvable, *The Undefeated Mind* is a book that exhorts us to stop hoping for easy lives and instead to focus on cultivating the inner strength we need to enjoy the difficult lives we all have. Though our ability to control what happens to us in life may be limited, our ability to establish a life state strong enough to surmount the suffering life brings us is not.

Knowledge vs. Wisdom

After a few days of giving serious consideration to dropping out of medical school, instead I became determined not only to retake Part I of the Boards and pass it, but also to score above the mean, something I'd never been able to do on any test I'd ever taken in medical school. Further, I resolved that no matter how much time I'd need to devote to studying for the test, my performance in the third year wouldn't suffer— rather, it would be stellar. I didn't just want to survive this obstacle; I wanted to triumph over it. I didn't just want to pass the test and learn the material; I wanted to transform the experience of failing into a genuine

benefit, into something I could one day say with conviction I was glad
had happened to me.

I had no real idea how this would—or even could—occur. Nevertheless, I chanted to bring forth the wisdom that would enable me to achieve
success. And then I took action: I studied every spare moment I had,
sometimes staying up late into the night, sometimes arising several hours
early in the morning. I studied at every meal. I stopped watching television, reading for pleasure, even socializing with friends. For the entire
year, I remained disciplined, focused, and relentless.

Then, ironically, on the day of the test I almost missed the eight o'clock
start time (which would have disqualified me from being allowed to take
it) due to an accident on the expressway that slowed traffic to a crawl.
Our eyes riveted on the clock, my mother and I cheered as my father sped
through two red lights to get me to the test center on time.

The test was scheduled to last two days—twelve hours in total. I finished the first day with a sense that I'd performed well. But then came
a crushing blow: the next morning, just before the start of the second
day, we learned that test security had been compromised by thieves who'd
managed to steal copies from a test center in Michigan and that officials
were considering invalidating the test results for the entire country. As I
glanced around at the horrified expressions in the room, I felt my will to
complete the exam draining away. But rather than close my exam booklet
and walk out as I felt the urge to do, instead I resolved to continue as I
had all year, in willful ignorance of the odds stacked against me, fighting
with all my might to overcome my impulse to give up.

My determination paid off. In the end, test officials decided not to
invalidate the results, and I not only passed the exam but also met my
goal of scoring above the mean. I went on to graduate medical school and
landed a residency at the University of Iowa Hospitals and Clinics.

But the true victory didn't come until years later, sometime after I'd begun working as a primary care physician at the University of Chicago, when a medical student came to see me one day distraught over having failed her third-year clinical rotation in internal medicine. Hoping to encourage her, I decided to divulge the story of my own failure. And as I told her what had happened and watched her expression shift from despondent to contemplative and then from contemplative to resolute, I felt my shame over having failed Part I of the National Boards finally evaporate. Only because I had failed, I realized, was I now in a position to offer someone else who'd failed in a similar way that most critical of psychological nutrients: hope. What's more, in telling my story to someone else for the first time, I realized that having to relearn all the material presented in the first and second years of medical school had made me a better doctor. It had not only broadened my knowledge base but also sharpened my reasoning skills, leading to an ability, I now saw, to make diagnoses I wouldn't have been able to make otherwise, as well as highlighted for me the importance of focusing not just on the diagnosis and treatment of disease, but also on the alleviation of the emotional suffering that disease often brings. I had indeed transformed the experience of failing the Boards into a benefit—twice.

After the student left my office, I found myself thinking about how quickly we pronounce final judgment on the things that happen to us, deciding whether they're good or bad in the first moment they occur—about how in doing so we surrender our own agency, abandoning the belief that we have the power to *create* meaning out of what happens to us. I'd always believed we did have that power—and had even encouraged others going through their own struggles to believe it—but hadn't known it was true myself until my own failure proved it to me.

Herman Hesse once wrote that wisdom, when spoken aloud, always sounds a little bit foolish.[6] Perhaps that's because when we hear something that makes sense to us, we think we already know it. But often we don't. At least not in a way that matters. We know it with our intellects, but not with our hearts. Not, as we say in Nichiren Buddhism, with our lives. For we can only be said to really understand a principle when we actually live by it.

So in full recognition that becoming more resilient is itself an arduous process, and that nothing as simple as reading a book could ever substitute for the difficult life experience that learning something with our lives seems to require, I offer *The Undefeated Mind* as a blueprint. A blueprint that if we make the effort to follow will enable us to assemble the most valuable of all commodities: the resilience we need to achieve victory in life.

1

The Meaning
of Victory

We are, all of us, meaning-seeking creatures. We may begin life as pleasure seekers and pain avoiders, but as our brains develop and language begins flowing from our mouths, we soon begin demanding to know the *why* of things, as any parent can attest who's been subjected to the inexhaustible energy children have for asking why the sun shines or the sky is blue. Yet the difficulty we face as parents in providing good answers becomes immediately apparent when we turn to science for help, perhaps murmuring something about thermonuclear fusion or the way the Earth's atmosphere scatters light. "But why do hydrogen atoms fuse?" we'll inevitably hear next. "Because of heat and pressure," we answer. "Why is there pressure?" they ask after that, and so on, each successive query sounding less like a follow-up question and more like a reprimand for our foolishly offering *how* answers to *why* questions, reminding us that when children ask why something is, they're actually asking to know its *purpose*.

At first glance this seems an innocent wish—even charming—so it's one we're willing to indulge. But if we chase the answer to any "purpose" question far enough down the rabbit hole, inevitably we'll come face to face with the frustrating truth that we can't answer the simplest one even to *our* satisfaction. We don't know why the sun shines or the sky is blue—or if such questions even make sense—any more than we know the ultimate reason for anything, including, most importantly, ourselves.

Which doesn't stop us from trying to figure it out. As we grow from toddlers to children and our thinking becomes more self-reflective, at some point we narrow the scope of our investigation into the purpose of things down to one overriding question: "For what purpose do *we* live?" And while some of us may only be asking how we'd like to *spend* our lives, others are asking about the meaning of life itself, seeking not just *an* answer but rather *the* answer, the ultimate reason for which we were all born. Undaunted by the possibility that no such ultimate reason even exists—that we simply *are*—some of us try mixing varying proportions of intuition, reason, introspection, philosophy, and religion in an attempt to uncover a purpose with which we've been endowed. Yet even if we eventually choose to place our faith in an omnipotent maker who's bestowed upon us the purpose we seek, belief in that maker's existence brings us no closer to knowing it. (Despite the protests of the faithful to the contrary, belief in a creator grants us no firsthand knowledge of that creator's intent.)

On the other hand, if we're willing to accept that we don't have an endowed purpose but rather an *evolved function*, we can begin from any one of the many desires that populate our everyday life and follow it back through all the desires that lie beneath it to find the answer we seek. We may rouse ourselves out of bed one day to study for a test, the next to help a troubled friend, and the next after that to run errands, but in every instance our motivation arises from some other, broader reason; and if we ask why *that* reason rouses us, we'll find the answer in yet another, even broader reason, and so on. We want to study for our test to pass it. We want to pass our test to get a good grade in our class. We want to get a good grade in our class to get into a good college. We want to get into a good college to get a good job. And if we continue asking why, like the child we once were, trying to excavate down to our most rudimentary ambition—a time-worn exercise—we'll eventually find all reasons lead to the same place, to the one core reason for living we'd sought all along, the core reason against which we measure the value of everything we do: to be happy.

Our Desire to Be Happy

Here, though, evolutionary biology would raise an objection, arguing that the ultimate end toward which all living organisms aim their activities is survival and reproduction. And though true for the vast majority of life on planet Earth, not so I'd argue for *Homo sapiens*. For when we evolved the ability to have thoughts and feelings *about* our thoughts and feelings (for example, the ability to recognize we enjoy football more than baseball), we gained the ability to form judgments about our experiences and make choices about which ones we'd rather have—choices, observation suggests, that are driven less by the desire to survive and reproduce than they are by the desire to become happy. (Though the desire to become happy undoubtedly evolved to *promote* survival and reproduction, with the advent of self-awareness, the relative strength with which we're motivated to become happy and motivated to survive and reproduce has reversed.) A sizable minority of people, for example, choose not to have children at all, believing that parenthood will lead them on balance to less happiness rather than more.[1] In addition, in circumstances in which the drive to survive is pitted directly against the drive to become happy—that is, when people perceive the need to make a choice between the two—the drive to become happy (or, at least, to avoid suffering) typically proves itself the stronger. We see this, for example, in patients suffering from intractable pain who have been known to make the reasoned choice—meaning in the absence of clinical depression or psychotic delusion—to end their lives. And though we may be tempted to believe that patients with chronic pain who choose to suffer it rather than kill themselves do so because they want to survive even at the cost of their happiness, the more likely explanation is that their personal degree of pain tolerance enables them to remain happy despite their discomfort. Either that, or their hope to be relieved of their pain is great enough to sustain their hope that they'll become happy one day in the future.

An Irresistible Pursuit

We actually have as little choice about wanting to become happy as the heart does about pumping blood. We're incapable of wanting *not* to become happy. The pursuit of happiness isn't merely an inalienable right with which we're endowed or an activity we're capable of choosing; it's psychological law we must obey. Even people who appear to want nothing to do with happiness, like those so immersed in self-hatred that their principle aim becomes self-sabotage, will say they haven't lost their desire for happiness so much as ceased to believe they deserve it. Similarly, people suffering from severe depression who seek their own destruction typically do so only to escape the pain they're feeling, not because they no longer *want* to be happy. They may no longer believe they *can* be happy and therefore stop *behaving* as if they want to be, but that's because depression often leads to a state of learned helplessness (once convinced that happiness is no longer possible, continuing to take action toward it becomes next to impossible). Just as the heart's function continues to be the pumping of blood even when it starts to fail, our minds aim toward happiness even when they appear to stop seeking it or even wanting it. Whether we want this to be true or even realize it is makes no difference. Like the heart, our minds are built a certain way to perform a certain function we can't change, one that by virtue of our sentience and self-awareness we just happen to be able to perceive.

But if happiness is indeed our primary function, why is it so difficult to achieve? Perhaps for at least two reasons. First, because merely desiring happiness more than anything else doesn't itself teach us how to achieve it. And as we're all capable of believing things without evidence, many of our beliefs about what makes us happy will simply turn out to be wrong. How many of us, for example, consider happiness to lie in the unmitigated pursuit of pleasure? Certainly pleasure plays an important role in *contributing* to happiness, but to appreciate how an existence can be overflowing with pleasure and still be miserable we only need look at people for whom certain pleasures (sex, gambling, drugs, and so on) send all other considerations spinning off into the distance and often cause the collapse of the very lives they delight. Further, too much pleasure can be paradoxically *unpleasant* (a few jelly beans are delicious, but too many make us sick), something happiness, by definition, can never be.

Loss Aversion

Which brings us to the second reason happiness is difficult to achieve: it requires not only the presence of joy (meaning a positive emotional state), but also the *absence of suffering*. Unfortunately, we often fail to appreciate these things as separate and focus most of our efforts on finding things that bring us joy rather than on preparing ourselves to withstand hardship. We may think things that bring us joy—a good job, money, a loving spouse, and so on—simultaneously immunize us against suffering, but if anything they actually make us *more* vulnerable to suffering by providing us more attachments to lose.

And avoiding the pain of loss is more important than experiencing the joy of gain. At least, that's how many of us behave when forced to choose between the two, a phenomenon psychologists term *loss aversion*. In the world of day trading, for example, most experts agree the best way to make money is by selling losing trades quickly and letting winning ones ride. But in one study, 62 percent of traders on average did just the opposite, selling their *winning* trades quickly and letting their *losing* ones ride.[2] Why? Because their desire to avoid the pain of loss, which they could only do by holding on to losing trades long enough for them to become winners and selling their winning trades before they became losers, was greater than their desire to experience the joy of gain (by riding out winning trades until they'd peaked).

A Sense of Impotence

Even the Buddha is said to have sought enlightenment out of a desire to resolve the problem of suffering. A famous Buddhist parable tells of Shuddhodana, King of the Shakya tribe, confining his son, Prince Siddhartha—who later became Shakyamuni Buddha—to the royal palace while he was growing up to shield him from the world's sufferings. On four separate mornings, however, Siddhartha managed to escape, venturing outside each time through a different gate. On the first morning, leaving by the west wall, he came upon a mother suckling an infant. On the second morning, leaving by the north wall, he came upon an old man sitting by the side of the road. On the third morning, leaving by the east wall, he came upon a leper begging for alms. And on the fourth morning, leaving by the south wall, he came upon a corpse.

These so-called four meetings are taken to represent the four inescapable sufferings of life: birth, old age, sickness, and death. The suffering of birth is taken to mean the suffering that arises simply as a result of our having been born—that is, of having desires that go unfulfilled, of encountering people and experiences we don't like, and of being separated from people and experiences we do. The suffering of old age refers to the suffering we experience as a result of the loss of our mental and physical vitality. The suffering of sickness is that which we experience as a result of illness. And the suffering of death arises from our awareness that we will one day die. Taken together, these four sufferings are said to encompass every kind of suffering human beings experience.

In response to these four meetings, Siddhartha pondered a question as relevant today as it was 2,500 years ago: How can anyone achieve happiness in life when it constantly brings us so much suffering? In an effort to find the answer, he adopted the life of an ascetic, depriving himself of all worldly goods, attachment to which was considered by many at the time to be the root of all suffering. After many years of begging for food, however, he concluded this approach was futile and discarded it. Frustrated but still determined, he eventually entered into a deep meditation under the branches of a pipal tree and found his answer in the attainment of enlightenment.

The answer he found wasn't, contrary to what many other forms of Buddhism suggest, that suffering arises from the frustration of our desires. Rather it was that suffering arises from our deluded thinking about the nature of life itself—specifically, from our deluded belief that we lack the power to overcome the obstacles that confront us. We don't suffer, according to Nichiren Buddhism, because we face obstacles; we suffer because we face obstacles *we don't believe we can overcome.* Even the state of continuous suffering—clinical depression—is considered to result from our being overwhelmed by a feeling of powerlessness.

In response to the reasonable objection that not all problems *are* solvable, including three of the four inescapable sufferings—old age, sickness, and death—and therefore that victory over these sufferings is impossible, Nichiren Buddhism would answer that not all problems are solvable *in the way we want.* This isn't a dodge, but rather a challenge to the notion of what solving a problem means.

Obtaining Benefit from Adversity

Life, a core principle of Nichiren Buddhism teaches, is win or lose. Right and wrong, success and failure, gain and loss—all constitute important and related issues to be sure, but nothing, according to Nichiren Buddhism, boosts happiness more than victory or causes more misery than defeat.

But in Nichiren Buddhism victory doesn't mean victory over others—no one else need lose for us to win—but rather victory over the obstacles that confront us. Yet victory over the obstacles that confront us isn't as much about liberating ourselves from adversity as it is about obtaining the greatest benefit possible as a result of having encountered it. Not just passing the Boards, but becoming a better doctor. Not just healing a broken heart, but learning to love oneself.

How do we know when true victory occurs? When the benefit we obtain from confronting an obstacle is enough to make us glad—or at least accepting—that it stood in our way in the first place. Which sometimes means solving problems *not* in the ways we want. What we want, after all, doesn't always represent the greatest benefit an obstacle has to offer. Had I gotten what I wanted by reconciling with my girlfriend, for example, I wouldn't have come to realize she had nothing I needed to be happy, the winning of self-love ultimately proving itself a far greater benefit than the winning of someone else's. Further, what we want often falls far short of our expectations. A new relationship, a new job, even a vacation—all are just a few examples of things we expect will resolve our loneliness, boredom, and stress but that just as often fail to deliver.[3]

This isn't to imply we shouldn't fight with all our might for the result we most desire. Just that we should remain open to the idea that the greatest benefit an obstacle has to offer us may be something other than what we expect. Sometimes, for example, the greatest benefit comes from failure—failure that forces us to pursue an alternative path we wouldn't have otherwise considered but that turns out to be the best way, if not sometimes the *only* way, our problem could have been solved. Or failure that leads us to a benefit that's even better than what we wanted and a victory even greater than we expected, as when I not only passed Part I of the National Boards but became a better doctor as a result of having to study for it twice.

At other times, the true obstacle isn't the obstacle in front of us but the obstacle inside of us. Perhaps it's our inflexibility, our arrogance, or our fear, but when victory over external barriers is contingent upon victory over internal ones, the greatest benefit a situation has to offer us is wisdom.

Adversity as a Catalyst

Such was the case with a patient of mine named Rick, who once came to see me with a lump in his neck. He stood at least six and a half feet tall with shoulders that seemed almost as broad. His lump, in contrast, was only two centimeters wide.

Wide enough, however, to warrant concern. It was firm rather than rubbery, fixed rather than mobile, and nontender rather than painful, all hallmarks of something potentially malignant. He'd noticed it only one month prior to coming to see me, which made me think it had grown rapidly, another bad sign. He'd had no infection during that time that he could recall.

I recommended a biopsy, to which he agreed, and set up an appointment for him to see a surgeon. A week later he called me to ask more questions. The conversation started calmly enough. He related how he'd gone to see the surgeon who'd immediately scheduled a biopsy—and then suddenly he was shrieking in my ear. He'd had to wait thirty minutes in the waiting room and then another fifteen in the exam room before being seen! He'd expected an office procedure and instead they'd taken him to the operating room! He'd wanted general anesthesia and instead they'd used a local block! What the hell was wrong with these people?

I could only listen in stunned silence, not just because I was taken completely by surprise, but because he offered no pauses during his dia- tribe—which lasted a full ten minutes—to allow me to respond. By the time he'd finished, however, I'd managed to regain my poise, and I sug- gested he come in to see me right away to discuss what had happened.

He arrived later that afternoon with his girlfriend and sat down in a much calmer state than he'd been before. He even laughed derisively as he related how someone had called the police after he'd gotten off the phone with me. Apparently, he'd been standing in a bookstore during his tirade, and his yelling had frightened someone enough that they'd called for help. He demonstrated no insight into why someone would have done that and thought it a completely inappropriate response to his "blowing off steam." He did, however, apologize for "being a little harsh" with me.

I accepted his apology and told him I was sorry about his experience with the surgeon. And then I told him, as gently as I could, that the biopsy results had come back and that they weren't good: he had Hodg- kin's lymphoma.

He looked at me in surprise. Then, after a prolonged pause, he asked tentatively, "That's treatable, right?"

I nodded. "Yes."

"Chemo?" he asked.

"Yes."

He paused again, thinking. Then he took his girlfriend's hand. "Okay, I can do that."

But his girlfriend pulled her hand away, saying in a trembling voice, "I'm sick and tired of you getting angry at me all the time. Either you get help to stop, or you're going to go through this alone."

He blinked, even more stunned, it seemed to me, than when I'd told him he had cancer. I expected a defensive, angry denial, but instead, after a moment, he only nodded and said, "Okay."

Five months later, after having finished a series of anger management classes, he came back to see me and announced that the lymphoma (which was now in remission) had been the best thing that had ever happened to him. He realized now, he said, that it had been only a matter of time before his anger drove his girlfriend away. But if he hadn't developed lymphoma, he wouldn't have felt a need for her support and therefore might not have been open to her suggestion that he needed help to control his temper. And if he hadn't gotten help to control his temper, though his life still would have been saved, he would have lost the very thing that he thought made it worth saving: the love of a good woman. He hadn't just won when he'd been cured of his lymphoma, he said. He'd won when he changed himself enough to be able to keep her.

Wisdom and the End of Suffering

Wisdom is so powerful, in fact, that it can even put a halt to suffering without changing the circumstances that cause it, as when I freed myself from suffering not when I resumed my relationship with my girlfriend but when I realized I didn't need to. Most of us deem a problem solved when it no longer confronts us, but from a Nichiren Buddhist perspective a problem is solved when it *no longer makes us suffer*, our escaping or overcoming oppressive circumstances representing only one particular means to that end. Certainly it may be the means we most prefer, and in many cases what we need to do to be able to declare true victory. But it's not the only means at our disposal. As Viktor Frankl wrote, "When we are no longer able to change a situation—just think of an incurable disease such as inoperable cancer—we are challenged to change ourselves."[4]

From a Buddhist perspective, however, this means neither denying our problems exist nor denying they make us suffer. Rather, it means learning to use suffering as a springboard for creating benefit. For when confronted by harsh circumstances over which we have no control, we become capable of enduring them only by finding a way to create value with them—as Frankl, a psychiatrist, did himself while a prisoner at Auschwitz by both attending to the suffering of his fellow prisoners and dreaming of the day he would be able to lecture about the lessons in psychology he learned from being imprisoned in a Nazi concentration camp.

Indeed, what Frankl's example teaches us is that the essence of victory lies in the act itself of refusing to be defeated. For whether our problems are diminutive or global, mundane or existential, resolvable in the way we want or not, winning doesn't just *require* we constantly attack with all our might: it *is* constantly attacking with all our might. That is, whether we can declare genuine victory doesn't depend only on the final outcome, but also on what we feel in all the moments leading up to it. After all, how can we say we've won even in achieving the best possible outcome if at every moment leading up to it we suffered at the hands of the belief that victory would never be ours? Given that we spend much more time fighting for victory than attaining it, what we feel during the former is even more important than what we feel during the latter.

Studies actually show that when most of us experience a significant loss—the death of a spouse or a parent, for example—we suffer for a while but then typically recover (becoming frozen in grief or outright depression following such an event turns out to be surprisingly rare).[5] But just knowing we're most likely destined to recover in the end doesn't automatically mitigate the suffering such traumas cause while we're going through them. For this reason, possessing an undefeated mind in which hope beats in time with every thrust of our pulse, a constant refrain in our body and heart, isn't just *necessary* for victory; it *is* victory. For in refusing to give up, we refuse to give in, not just to oppressive circumstances, but to the moment-by-moment experience of suffering itself. Resilience, in other words, doesn't consist only of returning to our original level of functioning after a loss; it also consists of not experiencing its decline in the first place.

Possessing an Undefeated Mind

This, then, is what it means to possess an undefeated mind: not just to rebound quickly from adversity or to face it calmly, even confidently, without being pulled down by depression or anxiety, but also to get up day after day, week after week, month after month, year after year, decade after decade—even over the course of an entire lifetime—and attack the obstacles in front of us again and again and again until they fall, or we do. An undefeated mind isn't one that never feels discouraged or despairing; it's one that continues on in spite of it. Even when we can't find a smile to save us, even when we're tired beyond all endurance, possessing an undefeated mind means never forgetting that defeat comes not from failing but from *giving up*. An undefeated mind doesn't fill itself with false hope, but with hopes to find real solutions, even solutions it may not want or like. An undefeated mind is itself what grants us access to the creativity, strength, and courage necessary to find those real solutions, viewing obstacles not as distractions or detours off the main path of our lives but as the very means by which we can capture the lives we want. Victory may not be promised to any of us, but possessing an undefeated mind means behaving as though it is, as though to win we only need wage an all-out struggle and work harder than everyone else, trying everything we can, and when that fails trying everything we think we can't, in full understanding that we have no one on whom we can rely for victory but ourselves. Possessing an undefeated mind, we understand that there's no obstacle from which we can't create some kind of value. We view any such doubt as a delusion. Everyone—absolutely everyone—has the capacity to construct an undefeated mind, not just to *withstand* personal traumas, economic crises, or armed conflicts, but to triumph over them all.

Attaining this state may seem impossible, an ability granted only to an extraordinary few like Viktor Frankl or that great champion of freedom, Nelson Mandela. But the tools those luminaries used to achieve their goals are available to us all. In fact, in his autobiography *Long Walk to Freedom*, Mandela describes achieving victory over a twenty-seven-year prison sentence by using several of the same principles described in this book.[6]

Extraordinary people may be born, but they can also be made. We need only look around at the number of people in everyday life who demonstrate the same resilience as a Viktor Frankl or a Nelson Mandela, some of whose stories I tell in the pages that follow, for proof that an undefeated mind isn't nearly so rare a thing as we think.

2

Find Your Mission

Nietzsche once wrote that he who has a *why* to live can bear almost any *how*. According to Nichiren Buddhism, however, not every *why* is created equal. To build the strongest life force possible—one that *can* bear the weight of any *how*—Nichiren Buddhism argues we need a *why* to live that in some way involves contributing to the well-being of others.

The first hint that my patient Steve had a problem related to the absence of just such a *why* came from, of all things, a series of sighs. Immediately after we exchanged names and shook hands at the start of our initial visit, he gasped as if poked by an invisible finger, sucked in a deep breath through his nose—then stacked a second, even more forceful breath on top of it, as if his lungs still weren't satisfied—before finally exhaling loudly from his mouth. Then, a few moments later as I was navigating to his record on my computer, he did it again.

After I pulled up his demographic information and quickly scanned it, I turned away from my screen, folded my hands in my lap, and asked why he'd come to see me.

"I'm having trouble sleeping," he said.

I took a moment to study him. Standing, he'd towered over me, but even sitting down he seemed a giant, his torso almost as long as his legs. He wore an expensive-looking suit, but sloppily, with his belt buckled too tightly, his pants wrinkled as if he'd recently lost weight, and his tie loosened at a sharp angle to the left.

I asked if he had difficulty falling asleep, difficulty staying asleep, or both. "I get into bed at ten o'clock and lie there until two or three in the morning, wide awake," he answered. In the last two or three months, he said, he'd averaged only a few hours of sleep a night.

"What time are you getting up?"

"Six o'clock. Even though I don't have to anymore," he added ruefully. "Old habits die hard, I guess."

"Why don't you have to anymore?"

He took in another deep breath and let it out slowly. "Lost my job."

He was the second patient I'd seen that morning who had. "I'm sorry," I said. He waved my sympathy away with his hand.

"When?" I asked.

"January."

Four and a half months ago—only slightly longer than he'd been having trouble sleeping. This was almost certainly the precipitating cause of his insomnia, I thought. But ever wary of my tendency to come to early closure, I forced myself to conduct a disciplined fleshing out of the details surrounding his complaint.

"How well were you sleeping before four months ago?" I asked him.

"Like a baby."

Did he ever get a normal night's sleep now, I asked, even one night out of seven? No, he said. In fact, two or three nights a week, he never fell asleep at all. Did he take naps? He did. Were they restorative? They were. How often did he drink alcohol? At most, a few beers on the weekend.

Had he ever used alcohol to try to induce sleep? Once or twice, but it hadn't worked. Did he use any other drugs recreationally? None, he said. He reported no significant past medical history, no allergies to any medications, and he took no medications on a regular basis.

"Have you lost any weight recently?" I asked him.

He admitted he had.

"Not hungry?" I guessed.

He shook his head no.

"On a scale of one to ten, how anxious would you say you've been feeling since you lost your job?"

His eyes widened slightly. And then, seeming as much to his surprise as mine, he began to cry.

Can Happiness Be Increased?

The *set-point theory* of happiness suggests that our level of subjective well-being is determined primarily by heredity and personality traits ingrained in us early in life and as a result remains relatively constant throughout our lives.[1] Our level of happiness may change transiently in response to life events, I told Steve, but then almost always returns to its baseline level as we habituate to those events and their consequences over time.[2]

"How long does that usually take?" he asked, wiping at his eyes.

"That's hard to say," I said. "It's different for everybody."

He sucked in another deep breath and shook his head. "I just don't understand it. I've got more than enough money. A great house, two cars—a boat, which I love. My marriage is great. My kid's not in any trouble. My health is good." He looked utterly bewildered.

I nodded. Habituation, a growing body of evidence now tells us, occurs even to things like career advancement, money, and marriage,

which was almost certainly why, I told him, none of the things he mentioned were able to carry him through his crisis.[3] They'd long ago lost
their capacity to boost his happiness, so had no power now to defend
him against significant loss.

And Steve's loss was clearly significant. Despite the numerous studies that support set-point theory, other research suggests a few events—
chief among them the unexpected death of a child and repeated bouts of
unemployment—seem to reduce our ability to be happy permanently.[4]
Few would have trouble understanding why the death of a child might
impair a parent's capacity to feel joy over the long term. But the reason
repeated bouts of unemployment erode happiness isn't quite as straightforward: research has also shown an excessive focus on material goals
like career advancement is actually associated with a slight *decrease* in
happiness.[5] Why, then, should repeatedly becoming unemployed prove
to be so scarring?

The answer, of course, is that money isn't the only reason we work,
as most multimillionaires and billionaires who still get up every morning for work well know. We also work to create value. In fact, according
to Tsunesaburo Makiguchi, an early-twentieth-century Japanese educa-
tor and founding president of the Soka Gakkai (the lay organization of
Nichiren Buddhists), creating value for others is the key to attaining happiness for ourselves. We may be more interested in worldly pleasures like
romantic love, sex, fine dining, or reading, but studies are beginning to
support the idea that the quantity and quality of value we create for others is what contributes to our happiness the most.[6]

In fact, recent research suggests not only that the set-point theory of
happiness needs to be modified—that we have more control over our
long-term level of happiness than current thinking suggests—but also
that it needs to be modified because Makiguchi had it right: we can, in
fact, make ourselves happier by helping others. According to one study

that analyzed data from the German Socio-Economic Panel Survey, a collection of statistics representing the largest and longest-standing series of observations on happiness in the world, the trait most strongly associated with long-term increases in life satisfaction is, in fact, a persistent commitment to pursuing altruistic goals.[7]

What's more, according to another study, altruism doesn't just *correlate* with an increase in happiness; it actually *causes* it—at least in the short term. When psychologist Sonja Lyubomirsky had students perform five acts of kindness of their choosing per week over the course of six weeks, they reported a significant increase in their levels of happiness relative to a control group of students who didn't.[8]

But why would creating value for others boost our happiness set-point beyond the point at which our heredity has set it when things like career advancement, money, and marriage don't? One possibility, I suggested to Steve, is that the more value we create for others, the more value we assign *ourselves*. Helping others, in other words, enhances our self-esteem.[9]

"I always knew my job was important to my self-esteem," Steve said. "I just didn't think this much."

"There's another possibility to consider as well," I said. "If the reason that value creation increases long-term happiness is because it enhances our self-esteem, then career advancement and wealth accumulation should, too. But they don't. So maybe creating value for others doesn't increase our long-term happiness because it enhances our self-esteem but because it enhances our sense of purpose."[10]

If our self-esteem determines the value we assign to ourselves (that is, how much we like ourselves), our sense of purpose determines the value we assign to our *lives* (that is, how significant or important we find our lives to be). And while a healthy self-esteem is well known to be necessary for happiness, increasing it beyond what's considered "healthy" hasn't been correlated with further increases in happiness (perhaps because any level of self-love beyond "healthy" strays, almost by definition, into the realm of narcissism). In contrast, the greater the sense of purpose we feel, the happier we seem to become.[11]

"And when we *lose* our sense of purpose—our ability to create value in the way that matters to us most—well," I concluded, "it's pretty hard not to become miserable."

Steve nodded. All he was able to think about, he said, was that he'd lost a job he loved and that he had no idea what he was going to do next or even who he was anymore. As a partner in a private equity firm, he'd been in charge of buying distressed companies, turning them around, and operating them or selling them off for profit. But when the economic crisis of 2008 hit, private equity funding dried up and banks not only refused to grant new loans but also called in old ones. Viable investments that would enable his company to provide its investors their returns became impossible to find, and as the portfolio of businesses they owned started to fail they found themselves having to return more and more of their investors' money, until eventually they went out of business. Which was how, at the age of fifty-six, Steve found himself jobless for the first time in his life.

"I just feel like I'm drowning," he said finally, heaving out yet another sigh.

"You keep taking these big gulps of air," I observed.

"That's the other thing," he said. "It's like I can't get a good enough breath in sometimes." As if to prove it, he sighed again.

A standard series of questions about what exacerbated or relieved his breathlessness confirmed my suspicion that the cause was neither heart nor lung disease. I could have arranged pulmonary function tests and an echocardiogram but didn't think either was necessary. I performed a quick exam—listened to his heart and lungs, palpated his abdomen—and then sat back down.

I paused to gather my thoughts. "The term I use for the kind of shortness of breath you're experiencing is air hunger."

"Yeah!" He nodded vigorously. "That's exactly what it feels like."

I nodded with him. "I think in your case it's caused by anxiety." For Steve, I suspected, the metaphorical had become the literal, his mind translating the image he had of himself drowning into the physical sensation of breathlessness. "It's also what I think is causing your insomnia and loss of appetite. Money may not be an issue, but not knowing who you are certainly is. I think anyone would feel anxious if he'd lost his sense of purpose and wasn't sure how he could get it back."

His eyes became unfocused, as if he was taking an internal inventory. "That sounds . . . just about right. . . ."

"The thing is, Steve, you *can* get it back," I said. "You just have to find something else to do that you think is important."

Steve shrugged. "I don't know what else I *can* do."

"Well," I said in my most pragmatic voice, "that's what you need to figure out then."

"I can't even figure out how to fall asleep," he said with a frustrated scowl.

I nodded. "Anxiety is a double-edged sword: a little is motivating, but a lot is paralyzing. So the first thing we need to do is get your anxiety under control. We don't have to *eliminate* it; just reduce it from paralyzing to motivating. I'm thinking medication might be a good way to do that, at least in the short run. We just need to calm you down enough so you can think a little more clearly and figure out what you want to do next. If you can do that—if you can find a renewed sense of purpose—I think there's a good chance your anxiety will resolve."

Steve sat motionless, thinking. Then with a slight shrug of his shoulders, he agreed.

"The medication I have in mind is called clonazepam," I said, reaching for my prescription pad. I told him I'd call him in two weeks to see how he was doing. If his anxiety hadn't quieted down by then, we could decide at that point to increase the dose.

"Think about what you liked best about your job," I said as he stood to leave. "What felt most meaningful and satisfying about it? Try to think of something else that offers the same rewards."

Two weeks later when I called him to follow up, however, he reported feeling even worse. "I'm racking my brain, but I just can't think of anything else I *want* to do," he said. He thought I'd identified the root cause of his problem, but two weeks of trying to solve it had only confirmed that he didn't know how, which had actually made his anxiety worse. He was still hardly sleeping and had little appetite.

I said I was sorry to hear it but that I wasn't, in fact, all that surprised. I told him I'd been reflecting on the advice I'd given him and realized I hadn't adequately explained the context in which I'd given it. I'd suggested he search for a new strategy for creating value. But what he really needed to do first, I believed, was define his mission.

Defining a Personal Mission

The word "mission" derives from the Latin *mittere*, meaning "to send," and was first used in 1598 by Spanish Jesuits to describe the sending of their members abroad. Later, in the early twentieth century, the armed forces began using it to describe the sending of aircraft on military operations. By the end of the twentieth century, then, businesses were creating mission statements to describe the purpose for which they existed.

"We had ours," Steve nodded as he sat down across from me at our second visit.

"So you know a company's mission is considered its broadest goal—a goal that defines the reason it exists."

"Sure."

"Well, to my way of thinking, people are no different. In my view, *our* purpose—our function—is to become happy."

"Our *function* is to become happy?" Steve echoed uncertainly.

I nodded.

"I don't know," he said, frowning. "I mean, I want to be happy as much as the next guy, but when you put it like that . . . it just sounds kind of . . . selfish. . . ."

"It's not selfish at all," I said, shaking my head. "You may not deserve happiness any more than anyone else, but neither do you deserve it any less. And since there's good reason to think that a significant part of our happiness depends on the contribution we make to the happiness of others, wanting to be happy ourselves ends up meaning the same thing as wanting others to be happy. Why do you think when a plane depressurizes we're told to put our own oxygen masks on before helping someone else with theirs? Only in taking care of ourselves first do we then become capable of taking care of others. It's certainly possible to contribute to the happiness of others when we're miserable, but we're much better at it when we're not." In fact, research suggests that our level of happiness not only influences the happiness of people *personally* close to us but also of people *physically* close to us.[12] Even more remarkable, our happiness seems to influence the happiness of others at a distance of up to three degrees of separation (not just the friends of our friends but *their* friends as well).[13] Emotions, it appears, are as contagious as infectious diseases.

Steve's expression became thoughtful. "Even if my *function* is to become happy," he said, "how does knowing that help me figure out what I want to do next?"

"For one thing, it stops you from thinking about what you want to do next as an *end* and starts you thinking about it as a *means*. As a strategy."

"For becoming happy, you mean."

"For fulfilling a mission that *makes* you happy."

Just like a corporation, I told him, he needed to delineate the broadest type of value he was interested in creating, to craft a statement that defined the end toward which all his value-creating *strategies*, like a job, would aim. "Something that defines the core *reason* you want to do what you want to do."

While Nichiren Buddhism holds that everyone's function is the same—to become happy—it also holds that everyone's mission is personal, meaning the type of value to which each of us chooses to dedicate our lives will vary according to our individual preferences. A mission isn't something, therefore, that an outside force or supreme being assigns us. It's something we assign ourselves.

"Once we figure out our mission," I said, "then we can turn value-creating activities that interest us into *strategies* with which we can accomplish it." Thus, I suggested, sculpting becomes a strategy *to fill the world with beauty*. Or teaching, a strategy *to inspire children to greatness*.

Certainly, I told Steve, he didn't *have* to define a mission for himself. The pleasures life brought him would still remain pleasurable even if he didn't. He could choose to view his job, his hobbies, or whatever he spent most of his time doing as just that: what he spent his time doing. Or as something he enjoyed. Or as a necessary evil, a means to some other end, like making money. But if he embraced a mission—his mission as a *provisional bodhisattva* (a bodhisattva defined in Buddhism as a person who dedicates himself to the happiness of others)—he would not only enjoy greater satisfaction in life, but also, according to recent research, gain something that the joy he felt from fleeting pleasures couldn't provide, something that most people failed to associate with a strong sense of purpose but that was nevertheless one of its principal benefits: increased strength.

"Why would a mission give me that?"

First, I told him, because strategies often fail. Companies go bankrupt.

Sculptures sit unsold. Teachers lose their jobs. A mission, on the other hand, endures. No matter how devastated we may feel when a strategy fails, no matter how much we may have loved doing it, if underneath that love also lies a commitment to the mission our strategy served, we'll eventually be able to pick ourselves up, dust ourselves off, and find another strategy we love just as much. Not that recovering from the loss of a strategy to which we're attached is easy. Such a strategy may have enabled us to create value we were exceptionally suited to create—like buying distressed companies and turning them around—or that only we ourselves were capable of creating (like a beautiful sculpture, a groundbreaking book, or a beautiful song). But the uniqueness of the value we create isn't as sustaining to our sense of purpose as it is to our egos, which, while certainly pleasurable, hasn't been shown to correlate with an increased happiness in the long term at all.

A Sense of Purpose

"So," I said, "if a sculptor's focus is as much on filling the world with beauty as on the act of sculpting itself, he'll have an easier time putting obstacles, like failing to sell a sculpture or an accident that shatters one, into their proper perspective. Even losing the ability to sculpt itself—say, from a stroke—though devastating, might then become a potentially surmountable obstacle."

"How?" Steve asked skeptically.

"Flower arranging?" I said. "Web design? I don't know. The point is that sculpting isn't the only way to fill the world with beauty."

Engaging in work we consider important rather than merely enjoyable also seems to increase our ability to tolerate stress. For example, though caring for patients with terminal illnesses is widely considered among the most nerve-racking jobs in all of health care, providers who do it report among the *lowest* levels of burnout.[14] Why? In a study of palliative-care nurses, the most commonly reported reason was the heightened sense of purpose they felt in providing comfort to the terminally ill.[15]

Perhaps even more remarkable is the increased ability to endure *physical* pain that a strong sense of purpose also seems to grant. In one study, psychologist Philip Zombardo administered a series of electric shocks to a group of college students to determine their pain tolerance. Then he offered a choice to some of them about whether to receive additional shocks while telling them that their continuing participation in the research would greatly advance scientific understanding (the experimental group). To the rest he gave neither a choice about receiving additional shocks nor a chance to gain a sense of purpose about receiving them (the control group). When he compared the responses of the two groups to subsequent shocks, not only did the experimental group report lower levels of pain, but also measurements of their galvanic skin resistance showed reduced *physiologic* responses to pain as well.[16]

Defining and embracing a mission can also greatly increase our sense of self-worth,[17] supplanting the image we have of ourselves as only one among faceless billions with one of ourselves as the important—perhaps even heroic—figures we all have the potential to be. Armed with a strong belief in the importance of our mission to others, we can also find the strength to keep fighting long past the point where others, lacking any reason to continue besides the satisfaction of their own desires, give up.[18] The inner strength that embracing a mission unleashes can be so great we may even find ourselves willing to risk our lives—to donate a kidney, for instance, or to be the first of our comrades to charge up a hill in a firefight.

Adopting a mission can also prevent onerous tasks from boring us. In fact, increasing our perceived level of life meaning decreases boredom even more than does improving our mood,[19] likely explaining why arming ourselves even with the humblest of missions—perhaps a mission to inspire others to excellence—can make even menial tasks interesting.

Which is why, as Martin Luther King Jr. famously advised, "Even if a man is called to be a street sweeper, he should sweep streets even as Michelangelo painted or Beethoven composed music or Shakespeare wrote poetry. He should sweep streets so well that all the hosts of heaven and earth will pause to say, 'Here lived a great street sweeper who did his job well.'"

Articulating the specific kind of value we most want to create in the form of a mission statement can also improve our ability to set boundaries. When asked to take on a task or perform a favor we'd prefer to decline, possessing a clearly defined mission can help us resist our need to please others and instead make the choice that's best for us.

Embracing a mission can also provide the determination, strength, and courage we need to survive obstacles that might otherwise shatter our spirit. As Frankl so poignantly demonstrated, the ability to create value out of even the most horrific circumstances is often what carries us through them, suffering ceasing to be suffering, he argued, at the moment it acquires meaning. In fact, Frankl maintained that only by choosing to transform his imprisonment in a Nazi concentration camp into a way to advance the world's understanding of the importance of meaning itself was he able to survive the experience psychologically intact.

Absence of a Mission

Certainly if we're already happy and successful, we likely won't lament or even notice the absence of a mission living and breathing in our lives. At least, until we reach the end of them, at which point we might find ourselves looking back with a sense that parts of the journey were enjoyable but also with a sense of dissatisfaction with the final result, as if each sequence had merely followed one after the other without any particular trajectory or purpose, without swelling to a satisfying climax or arriving at a gratifying conclusion. But if we can manage to connect our mission not only to extraordinary events but to ordinary ones as well, we'll find our mission becoming an organizing principle that transforms our choices into a whole greater than the sum of its parts. For when we make our choices in the service of a mission, what feels like a succession of isolated events becomes a series of interconnected plot points that delineate a coherent narrative—a narrative that grants a sense of weight to even apparently inconsequential actions (throwing a birthday party for our spouse, visiting a sick friend, even allowing a stranger to merge into traffic in front of us). In other words, armed with a mission, we'll be able to feel that our life is important *at every moment*.

Ultimately, I told Steve, adopting a mission can help sustain us through loss, improve our ability to endure stress, enhance our sense of self-worth, diminish our inclination to give up, make mundane tasks more enjoyable, help us to say "no" more easily, defend us against despair, and imbue the events of our lives with heightened significance. Few things, I concluded, had the same power to make us as resilient.

Steve looked at me, despondent. "Believe it or not, for me, working in private equity was one of them . . ."

"Until it was taken away," I pointed out.

To this he had no response.

"Look," I said, "I'm not saying things like working in private equity or sculpting or teaching aren't important, or that we shouldn't become attached to them. I'm saying that if those things are *all* we're attached to, we're failing to take advantage of an effective way to defend ourselves against suffering." I suggested to Steve he'd followed a commonly trodden path, expecting to find fulfillment from the execution of a specific strategy, his job in private equity, rather than from a clearly defined mission. He'd been more attached, in other words, to *what* he'd been doing than *why* he'd been doing it.

"But I know why," he told me. "I loved it."

"And because that's *all* you loved," I said, "losing it brought you to me."

Commitment to a Mission

To contribute to the construction of an undefeated mind, we need to fall as much in love with our mission as we are with the strategies we use to fulfill it. We need to love it like a parent loves a child, at some level always keeping it in our thoughts, always seeking to support and advance it, and always standing at the ready to sacrifice for it.

Makiguchi argued that this level of commitment to a mission is only possible when the strategies available to help us fulfill it also provide some kind of benefit to *us*. For if our activities feel more like sacrifices than personal gains—even if our gain is merely engagement in something we find intrinsically enjoyable—we'll fail to maintain an interest in and commitment to them in the long term. Dedicating our lives to the Peace Corps, for example, would seem a wonderful strategy to create value for others but isn't something we'd likely continue unless we had some other way to support ourselves.

Unfortunately, some people approach the task of finding their mission by first deciding what they think it *should* be—a choice often influenced by parental expectations or a need to project a certain image to others—and then attempt to stir up a requisite amount of passion for it. But forcing ourselves to feel something we don't is probably futile. We might find a better approach in attempting to articulate a value-creating statement about which we *already* feel the most excited. For that value-creating statement, whether we realize it or not, represents the mission to which we're *already* committed. As if a precious jewel had been sewn into our clothing without our knowledge, we only need to realize it's there to take advantage of its full worth.

Though by no means easy, this part is at least relatively straightforward. All we need do is trace our way back through the strategy to which we're already the most attached—whether a hobby we like, the job we have, or a job we want—to identify, or "reverse engineer," the mission that lies underneath it. We shouldn't try to imagine things we think *would* excite us. We should examine our experience to find what actually *has* excited us. Or go out and try a new experience to see if it does.

"What's more challenging, then," I said, "is finding a way to articulate the *reason* those experiences excite us, a reason that feels important enough to serve as our mission."

Steve nodded.

"So tell me," I said, folding my hands in my lap, "what felt most meaningful about working in private equity?"

"So many things," he replied. "Finding businesses in trouble. Evaluating their strengths and weakness. Figuring out how to rescue them. Or if we couldn't, how to break them up and sell off the pieces—"

"That might be a little too narrow. What felt most meaningful about your job in the broadest sense? What made you get out of bed singing?"

"Singing?" Steve mused uneasily. "When I saw a company we took over start to turn a profit."

"Even broader," I urged.

"When I saw a company start to fulfill its potential."

"Does it have to be a company?"

He paused. "No . . . the people in the company, too. When they started to become really excellent at what they were doing."

"Now that," I said, "is beginning to sound like something we can use: helping others to fulfill their own value-creating potential."

Steve stared for a moment. "That sounds great, but . . . I don't know how much I really—I don't know if I'm going to be as excited about that as I was about private equity. . . ."

"You're not looking for something that excites you," I reminded him. "You're looking for something that gives your life meaning, which you can best discover *by means of* something that excites you. I don't know if even a sculptor gets *excited* about filling the world with beauty. He gets excited about sculpting—but only because that's how he fills the world with beauty, the activity that makes his life feel the most significant."

After a pause, Steve said I'd given him a lot to think about, but he wasn't exactly sure it had helped his anxiety. I suggested that he sit with it a while and sent him out with a prescription for double the original dose of clonazepam, suggesting that if it didn't start to help soon he might also consider psychotherapy, all the while hoping our discussion would somehow combine with a tincture of time to produce the breakthrough he needed.

A Mission Found

My first hint that such a breakthrough had occurred came when I entered an exam room at Steve's next appointment a month later to find him wearing jeans, a T-shirt, and a bright smile instead of a worried frown and a rumpled suit. He stood up and thrust his hand out to shake mine. We exchanged greetings, and I sat down and asked him how he'd been doing.

"Much better," he said. "So much better I can't even tell you."

"What happened?"

"Ever since our last visit I've been thinking about what we talked about. I haven't been able to stop thinking about it. It was even making my insomnia worse for a while. Everything you said made perfect sense, but I just couldn't get myself excited about the mission you talked about. So I figured I had to be thinking about it wrong, that I just needed to keep at it. So I kept asking myself, *What's my mission? What's my mission?* But I kept coming back to what we said it was, helping other people fulfill their value-creating potential, and it just wasn't doing anything for me. And then—I don't know—maybe I just started to get used to the idea that I'm not going to be in private equity anymore. But I woke up one day with this idea in my head: that my mission is to help people fulfill their value-creating potential *in business*. That's what I'm good at. That's what I know. I know it sounds silly—it's such a small difference—but when I added that to what you said . . . I started to get"—and here he smiled even more broadly—"excited."

I felt a surge of excitement myself. "It's not a small difference at all," I said. "It's huge."

"That's how it felt to me," he said. He laughed awkwardly. "It still sounds a little corny when I say it out loud. 'My mission.'"

"It does to me, too, sometimes," I said. "But don't let that stop you from holding it fast to your heart."

"This was two weeks ago, and I'm still pretty excited," he reassured me. "But I wondered if you thought it was broad enough. I really want to make sure I've got this right."

"It sounds like it to me."

He smiled again. "Yeah, me, too."

Entirely gone was any hint of the passivity he'd displayed previously that I so commonly observed in people distracted by chronic anxiety. "Don't forget how this feels," I told him. "Right now it's thrilling partly because it's new. But the thrill will fade unless you make a determination to remind yourself about it every day. It can be exhausting to keep a mission constantly at the front of your mind, but it's absolutely worth the effort. Try to connect everything you can to it, to turn as many things into strategies that support it as you can, even if only in tiny, indirect ways. Try to figure out a way to do at least one thing to advance it every day. That's how you keep it alive. And when adversity strikes, reminding yourself of it will give you strength."

"What's *your* mission, if you don't mind my asking?" He seemed giddy with the thrill of discovery, hungry to bond over our shared understanding.

"To help people become healthier," I said.

He nodded. "That's why you're a doctor."

"And why I write," I said. "It's not why I started either, but now it's the main reason I do both."

"What about people who don't have a passion for anything?" he asked suddenly. "My son is about to graduate college and doesn't have the first clue about what he wants to do. Nothing seems to excite him."

"Everyone has dreams," I said. "Or at least *a* dream. It may be buried so far back in his childhood he can't remember it, or may seem too childish for him to take seriously now as an adult. Or it may seem so hard to accomplish he stopped himself from even wanting it a long time ago. Or maybe going after it now risks so much that fear stops him from even trying. But everyone has an interest in doing *something*—or did once. So I'd say to your son and anyone else who's struggling to figure out what to do with their lives: even if they aren't ready to pursue it today, they can still use whatever they dream about doing, or dreamt about doing in the past, to work backward to find an underlying value-creating idea that they can embrace as a mission, just like you did with your job in private equity. Then they can work their way forward again to figure out what specific strategies they're actually prepared to use to accomplish it. And who knows? Maybe in the act of finding their mission they'll also find the courage and determination to chase the dream that led them back to it in the first place."

"I shouldn't say *nothing* excites him," Steve added. "Money excites him. Making lots of money." He smirked. "I guess it's silly for a parent to worry that his kid is too concerned about making a living."

"Nothing wrong with wanting to make a lot of money," I said. "People rarely do anything for only one reason, and making a living is important. But if the *central* reason we live isn't to create value for others—well, it may be trite, but it's true: past a certain point, more money really doesn't buy more happiness.[20] And no amount of money can purchase an unde-feated mind."

"No," Steve agreed.

"Figuring out your mission can take years," I said. "You just have to pay close attention to how you react to your own experiences."

"Learn by doing," he affirmed.

"That's what worked for me. Also, when I was in college, I found that constantly thinking about what I wanted to do led me nowhere. But when I reframed the question, asking myself instead *what kind of value I wanted to create*, ideas began popping up. In fact, here's another idea: Have your son try writing down the fifty or so experiences he's had so far that have brought him the most joy, and then have him figure out which ones involved contributing to the well-being of others and the mission statements he would craft out of each of them. Then ask him to imagine being given an award by the president at the age of ninety for having spent his entire life dedicated to whichever one seems to him the most consequential. Whichever 'award' fills him with the greatest sense of pride—whichever makes him feel the greatest sense of satisfac-tion—then that's the mission he should probably spend his life trying to fulfill."

"Hmm," Steve mused. "Maybe I'll suggest that."

"I think it's also important to remember that not every value-creating strategy has to be colossal. Even a smile can create value," I added, smil-ing. "Anyone who imagines that nothing he does creates value for others should remember that even a well-tended garden has the power to lift the spirits of someone walking past it. And a mission to raise happy children is made no less important by the fact that it's ubiquitous."

Steve smiled, too. "What about teaching disadvantaged children eco-nomic literacy?" He went on before I could respond: "I found out about it online. No one even shows these kids how to balance a checkbook.

Forget about keeping a budget or even just the value of money. But it's right up my alley."

"Steve," I said, "I think that's great."

His smile grew wider.

"You sure seem to be feeling a whole lot better," I observed.

"I am. It's been amazing. Like you said, I just had to figure out my mission."

"And take clonazepam," I reminded him with a smile. "We should talk about weaning you off it. It doesn't sound like you'll be needing it anymore."

"Actually," Steve confessed sheepishly, "I never started it."

My eyes widened in surprise. "Why not?"

He shrugged. "When you said anxiety was motivating, I started wondering if I was making mine out to be worse than it was. I guess I was worried that if I started it I'd never get off it. I don't like taking medication."

"And your anxiety now?"

"Gone," he said.

"And you're sleeping all right? You're breathing okay?"

"Like I used to before I lost my job."

"Since when?"

"Since right after I taught my first class," he said. "That night."

I leaned back in my chair and folded my arms across my chest, marveling at the power of the human mind to mend itself simply by altering its perspective, a process that once again struck me as both wonderful and inscrutable. Yet the evidence before me was irrefutable: Steve had indeed managed to quell his anxiety by finding a *why* to live. And though no panacea, this finding of a mission, the life he was now poised to create as a result, like the microscopic beginning of a human embryo, would, I could only imagine, eventually yield something utterly magnificent.

3

Make a Vow

People all over the world know the story of Helen Keller, the deaf and blind girl who learned to communicate when her teacher Annie Sullivan began spelling out words on her hands. But what many don't know is how Helen's parents found Annie Sullivan in the first place. Helen's mother had read about the successful education of another deaf and blind girl, Laura Bridgman, in Charles Dickens's book *American Notes*. So in 1886, Helen and her father traveled from their home in Alabama to Baltimore to see otolaryngologist Dr. Julian Chisolm for advice. Chisolm examined Helen and confirmed she would never see or hear again (she'd lost the capacity for both at nineteen months after contracting an illness described as "an acute congestion of the stomach and brain"). However, Chisolm also believed she could be educated. So he referred her to Alexander Graham Bell (the inventor of the telephone), who was teaching deaf students at his School of Vocal Physiology and Mechanics of Speech. He in turn advised them to visit the Perkins Institute for the Blind (the first school for the blind established in the United States) where Laura Bridgman herself had been taught. Helen and her father then traveled to Boston to meet with Michael Anaganos, the school's director, who at their request asked a former student, Annie Sullivan (herself visually impaired and only twenty years old), to become Helen's teacher.[1]

Take a moment to consider all the obstacles Helen's parents had to overcome to follow this convoluted path to Annie Sullivan: not only the great distances they had to travel and the difficulty involved in finding people knowledgeable about treatments available for deaf and blind children in the late 1800s, but also the prevailing belief that deaf and blind children were uneducable. Yet they faced these obstacles without complaint and without any thought of giving up. Which suggests they had an abundance of the very same stuff that enabled Helen herself not only to learn to communicate, but also to become the first blind person to earn a bachelor of arts degree in the United States (at Radcliffe); to read Braille (not only in English, but also French, German, Greek, and Latin); to write and publish numerous books; to campaign for women's suffrage, workers' rights, and socialism; and even to help found the American Civil Liberties Union—namely, her *resolve*.

The Ability to Soldier On

Oxford Dictionaries Online defines resolve as "a firm determination to do something," but a better definition might be "a firm *decision* to do something," for resolve doesn't merely come from the decision to act; resolve *is* the decision to act. Or rather, the *recurrent* decision to act, for the consistency with which we choose to continue toward a goal when obstacles arise is, in fact, the best measure of resolve we have.

If we think of a mission as a car that can take us to a more resilient place, then resolve, or commitment, must be considered the engine that makes it go. Indeed, the ability to soldier on when obstacles block our way to any goal, whether our life's mission or our most trivial wish, has to be considered as much a part of resilience as the ability to survive and thrive in the face of adversity.

Yet many of us fail to grasp the full extent to which our resolve determines our ability to solve problems, and as a result we often fail to focus on the mustering of resolve when setting out to accomplish a goal. Indeed, when asked to forecast the likelihood that someone will free himself from an addiction, many people will exclude from their calculations the power of resolve entirely and instead rely on the principle that the best predictor of future behavior is past behavior (which would suggest that if someone failed in their attempts to quit smoking in the past, for example, they're more likely than not to fail in their attempts to quit in the future).[2] If the relevance of resolve is acknowledged at all, it's often with a dismissive platitude ("They must not have wanted to quit badly enough"). But people who try to kick nicotine, drug, and gambling habits typically suffer terribly at the hands of their failures, suggesting in fact they wanted to succeed a great deal. Which raises an important question: Why can only some of us maintain our resolve in the face of the most intractable obstacles and irresistible temptations while others crumble at the appearance of even the most minor setback?

Barriers to Mustering Resolve

To my chagrin, I realized that resolve was an issue I'd never once thought to discuss with my patient Tanya, a twenty-nine-year-old Hispanic woman from northwest Indiana, until she appeared in my clinic for her three-month diabetes checkup one day weighing a full twenty pounds less than her usual weight for the first time since I'd known her. At five-feet-five, she'd been obese since childhood and had never been able to achieve anything other than modest weight loss—never anywhere close to twenty pounds—always invariably regaining the weight she'd lost and then some. But here she was having lowered her weight from 275 to 255 in only three months.

Delighted, I asked Tanya how she'd done it. In response, however, she only glanced down at the floor and shrugged indifferently, as if either she didn't know or didn't care to explain.

"Why so glum?" I asked.

She sighed uncomfortably, a frown arching down over her perfectly round face. "Someone asked me out," she said finally.

"Hey, that's great!" I said.

Her only response to this, however, was to glare at me silently.

"Isn't it?" I asked.

She smiled but shook her head. "No, *señor*, it is *not.*"

The problem, she explained, was, in fact, her success. She had little expectation she could maintain her current weight, much less drop any more, and having at last attracted someone's attention, she was desperately afraid of losing it as her size inevitably increased. Better, she said, never to have attracted it at all.

Weight-Loss Studies

A common belief, even among doctors, is that almost no one succeeds in losing weight in the long term. Most of us believe that the vast majority of people who manage to lose weight inevitably not only regain what they've lost but also become heavier than they were in the first place. Yet recent studies have put this assumption in doubt.

Because most of what we know about weight management comes from research on subjects recruited specifically for their *inability* to control their weight (people already successful at weight loss have no incentive to join studies designed to compare weight loss interventions), such studies have largely examined groups of people self-selected for failure. For this reason, researchers Rena Wing and James Hill wondered if successful long-term weight loss is actually more common in the general population than currently believed. So in 1994 they created an online database, the National Weight Control Registry, to find and learn from people who'd *already* achieved long-term weight loss success. To be eligible for entry, participants needed to have lost at least thirty pounds and to have maintained their weight loss for at least one year.

When they examined their registry data six years later, however, Wing and Susanne Phelan, another researcher, found its participants—by then over 4,000 strong—had lost on average *60* pounds (ranging between 30 and 300 pounds) and maintained their weight loss on average for *five and a half* years.[3] Though the diet and exercise regimens they used varied, 89 percent of participants employed some form of both, while 10 percent employed diet alone and only 1 percent employed exercise alone. No difference in outcomes was found between participants who lost weight on their own and participants who used a formal program. Participants also tended to weigh themselves regularly—in some cases daily—and eat breakfast.[4]

To estimate what proportion of the general population might enjoy the same degree of success as their registry participants, Wing and Hill then conducted a random-digit telephone survey in which they asked 474 adults to provide information about both their lifetime maximum weight and current weight. If a subject's current weight was more than 10 percent below their lifetime maximum weight for longer than a year, they were classified as weight-loss maintainers. In contrast to traditional studies that show only a 3 percent likelihood of maintaining long-term weight loss,[5] Wing and Hill's study found that the proportion of people who maintained long-term weight loss in the general population was *20* percent.[6] What's more, the average length of time they'd managed to maintain weight loss wasn't one year. It was eight.[7]

"Really?" Tanya said tentatively. She sounded unsure whether to be encouraged or suspicious.

"I'm not trying to tell you a twenty percent success rate translates into *easy*," I said, wondering if her blood sugar control had improved as a result of the weight loss she'd already achieved. "Or that everyone has an equal chance of success; we know genetics matter. But I am saying success appears to be more likely than most people think."

She looked down at her lap and shrugged. "It's just that the stakes are so much higher now."

Sometimes, I suggested gently, dwelling on how badly we want something only highlights how difficult it is to get. And when we focus more on the obstacles than the goal, we often find ourselves ruminating more about all the ways we might fail. "Try instead to keep your focus on how you might succeed," I urged her.

She nodded absently, still staring into her lap. Then she brought out a wan smile. "I just wish I could have met him six months from now."

It was a heartrending admission. Her suitor's interest had only served to draw her attention to the weight she hadn't yet lost, she seemed to be saying, to how attractive she didn't yet feel, and had transformed her sense of accomplishment into a sense of futility. I leaned back in my chair, groping for something more helpful to say, something that would spark her self-confidence back into life.

"The other thing you should know," I added, "is that before they lost enough weight to qualify for entry into the registry, over ninety percent of the registry participants reported having tried unsuccessfully to lose weight for years."

"Really?" she said again. This time she sounded more startled than anything else.

I nodded. "It's like quitting smoking. You just have to keep trying. You never know when it's finally going to stick."

"I've tried and failed so many times I've lost count."

"Tanya," I emphasized, "*so did they.*"

When Self-Confidence Is Undermined

Nothing dismantles our resolve more quickly than the loss of self-confidence. For this reason, we have much to gain from conceiving of self-doubt not as a character flaw but as a mortal enemy. In fact, preserving our self-confidence represents the single most important and challenging part of any attempt to accomplish a goal, a fierce moment-by-moment struggle that requires us to smash to pieces even the most fleeting of our negative beliefs.

When obstacles arise and we don't immediately see a way to overcome them, even the most determined of us will often decide that overcoming them isn't possible. And whether true or not, once this belief takes root in our minds, a thunderstorm of self-doubt inevitably descends. Because of this, when we're held hostage by the conviction that victory is impossible, we shouldn't aim to *prevent* self-doubt, which, like anxiety, typically only becomes worse when we try to suppress it,[8] but rather to accept the disappearance of our self-confidence as a reflexive response over which we have little control and to focus instead on *regaining* it as quickly as possible.

Before we can regain self-confidence, however, we first need to recognize we've lost it. Though many might think it unlikely that they wouldn't recognize something they were feeling, it turns out that slightly more than 10 percent of the population struggles with exactly that.[9] Termed *alexithymia*, the inability to correctly identify feelings is especially common in people suffering from depression, many of whom have difficulty even recognizing they're depressed.[10] For many of us, then, a real danger lies in misattributing our faltering resolve to a genuine (if unexplained) loss of interest in pursuing a goal rather than to the fact that we've simply become discouraged. So when our resolve wanes, we might have something to gain by pausing to ask whether it's merely as a result of our interest having moved elsewhere or as a result of a failed belief in ourselves.

If recognizing that we're discouraged is sometimes difficult, recognizing *why* we're discouraged can be even harder. Though sometimes we become discouraged because of an accumulation of problems that makes us feel as if we're trying, hopelessly, to prevent a large plate with too many objects piled on top of it from tipping over, sometimes we become discouraged because a single problem lands on us with such crushing force we suddenly feel too weak to withstand the weight of any. And once an obstacle has stripped us of our self-confidence, even problems we'd previously felt we could overcome may abruptly appear insurmountable, concealing which one caused our self-confidence to falter in the first place.

We're actually quite frequently confused about the reasons we feel things in general. Though we manufacture what seem like valid explanations for our feelings all the time and accept them as irrefutably true almost as soon as we think them up—from why we become infuriated when criticized to why we become embarrassed when praised—in reality these explanations often amount to little more than reasonable guesses.[11] As a result of the vast and often unpredictable influence our unconscious mind can exert on our conscious one, the true reasons we feel as we do are much harder to pin down than we realize.[12] What's more, in attempting to correctly identify the causes of our feelings we often come up against a surprising temporal disconnect between emotion and thought: research suggests that even a single random idea (for example, "competition for college scholarships is fierce") can leave us bathed in a corrosive emotional residue (for example, discouragement) long after we've forgotten we even thought it.[13]

Identifying Obstacles

All this is to say that we may need to become a bit more proactive to figure out just which obstacles are responsible for discouraging us. Luckily, once we've decided to do so, it becomes relatively easy: given that such information sits just beyond the edges of our consciousness, to grasp it we need only do something to *notice* it. Though it requires some degree of effort, we can, for example, make a list of every obstacle that comes to mind. Much in the same way we often don't know exactly what we think until we commit our thoughts to paper, we may not be able to tell precisely why we're discouraged until we're literally staring at the answer.[14] Alternatively, we could speak the same list out loud to someone else, attending not to their reactions, but to our own. Knowing which obstacles have discouraged us, then, enables us to isolate them in our minds from all the other obstacles that haven't, an exercise that typically empowers and uplifts, perhaps by helping us recognize that the size and number of discouraging obstacles are limited and therefore manageable, and also that the number of obstacles we *can* overcome is usually greater than the number we can't.

However, the real reason to identify the obstacles we believe we can't overcome isn't to mark them for more scrutiny, but rather for *less*. For whether we find ourselves discouraged by problems we don't know how to solve (in my case, finding time to study for the Internal Medicine Boards during the third year of medical school), by problems we do know how to solve but don't think we're up to solving (like marketing and promoting a book), or by problems we don't think can actually be solved at all (such as overcoming the fear of death), ruminating about them isn't likely to eliminate self-doubt, but rather make it worse.[15] Certainly, thinking over and over again about an obstacle standing in our way *could* produce a new perspective or plan about how to get past it that restores our self-confidence (that tantalizing possibility undoubtedly one of the reasons we're enticed to ruminate about problems at all), but if we hadn't *already* exhausted our supply of good ideas we wouldn't have become discouraged in the first place.

Regaining Self-Confidence

Ironically, the best way to regain our self-confidence when we find ourselves facing a problem we have no good idea how to solve may be by flinging ourselves, however blindly, into action, doing whatever we think we *can*. This isn't to say we shouldn't use our best judgment, or even best guess, when deciding what action to take, or that we shouldn't remain alert for novel solutions to challenging problems, but rather that the point at which rumination becomes harmful is reached more quickly than most of us realize. Our initial attempts will likely fail (we are, after all, out of good ideas). But as every inventor or artist learns who's ever tried to create something new, attempting things that *don't* work often represents the best way to discover the things that do, something worth remembering whenever we find ourselves looking at our circumstances through a pessimist's lens.[16] We should simply never presume to know whether something will fail without performing the experiment to find out. For even if it does, what we get from trial and error—that is, from trying and failing—that rumination can't provide is the chance to view things from vantage points we can't acquire through theorizing alone. Viewing things from novel vantage points may help disrupt our preconceived notions about how to solve a problem, thus increasing the likelihood we'll *discover*—rather than have to invent—a novel approach that works.[17]

Action Creates Feelings

Unfortunately, as a result of becoming discouraged, we often lose the *desire* to take action. Perhaps a failed romance ruins our interest in dating, or a failed business ruins our interest in entrepreneurship. When this happens, people often naturally assume they need to focus first on rekindling their feelings before attempting further action. But research suggests that action *creates* feeling almost as often as feeling creates action. When we make ourselves smile, for example—or even better, when we make ourselves laugh—we actually begin to feel happier.[18] Further, when we put ourselves in positions that demonstrate power (for example, leaning forward on a desk with hands spread apart) we actually begin to feel more powerful.[19] Taking action, then, doesn't only lead us to new solutions; it may also help reignite our desire to find them.

Unfortunately, taking action also risks an even greater diminution of self-confidence than the rumination it's meant to halt: the experience of failing, after all, is far more discouraging than the experience of merely finding ourselves not knowing what to do next—appearing to confirm, as failing does, that we *can't* succeed. When we don't know what to do next, we can at least hold out hope, however small, that we still *might* succeed.

On the other hand, failure is also what once helped us all learn how to walk, something some of us remember more clearly than others, according to psychologist Dean Simonton. In Simonton's words, "Creativity is a probabilistic consequence of productivity," meaning not only that the more ideas we have the more likely we are to come up with good ones, but also that the more attempts we make to solve a problem the more likely we are to succeed. What separates people who ultimately succeed from those who fail, according to Simonton, is simply a larger number of tries and a willingness to keep failing. People who succeed, in other words, don't succeed because they're necessarily smarter or more creative than people who don't (that is, their ratio of successes to failures isn't better than everyone else's). They succeed because they have an increased tolerance for failure, paradoxically suffering even *more* failures than people who *don't* succeed.

Persistence and Success

Not that persistence is necessarily more important than talent, I told Tanya. Likely no amount of persistence in the absence of talent will lead to brilliance. But brilliant or not, success typically comes only to those who persist.[20]

"That's exactly why I keep failing," Tanya said in a self-deprecating tone. "I keep giving up." She shook her head in self-disgust.

"But then you try again," I pointed out. "Like you are now."

"And then I quit again," she said. "Like I want to now."

I nodded my acquiescence. This was an argument I couldn't win—nor that I even wanted to win. She needed her spirits buoyed, not her thinking criticized. "I'm sorry you're feeling so demoralized," I said. "I thought telling you about the National Weight Control Registry would encourage you."

"Why?" she said derisively. "Because they've all been able to do what I can't?"

"No," I said. "Because they're all *just like you.*"

Social Comparison

Despite abundant warnings that we shouldn't measure ourselves against others, most of us still do. We're not only meaning-seeking creatures but social ones as well, constantly making interpersonal comparisons to evaluate ourselves, improve our standing, and enhance our self-esteem. But the problem with social comparison is that it often backfires. When comparing ourselves to someone who's doing better than we are, we often feel inadequate for not doing as well. This sometimes leads to what psychologists call *malignant envy*, the desire for someone to meet with misfortune ("I wish she didn't have what she has"). Also, comparing ourselves with someone who's doing worse than we are risks scorn, the abstraction of others into something undeserving of our beneficence ("She's disgusting and beneath my notice").[21] Then again, comparing ourselves to others can also lead to *benign envy*, the longing to reproduce someone else's accomplishments without wishing them ill ("I wish I had what she has"), which has been shown in some circumstances to inspire and motivate us to increase our efforts even in the wake of a recent failure.[22]

What causes social comparison not to divide us but to drive us? According to recent research, the trick may lie in comparing ourselves to people with whom we personally identify and who followed a path to success we believe we can follow ourselves.[23] Also important is our conviction that the people with whom we compare ourselves succeeded not because of some special ability, position, or luck but because of their own efforts.[24] In fact, effort is such an important issue that even *negative* role models can inspire and motivate us if we believe they failed because they *didn't* work hard enough. So not only can the strict dieter who exercised three times a week and lost a hundred pounds bolster our motivation and enthusiasm, so can the couch potato who's remained stuck, due to a lack of effort, at the same weight for years.[25]

On the other hand, if we pick a positive role model who took a path to success we *don't* think we can follow, or if the people with whom we compare ourselves seem endowed with special abilities we think we're missing, not only won't social comparison work, it may leave us feeling more discouraged than before. Further, if, instead of comparing ourselves to others whose accomplishments we admire, we compare our specific *results* to theirs—focusing not on the fact that they lost weight, published a book, or earned a raise, but on the *number* of pounds they lost, the *quality* of the writing they published, and the *amount* of the raise they earned—the effects of social comparison will likely reverse. Instead of encouraging us, upward comparison will likely *discourage* us, lending as it will to our work the patina of dross ("His writing is so much better than mine I might as well not write at all") and downward comparison will likely *encourage* us, lending as it will to our work the patina of gold ("I can certainly write better than *that*").

So whenever we become discouraged, I told Tanya, we can encourage ourselves by looking for examples of successful work we consider inferior to ours (however mercenary such a strategy might seem), or by finding a role model who found a path to success we think we can follow ourselves. "Which is why I brought up the registry," I concluded. "Because it isn't filled with triathletes and tennis pros. It's filled with housewives and teachers. And women from Indiana."

Tanya stared at me for a few moments in silence. "But what if I really can't do it?" she said finally. "Sometimes ability, position, and luck *do* play a role in success."

"Maybe you can't lose as much as someone else," I said. "But lose weight at all? Of course you can. You just need to believe it's possible."

She exhaled a long breath. "You have a pill for that?"

Believing in Our Ability

In 1999 David Dunning and Justin Kruger published a study in which they asked sixty-five Cornell University undergraduates to rate the quality of a series of jokes. When they then compared the ratings to those of a cohort of professional comedians (who presumably represent a gold standard), they found, not surprisingly, that some students were better than others at judging which jokes were funny. But when they next asked the students to rate how good they thought they were at the task of joke rating itself, they found the students who were bad at recognizing which jokes were funny were also bad at *recognizing they were bad at it*. Because humor is largely subjective (as evidenced by the variability in the ratings of the jokes even among the professional comedians), they confirmed their findings in subsequent studies of two other, more objective domains, logical reasoning and grammar. In these areas, too, performers at the bottom quartile were the most likely to overestimate their abilities relative to their peers. "People who lack the knowledge or wisdom to perform well are often unaware of this fact," Dunning and Kruger concluded. Their explanation? The same incompetence that causes them to perform poorly also causes them to overlook their own incompetence.[26]

Interestingly, as a result of this cognitive distortion, incompetent people are also paradoxically more optimistic. Their expectations for success are inflated not only because they think they're better than they actually are, but also because the same poor judgment that makes them think so also increases their susceptibility to a peculiar reporting bias. When looking for role models for inspiration, we don't find a dearth of successes from which to choose but rather a dearth of failures—not because so many more people succeed than fail, but because people tend not to publicize their failures nearly as much. The net effect is that success seems more common than it is and therefore, in the eyes of low performers, more easily obtained than high performers know it to be.

"Well, *that's* encouraging," Tanya said.

"No," I said, "it's actually good." Naive optimism may have its pitfalls, dissuading us from taking important precautions like purchasing health insurance or making reference calls on prospective employees, but research also suggests that the greater our belief that we can do something, the greater the likelihood we can actually do it. In one study of smokers, for example, subjects who rated themselves even moderately confident that they could quit were ten times more likely to succeed than subjects who didn't.[27]

Optimism Yields Persistence

The reason optimism yields results isn't that we necessarily tend to try *harder* when we think a goal is achievable; rather, we tend to try *more often*. Optimism, in other words, yields persistence, for nothing seems to keep us going like believing success is possible.[28] And nothing keeps us believing success is possible, even in the face of failure, like overestimating our abilities.

This would seem to lend low performers an ironic advantage, one that should enable them, if Simonton has it right and success is largely a function of the number of times we try, to enjoy unexpectedly *high* rates of success. We might even expect their rates to be higher than those of high performers, who in Dunning and Kruger's study consistently *underestimated* their abilities relative to their peers (apparently assuming that if they could do it, so could everyone else), and who, therefore, we'd expect to be less optimistic than low performers and therefore less likely than low performers to keep going when they fail.

But when we look at the actual rates of success of low performers, we find, of course, that they *don't* outperform high performers. Though it grants them the advantage of higher levels of optimism, the Dunning-Kruger effect also hamstrings low performers with an even greater *disadvantage*: being less aware of their failings, they remain less likely to see the need, and thus to make the effort, to improve themselves. It's not that Simonton had it wrong—just that success is a "probabilistic function of productivity" only when our productivity is of sufficiently high quality. Optimism may yield persistence, but persistence isn't enough when optimism is blind. Low performers may keep trying, but they're also more likely than high performers to keep failing.

Importantly, though, studies also show that when high expectations for success *are* warranted—that is, when they're based on *accurate* appraisals of both our abilities and the circumstances we face—such optimism does in fact become a self-fulfilling prophecy, increasing the actual likelihood of success.[29] In other words, optimism does help us to succeed, but only when it's been earned.

"So how do I earn it?" Tanya wanted to know.

"Not by fooling yourself into thinking you're better than you are," I answered. "By turning yourself into someone who actually is."

Waging a Campaign

Over dinner one night in 2002, my brother and his wife announced they were going to have a baby. I was thrilled. This would make them the first of our generation to become parents, which was an exciting development for our entire family. But by the end of the evening I also found myself feeling vaguely uneasy. The contrast between my life and theirs never seemed starker, and by the time I arrived home, I found myself brimming with a strange sense of urgency. The next morning, my mind filled with thoughts of life stages and transitions, I decided it was time for me to get married.

In Nichiren Buddhism, practitioners chant *Nam-myoho-renge-kyo* to acquire the wisdom that enables them to achieve their goals. So I decided I would chant *Nam-myoho-renge-kyo* one million times ("a one-million-*daimoku* campaign") to acquire whatever wisdom I needed to find my wife. I'd waged such campaigns several times in the past, so I knew it would take 300 hours, which, given my schedule at the time, meant approximately nine months.

Later that same night I received an e-mail from a woman to whom I'd reached out weeks earlier on Match.com, an Internet dating site. Her name was Rhea, and her profile was as articulate and bold as her picture was beautiful. We corresponded by e-mail briefly, then talked one night on the phone for several hours. The conversation flowed effortlessly, and at the end of it we made plans to meet for dinner that weekend.

The date was electric. We ended up spending the entire week together and soon were dating seriously. Five months later, on Christmas Eve, she moved in with me.

Soon after, though, I began experiencing intense bouts of anxiety, mostly in the morning right after waking up. I thought it arose from my continued uncertainty about the future of our relationship, so I continued my *daimoku* campaign, still unclear about whether I wanted to marry her. On an intellectual level, nothing seemed to be standing in the way. Though far from perfect, she was outstanding: smart, beautiful, emotionally healthy, happy, and fun, someone I not only enjoyed but from whom I could learn. Yet I still seemed to be waiting for some invisible switch to flip, some internal confirmation that she was the one for me. I knew I was hesitating at least partially because to choose her was simultaneously to reject everyone else. But I also recognized that most of the other 3.5 billion women in the world would never make their way in front of me to become potential choices. And though somewhere out there among them was probably someone else more wonderful than she (as somewhere out there someone else was undoubtedly more wonderful than I), for me Rhea was more than wonderful enough.

Eventually my brother and his wife had their baby, a boy. The morning of the bris, however, Rhea and I had a terrible fight, and by the time we arrived at my brother's place we were barely speaking. When we came home, she went downstairs to be alone, and I went upstairs to chant.

I still didn't know if I wanted to marry her. Fuming from our argument, I decided that I'd had enough: two hours were left in my *daimoku* campaign and by the end of that time, I decided, I was going to have my answer. At first, all I felt as I chanted was anger. But gradually my anger abated and my thinking began to shift. I began to wonder just why at the age of thirty-four I was still unmarried. I didn't think a marriage was necessary for a happy life, but I'd always envisioned myself being in one. So why wasn't I? Had it merely been a matter of not finding the right person? Or perhaps, I wondered, there was something I needed to change about myself?

Abruptly, I found my thoughts drifting back to a point in my life years earlier when I'd been a first-year resident. It was the first time I'd ever lived completely alone, and as I thought back on it, I realized it had been one of the happiest periods of my life. When I returned at the end of each day, I'd come home to an empty kingdom, one in which I had complete freedom to do whatever I wanted. No one else lived in my personal space to ask favors of me or require my help or have an opinion about what to do that was contrary to my own. That freedom, I suddenly realized, was what I wanted more than anything else. And at that moment, at the very end of my million *daimoku* campaign to find my wife, I discovered to my surprise that the true reason I was still single was simply this: *I wanted to be.*

Despite my surprise, I understood the reason almost immediately: being alone was the strategy I used to protect myself against the demands placed on me by others. I'd learned from my relationship with my first girlfriend that I didn't need a woman to love me to be happy, but conflict, I realized now, still made me uncomfortable and anxious. So how did I manage that anxiety? *By preventing it from occurring in the first place.* By reserving private time and space in which no one could demand anything of me.

This, then, I realized, was the reason I'd felt so anxious once I'd started living with Rhea. She had no compunction at all about expressing her desires about what she wanted to do ("Let's go shopping," "Let's go for a bike ride," "Let's watch a movie"). And though I didn't dislike any of those things, I often didn't want to do them at the same time she did. But I found myself unable to tell her so. I felt anxious, therefore, because I felt helpless in general to determine the direction I wanted my life to go as long as she was in it. Up to that point, remaining unattached was the only strategy for maintaining my autonomy that I felt capable of executing. So I'd remained unmarried.

In that moment of understanding, however, I decided I didn't want to remain as I was. I needed to learn to take care of myself, of my needs, in the *midst* of a relationship, not apart from one, so that not only could I actually have one but also so that I could enjoy it. Rhea, I realized, wasn't just the woman I loved. She was also an opportunity for me to forge myself into a stronger, happier person. And in that moment I realized what my million-*daimoku* campaign had actually been about all along: not finding a wife, *but turning myself into a person who could have one.*

One week later, I asked Rhea to marry me.

Self-Transformation

According to Nichiren Buddhism, I told Tanya, when facing a problem we don't know how to solve, the key to victory lies in self-transformation. That we don't know how to solve a problem doesn't mean it's not solvable; it means we can't solve it if we remain as we are.

Self-transformation needn't be dramatic, though, to have a dramatic effect. It often means simply opening our minds to something to which they've been closed: perhaps to learning a new skill or sharpening an old one; to seeking expert help; to conquering self-doubt, fear of failure, or fear of success; or to developing a new attitude, adopting a new way of doing things, or forsaking a deluded belief. Even if we don't know *how* we need to change, the simple act of looking inward with a mind fully accepting of responsibility for strengthening what weaknesses it finds and correcting what misconceptions it holds frequently yields remarkable results.

"So, for example, if your marriage is in trouble," I told Tanya, "it may mean you need to learn to control your anger. Or if your marriage fails, it may mean you need to abandon your belief that you need a spouse in order to be happy. Or if you can't lose weight," I finished, "it may mean making sure there isn't some secondary gain keeping you from giving it your all."

She looked at me quizzically. "Secondary gain?"

"A hidden reason for wanting to be overweight," I clarified.

"Why would anyone *want* to be overweight?"

"It depends." Some studies, I said, suggest that overweight women with a history of sexual abuse may resist weight loss because obesity offers them protection against unwanted sexual attention.[30]

She cocked her head back sharply and shook it. "Not me."

I held up my hand in a gesture of appeasement. "I only meant that sometimes people don't realize they're working at cross-purposes with themselves."

"I'm pretty sure I only want to be thinner."

"Okay." I nodded. "Then you need to figure out what's been stopping you from losing as much weight as you want."

"That's easy," she said. "Overeating."

A Promise to Ourselves

Prayer in Nichiren Buddhism isn't a solemn request made of a supreme being to grant us something we fervently desire, but rather a vow, or promise, we make *to ourselves*. As such, it signifies a reaching out not to an external force, but rather to the wisdom and strength that exist within our own lives, a summoning of internal resources that poises us, like a sprinter lining up at a starting block, to launch ourselves forward under our own power.

Apart from what it may or may not accomplish in the realm of the supernatural, prayer in the Judeo-Christian tradition, in contrast, is more akin psychologically to wishing. And though most of us consider wishing harmless, it may not in fact be so. In one study, subjects who were even *reminded* of God demonstrated decreased motivation in pursuing goals, even if they weren't religious.[31] Another study showed wishful thinking was positively correlated with a *failure* to carry out New Year's resolutions.[32] And in yet a third study, entertaining positive fantasies about a desired future was actually found to sap the energy available to make it come true.[33] Not that imagining ourselves reaching a goal or daydreaming about it isn't fun and even sometimes useful, but if we allow it to take us over, it may actually inhibit us from taking action. Because wishing signifies a handing over of at least partial responsibility for the accomplishment of our goals to an outside power, it reinforces the belief, however subtly or subconsciously, that we're unable to realize our goals on our own. As a result, wishing hazards an important unintended consequence: passivity. Though it may not be a passivity significant enough to hamper our initial ambitions when our enthusiasm is high, the subtle drag it places on our drive may mean the difference, whenever things start to seem hopeless, between our continuing to rack our brains for solutions and our throwing up our hands in defeat.

Making a vow, or determination, on the other hand, produces the opposite effect: it prevents us from expecting others to act on our behalf and from making excuses for our own inaction. It reduces our patience for waiting to see if circumstances will bend in a more favorable direction and activates us instead to bend them ourselves. And when unforeseen obstacles appear and our spirits sag, remembering we always have the power to refresh our determination can reinvigorate us. (Though the strength of our determination may not be infinite, it is *indefinite*, meaning that when we look for its limit, we can't precisely find it; that is, we can always find a way to extend it.) When circumstances change, we may not be able to continue at the same rate or in quite the same way, but the choice to continue itself can never be taken from us. And when our response to failure is to summon an even greater determination to succeed, vowing to get back up after being knocked down not just once but again and again and again each day and with every obstacle that rises up to challenge us—attacking them, as Nichiren Daishonin wrote, like a "lion king who unleashes the same power whether he traps a tiny ant or attacks a fierce animal"[34]—then we'll have found a treasure even more valuable than any apparently foolproof plan to reach our goal: the determination necessary to seek a better one when it fails. For in demonstrating to *ourselves* that we can always summon more of it, our determination becomes to us like a good friend, its steady presence and our faith in its power imbuing us with confidence that no matter how many times we've failed, no matter how much we may want to quit, victory can still be ours.

"When your determination changes," Daisaku Ikeda, the third president of the Soka Gakkai, writes, "everything will begin to move in the direction you desire. The moment you resolve to be victorious, every nerve and fiber in your being will immediately orient itself toward your success. On the other hand, if you think, 'This is never going to work out,' then at that instant every cell in your being will be deflated and give up the fight. Then everything really will move in the direction of failure."[35]

"That's *exactly* what's going on with me," Tanya said.

I nodded. "But no matter how many times you've failed in the past," I told her, "you can always renew your determination to try again."

"And if you just keep failing?"

"Then you try something different."

She looked at me glumly. "Like what?"

"The way you define your goal, for one thing," I offered. "In fact, let's talk about that. What exactly do you want to accomplish? How much weight do you actually want to lose?"

She paused as if she hadn't considered the question until just that moment. "I don't need to be a swimsuit model," she said. "I just want to look good. The best *I* can look."

"That sounds reasonable," I said with a nod. "But you might consider getting more specific." Studies show that the more concrete our goals, I told her, the more likely we are to reach them.[36] So we shouldn't aim just to "exercise more." We should plan to lift weights three times a week, or run five miles a day. Likewise, she shouldn't just aim to "look good," I said. She should pick a specific weight she wanted to reach.

Tanya shuddered. "No way," she said. "I'd just be setting myself up for failure."

"Aiming high does risk greater disappointment," I acknowledged. "On the other hand, *too big* is just about the right size for dreams. What we're able to achieve in life is only a fraction of what we set out to. So if you start out with expectations that are too low, you'll end up not being able to accomplish much at all." Research also shows, I emphasized, that people are more likely to regret the choices they *didn't* make—the things they *didn't* try—than those they did.[37]

Further, studies show that *unrealistic* goals inspire greater effort than do goals that are more pragmatic.[38] In one experiment, for example, when women were exposed to advertising that induced unrealistic expectations about the effects of dieting, they were more likely to restrain their food intake.[39] Research also shows that people who take on difficult goals outperform people who take on easy goals, placing difficult goals, in many cases, paradoxically within *closer* reach than easy ones.[40] "Not that you shouldn't march toward ambitious goals in small, manageable steps," I said. "Just that you're more likely to give it your all when you try to lose fifty pounds than when you try to lose five."

Panic rose in Tanya's eyes. "Right now I'm not even sure I could lose two."

"You've already lost twenty. You know what you *need* to do. You've just lost confidence that you can keep doing it."

"Something always gets me off track," she said.

"There's no reason to think what you've been doing will suddenly stop working just because someone asked you out on a date. We just need to figure out a way for you to feel like you can keep doing it. So why don't you start by telling me what's been working so far, and we'll go from there?"

She paused to take stock. "Well, I stopped eating pasta," she said. "And bread. And McDonald's." She rolled her eyes at the pain of the sacrifice. "¡Ay, caramba!"

"Fast food's a tough one," I said.

"Don't remind me."

"How'd you manage to give it up?"

She shrugged. "I just made myself."

"What about the pasta and bread? Carbohydrates are everywhere."

She rolled her eyes again. "Tell me about it."

"So you just made yourself give them up, too?"

"Pretty much."

"What do you do if that's what's being served?"

She shrugged. "Eat a salad."

I glanced briefly at my computer screen to remind myself what her most recent lab tests showed, noting her cholesterol was still high. "I'm glad that's been working for you, but here might be something you could do a little differently," I said, turning back to her. "The problem with using willpower to resist temptation is that it often doesn't work. People beat themselves up constantly for what they perceive to be their lack of it, but as far as mental forces go, willpower is actually pretty weak." In fact, studies show that willing ourselves to avoid thinking about a temptation is actually associated with an *increase* in the likelihood of surrendering to it (suppression of food-related thoughts, for example, is associated with an *increase* in food cravings and binge eating).[41] Additionally, how effectively we can use willpower to resist a temptation depends largely on our degree of *visceral activation*—meaning that how hungry, tired, thirsty, drug-craving, physically uncomfortable, or sexually aroused we are at the moment temptation confronts us, the greater our degree of activation and the less effective our willpower will be.[42] "Which is why the hungrier we are when we're confronted with a delicious-looking piece of cake, the less able we are to resist eating it."

What's more, research also suggests that the more we use our will-power, the weaker it becomes. In one study, subjects were asked to eat a plate of radishes while being denied a plate of freshly baked chocolate chip cookies and then asked to solve a puzzle (which unknown to them was unsolvable, enabling experimenters to use the length of time they continued to try as an index of their willpower). In comparison to the control group that was asked only to solve the unsolvable puzzle (and therefore didn't need to exert willpower to resist eating chocolate chip cookies prior to trying), subjects prevented from eating the cookies gave up on the puzzle almost twice as quickly.[43] Other studies have shown that willpower wanes when it's used to suppress stereotypes, control prejudicial reactions, accommodate unpleasant behaviors in romantic relationships, manage impressions of others, and restrain eating.[44] Just why this happens, however, isn't clear. Though some researchers have argued that willpower relies on a single fuel source—namely, glucose—and that as glucose levels diminish so does the strength of our will, the data don't entirely support this.[45] (Additionally, when either our mood or our motivation is increased in between tasks requiring self-control, the strength of our willpower *doesn't* decrease.[46]) Thus, though willpower may represent an effective tool with which to fight temptation for a fortunate few, willpower's effectiveness for the majority of us must be considered inconsistent at best.

"So where does *that* leave me?" Tanya asked despondently.

Distraction and Avoidance

In 1970 psychologist Walter Mischel famously placed a cookie in front of a group of children and gave them a choice: they could eat the cookie immediately, or they could wait until he returned from a brief errand and then be rewarded with a second. If they didn't wait, however, they'd be allowed to eat only the first one. Not surprisingly, once he left the room, many children ate the cookie almost immediately. A few, though, resisted eating the first cookie long enough to receive the second. Mischel termed these children *high-delay children*. How did they succeed? "Instead of focusing prolonged attention on the object for which they were waiting," he writes, "they avoided looking at it. Some covered their eyes with their hands, rested their heads on their arms, and found other similar techniques for averting their eyes from the reward objects." In other words, Mischel concluded, *distraction* is superior to willpower for delaying gratification.[47]

"Willpower," I told Tanya, "is just one *tool* of our determination, and a poor one at that. So when the urge to overeat, or to smoke, or to have sex, or to do anything you find yourself craving but don't really want to do comes over you, don't use willpower to try to *resist* it," I said. "Use something else to *distract* you *from* it."

Tanya looked at me helplessly. "What?"

"One of the most distracting things there is," I said. "*Another pleasure*." In a second study, Mischel placed two marshmallows side by side in front of a different group of children to whom he explained, as in the previous study, that eating the first before he returned to the room would mean they couldn't eat the second. He then instructed one group of them to imagine when he stepped out of the room how much marshmallows are like clouds: round, white, and puffy. (He instructed a control group, in contrast, to imagine how sweet and chewy and soft they were.) A third group he instructed to visualize the crunchiness and saltiness of pretzels. Perhaps not surprisingly, the children who visualized the qualities of the marshmallows that were unrelated to eating them (that is, the way in which they were similar to clouds) waited almost three times longer than children who were instructed to visualize how delicious the marshmallows would taste. Most intriguing, however, was that picturing the pleasure of eating *pretzels* produced the longest delay in gratification of all. Apparently, imagining the pleasure they'd feel from indulging in an *unavailable* temptation distracted the children even more than cognitively restructuring the way they thought about the temptation before them.[48]

"So when you want to avoid something tempting," I offered, "go shopping instead. Or watch a movie. Or listen to music. Something you find genuinely pleasurable. Or if for some reason you can't engage in an alternative pleasure, or shouldn't for some reason, *think* about doing it instead. For example, when you see a pizza, *think* about eating ice cream. Or," I added, "turn your focus to a problem you're trying to solve. Problem-solving is incredibly engaging, and engagement is the key to distraction."

"Huh . . . ," Tanya said thoughtfully.

"Also, whatever you decide to do when temptation strikes," I said, "have it planned out ahead of time." Studies show that making decisions—even simple ones—*also* depletes willpower.[49] "If you're constantly deciding what alternative pleasures to think about or pursue each time you face a temptation, you become progressively less likely to be able to make the strategy of distraction work. Which is when rationalizations gain the power to convince you it's okay to do what you're trying so hard not to. The key is having your response ready. To make it a *rule* instead of an on-the-spot decision. Something that doesn't require conscious thought." For example, I told her, she should figure out ahead of time what she was going to have for lunch at work every day *before* she entered the cafeteria, and simply make eating it an automatic rule.

Research shows we're most likely to succeed in maintaining a new behavior when we do it without thinking.[50] Not that getting ourselves to engage in a behavior consistently enough to turn it *into* a habit is easy. For one thing, the time required to establish a new habit varies tremendously, in one study taking anywhere from 18 to 254 days.[51] For another, and

not surprisingly, the more complex the desired behavior, the longer turning it into a habit seems to take, decreasing the likelihood that we can
turn it into a habit at all.[52] Finally, when confronted with the need to
choose between competing behaviors, we tend to follow the path of least
resistance, the path that requires the least amount of energy, which isn't
necessarily the path along which our desired behavior lies.

Here, however, is where the creative use of willpower *can* help us: not
to resist temptation directly, but to lower the energy required to initiate a desired behavior (like exercising) while raising the energy required
to initiate competing, undesired behaviors (like watching television). In
this way, we *decrease* the effort required for us to act in the way we want
and *increase* the effort required for us to act in a way we'd rather not. We
might, for instance, choose to move our treadmill up from the basement
into the living room where we spend more of our time while simultaneously removing the batteries from the television remote control and placing them in an inconvenient location. By placing the desired behavior
along the path of least resistance, we turn it into the behavior we're most
likely to repeat. And the more we repeat it, the more likely it is to become
a habit, and the less and less we need it to lie along the path of least resistance. The key lies in recognizing that the energy required to initiate a
desired behavior often needs to be even lower than we expect. "Which is
why the reason moving a treadmill from the basement to the living room
may mean the difference between using it and not. Despite our believing it shouldn't, having to walk that small extra distance to the basement
often requires a level of energy that's beyond us, especially when other
habits, like television, beckon within easier reach."[53]

"Huh," Tanya said again.

"You also need to think about what you want to have *cue* your habits," I said. Research shows that habits are tremendously context dependent, meaning they tend to break down when their cues are changed or

removed. In one study of college students, the strongest predictor of a failure to continue a program of regular exercise when transferring schools
was the choice to exercise in a different location than they had at their old
school (for example, in their dormitory rather than the school gym).[54]
"So make sure whatever cues you pick—where you exercise, what time
of day you exercise, if you're going to exercise with a partner or not—are
things you can keep relatively constant."

"Got it," Tanya said.

I paused. "The other thing to try is avoidance." In another part of his
first study, Mischel also tempted children with a cookie, but this time
took it away from half of them when he left the room (telling the children
from whom he took it that they could signal their desire to eat it immediately by ringing a bell). What he found was that the effect of *removing*
the temptation was even more striking than visualizing an unavailable
pleasure: six out of eight children who couldn't view the cookie waited a
full fifteen minutes before signaling their desire to eat it; those who could
view it, on the other hand, waited on average less than a minute.[55]

I found this strategy worked well for me, too, I told Tanya. When it
came to writing, I'd always been hamstrung by my need to achieve perfec-
tion. From blog posts to magazine articles to book manuscripts to screen-
plays, my dogged pursuit of flawlessness was the single greatest obstacle
to my completing almost every creative work I'd ever started. I'd sometimes even found myself fiddling with a single sentence for hours. I continued to have trouble finishing almost everything I started until one day
I realized that word processors had made rewriting simply too easy and
therefore too hard to resist. So I solved my problem by *avoiding* its cause:
I turned my computer off and began composing my first drafts on paper.

The strategy of avoidance even seems to work for drug addiction.
Studies have found that when drug addicts avoid situations that cue their
desire to use cocaine, for example, it increases their likelihood of abstain-

ing.[56] "So if you really want to stop eating at McDonald's," I concluded, "you stop *going* to McDonald's. You don't even drive down the street it's on. If you want to stop snacking on bagels in front of the television, you stop *buying* them. If you want to stop smoking, you stop going to bars and parties where people are going to be smoking. You stop letting people smoke in your house. You get someone else to buy your groceries so you're not confronted with rows of cigarette cartons at the checkout counter. You stop hanging out with people who smoke."

"Wow," Tanya said. "Really?"

I nodded.

"You don't think that's kind of harsh?"

I shrugged. "It all depends on how badly you want to quit."

Commitment

In the Stephen King short story "Quitters, Inc." a man encounters an old college friend in an airport bar who tells him about a company—Quitters, Inc.—that boasts a 98 percent success rate in getting people to quit smoking. Intrigued, he goes to their offices, listens to their marketing pitch, and signs their contract—only then to be told the grisly secret of their success: from that moment onward, they inform him, he'll be maintained under twenty-four-hour surveillance. The first time one of their operatives sees him smoke a cigarette, his wife will be brought in and, without malice or prejudice, administered a painful electric shock. With each subsequent infraction, then, the voltage will be increased until he either quits smoking—or his wife dies. Needless to say, after only one slip (followed by one electric shock), he manages to quit. (At which point they decide he's too heavy and put him on a weight loss program whose milestones they tell him he has to meet unless he wants to see his wife's fingers cut off one by one.)[57]

Certainly people do things all the time without being committed to them. But if we lack a strong commitment to our goals, we'll lack a critical ingredient for success that desire alone, no matter how consuming, won't provide us: *a willingness to work at it.*

This is especially true of our ultimate goal, happiness, which comes within reach not because we *desire* it but because we *commit* to pursuing it. A sustained increase in happiness never occurs by accident or without effort, despite the prevalent belief that it will inevitably appear as a byproduct of doing things we enjoy. And though some also think that actively aiming to attain happiness will somehow drive it further away like a tepid lover being repelled by too much attention, nothing could be further from the truth.

To accomplish a great goal, then, we have to begin with a great determination. But a great determination requires an equally great motivation. Without the will to use it, even the most powerful force in the world will accomplish nothing. As Nichiren Daishonin wrote, "A sword is useless in the hands of a coward."[58]

Finding the Motivation

So how do we muster enough determination to transform ourselves into people who can achieve the things we want? The same way we create new habits, resist irresistible temptations, and continue fighting when victory seems impossible. "By caring about our dreams so much," I said to Tanya, "that whatever we have to do to achieve them seems a small price to pay."

Tanya remained silent but nodded her agreement. I leaned my chin in my hand. "So tell me," I said, "why exactly do you want to lose weight?"

"Because I'm too fat," she replied with a strained smile. "I want to look better."

"Fair enough," I said. "But when obstacles arise, being able to bring to mind the *most* compelling reason we started marching toward a goal often means the difference between our deciding whether to continue or to quit. So I don't mean to be intentionally obtuse about this, but is wanting to look better your *most* compelling reason?"

"I don't know . . . ," she said, exasperated. "I also want to be healthier," she offered. We'd discussed many times in the past how weight loss would likely improve her diabetes, she reminded me.

"That's always a good reason," I said, but her tone left me thinking it wasn't one she found particularly rousing. "Is there anything else?"

She sighed. "Dr. Lickerman, what *isn't* there? I can't go on airplanes. I can't ride a bicycle. I can't even sit comfortably in a movie theater. My weight is the most defining characteristic of my life." She said all this without emotion, however, as if she'd so long been accustomed to these facts that they no longer bothered her.

Despite feeling a sudden burst of unpleasant lightness in the pit of my stomach, I pressed on. "What about dating?"

She flushed, and with a self-conscious flick of her eyes to the side answered, "Sure. Eventually."

"Do you think *that* might be your most compelling reason?"

"It's up there."

"But not number one?"

She looked away, her expression troubled, as if she were debating whether to answer. "No," she said.

"No?" I asked, surprised.

She looked away again. Then she turned back to me. "There *is* something else," she said. Then she added, "Everything I say in here is confidential, right?"

I nodded somberly, pulled abruptly between amusement and concern that a reason she wanted to lose weight might be sensitive enough to require my confidentiality.

She took a deep breath. "I want to be a mom."

I paused, unsure for a moment how to respond. "You think for that to happen you have to be thin?"

She sighed. "I don't know." Yet over the years, she admitted, she'd distanced herself from her desire because as she continued to fail at losing weight she gradually stopped believing she would ever find someone who wanted to marry her.

"Even though you know—" I stopped myself. "You know overweight people get married and have children all the time."

She nodded absently. "You know what the hardest thing is?" she asked suddenly. "Accepting my body like it is at the same time I'm trying to change it. How do you motivate yourself to lose weight when you're also trying to like the way you are?"

I grimaced sympathetically. "Yeah," I agreed. I thought about how studies also show that food can be as addicting as cocaine to the brains of people who are obese,[59] as well as how food also seems to help fend off negative emotions, not only through the distracting effects of pleasure but also through mechanisms entirely independent of it.[60] "Losing weight is just really, really hard," I said.

"I guess I really *am* at cross-purposes with myself," she muttered.

The Reasons We Care

All the more reason, I said, to be clear about what was fueling her determination. For in the same way we may not be aware why we've become discouraged, we may not be aware of the reasons that motivate us the most. It may be, for example, a reason about which we feel conflicted, embarrassed, or even repulsed. So we simply ignore it, or even lie to ourselves about it. But this is a mistake. Even if we think we *shouldn't* be motivated by something, if we actually are, we shouldn't hesitate to use it when our determination starts to wane.

So I wondered, I told Tanya, if she shouldn't *embrace* the idea that she needed to be thin to become a mother. The reason, I said, was this: Another way we can fan the flames of our determination is by flinging ourselves into a situation that urgently demands escape, but which we can only effect by accomplishing our goal—that is, in contrast to the way in which Stephen King's hapless protagonist was trapped, *by intentionally trapping ourselves.* For example, by committing to a rigid deadline someone else requires us to meet, someone who wants us to be successful not for our benefit but for their own. (As discussed in Chapter 1, our aversion to loss—in this case, to the loss of the respect or goodwill of someone else whom we disappoint by failing—is a far more potent motivator than the promise of gain.) Or, I suggested hesitantly, we can trap ourselves with a motivating belief. "In your case," I said, "that you can't become a mother unless you lose weight."

"So you're saying—I should—what exactly?" Tanya asked.

"Make wanting a child matter as much as you can. In every *way* you can." Whenever she got discouraged in her attempts to lose weight and wanted to give up, I explained, she should imagine as vividly as possible the child she wanted *never being born.* Her desire to look better, to be healthy, and to find a mate were all potent incentives for her to lose weight, to be sure. But if her desire to have a child was the thing about which she felt the most passionate, consciously and firmly lashing it to her desire to lose weight would propel her forward in her efforts more powerfully than any of them.

Her first reaction was to express reluctance, not so much because of a concern that making motherhood mentally contingent on losing weight was psychologically unhealthy (we both agreed it was), but because she thought that failing to lose weight *and* having her hopes to become a mother dashed at the same time would be too much to bear.

"I understand completely," I said, feeling ambivalent about the suggestion myself. "It was just an idea." And certainly not one, I was careful to add, that would by any means guarantee success, nor one that I was arguing was required for it. But if raising a child represented her greatest dream, I said, it might also represent a lever she could pull to accomplish her greatest personal transformation.

The Power Of Feedback

Three months later, Tanya returned to see me having lost an additional 15 pounds. Now weighing 240, she'd set her sights on an even more audacious goal: 175. But she'd decided she was going to give herself two years to do it. Also, she planned to lose the weight in stages. With each 20-pound drop she planned to pause "just to make sure she was still happy." If she was, she said, she'd keep going.

She told me that thinking about the child she wanted to have when temptation would strike had actually been helpful. She'd also stopped shopping for food she didn't think she should eat, now avoided social functions where the "wrong" food would tempt her, and had made a habit out of swimming every day after work.

She'd also begun making effective use of feedback. Some investigators, I'd told her previously, have argued that positive feedback increases our confidence and negative feedback undermines it. But other investigators have said that by making us feel successful, positive feedback sends us the signal that less effort is necessary and actually *decreases* our willingness to work hard. Negative feedback, in contrast, signals that more effort is needed and actually *increases* our willingness to work hard.

"So which is it?" she'd asked me.

"Both," I'd answered. Negative feedback, research suggests, helps when it signals insufficient *progress* (as opposed to insufficient *commitment*). For example, if a dieter chastises herself for her insufficient progress when she fails to follow her diet at breakfast, she's actually *more* likely to follow her diet at lunch. On the other hand, if she chastises herself for her lack of commitment when she fails to follow her diet at breakfast, she's *less* likely to follow her diet at lunch. Positive feedback, in contrast, helps when it signals a strong *commitment* (as opposed to sufficient *progress*). If a dieter congratulates herself for her strong commitment when she faithfully *follows* her diet at breakfast, she's actually *more* likely to follow her diet at lunch. But if instead she congratulates herself on her outstanding progress when she faithfully follows her diet at breakfast, she's actually *less* likely to follow her diet at lunch.[61]

"Wait," Tanya had said. "So positive feedback isn't what—wait—I'm confused."

"Just remember it this way," I'd said. "Let success mean only that you're committed, and failure only that you've made insufficient progress."

In the last month, however, she now informed me, her progress had all but ceased. "I'm doing all the same things I was," she said. "I just don't get it."

I told her that this often happened to people as they tried to lose weight; their bodies are willing to surrender pounds at certain weights but not at others, and that if she redoubled her efforts she might yet be able to find a way to slip down from her current weight-loss plateau. I also encouraged her to make her goal not continuing to lose weight but *continuing itself.* "That way," I said, "when everything seems hopeless, you'll still have something to celebrate: your success at being able to persevere. Even when your true goal seems hopelessly out of reach, you can always succeed at not giving up. And if you succeed at not giving up long enough, your true goal will follow eventually as a matter of course."

Never Be Defeated

Each time I saw Tanya over the following nine months she weighed less than she had the visit before. Two hundred thirty pounds. Two hundred twenty pounds. Two hundred sixteen. She was like a slowly deflating balloon; each time she appeared her clothes looked again one size too big. Soon her blood sugars normalized, and I took her off her diabetes medication.

Then she appeared one day in my office in tears. "We broke up," she told me, meaning she and Tom, the man who'd asked her out just as she'd first begun to lose weight and whom she'd been dating ever since.

"Tanya, I'm so sorry."

Dabbing at her eyes, she waved my concern away. "It's for the best," she said. Tom hadn't wanted children, she now confessed. And though she'd accepted this initially, as her weight had dropped, her resolve to become a mother had grown. In the end, she told me, *she'd* decided to break up with *him*.

"The other thing is, I'm moving to Texas."

She'd found a job in Houston teaching at a Montessori school. She'd chosen to move out of state, she said, because she wanted to live in a place where no one had ever known her as obese. I glanced down at her vitals and saw my nurse had drawn a circle around her current weight: 198 pounds. I looked up and smiled.

"That's a lot of change to handle all at once," I said. "How are you holding up?"

"You know, I'm okay," she said. "I'm actually feeling kind of strong these days."

I nodded. "That's the great thing about making a strong commitment: it doesn't just enable you to accomplish the goal you're committed to; it engenders hardiness in general."[62]

"It totally does," she agreed.

I told her my office would make copies of her medical records and send them to her new address. "Don't ever quit," I said as we parted for the last time. She thanked me for my compassionate care and left.

One year later, she sent me a letter. She'd learned of my son's birth from another patient of mine, she wrote, and was dropping me a quick note to offer her congratulations. She said she was doing well and liked Texas very much ("minus the heat").

Inside the envelope she'd also included a wallet-sized photograph picturing a man in a black tuxedo and bow tie. And next to him, smiling back at me in a white strapless wedding dress, her face gently pressed against his, was a Tanya I barely recognized. And as my gaze dropped lower, I found the explanation for my brief inability to place her in something she'd circled several times in thin black ink at the bottom of the photograph, a testament to the amazing power of her resolve and a final declaration of her victory: "168!"

4

Expect Obstacles

Once we make a determination, whether to pursue our life's mission or merely our most trivial wish, we typically begin to take action. At which point, wrote Nichiren Daishonin, "The three obstacles and four devils will invariably appear, and the wise will rejoice while the foolish will retreat."[1] Action almost always elicits resistance from our surroundings because people, places, and things are saturated with inertia and reflexively resist change. The wise, however, know not only to anticipate such obstacles, but also to welcome them, recognizing barriers not only as inevitable but also as precursors to success.

In fact, according to Nichiren Buddhism, encountering obstacles after we've made a determination isn't just an indication we're making progress. It's often the very thing required for victory. An oft-quoted metaphor compares the process of pursuing a goal to an airplane accelerating down a runway. Once the airplane starts moving, wind resistance builds rapidly, making it progressively harder for the airplane to reach the speed required for takeoff. But because of the shape of its wings, the plane is able to use this resistance to generate the very thing that enables it to become airborne: lift. Similarly, according to Nichiren Buddhism, though obstacles invariably arise in the course of goal pursuit, because of our innate capacity to learn from them, we're able to use them to generate the very thing that enables us to overcome them: strength. In Nichiren Buddhism, encountering obstacles is thus considered, paradoxically, the path to a life of "comfort and ease." For only in facing a strong enemy are we able to become strong ourselves. And only in developing strength can we navigate life's challenges with a sense of confidence and calm.

Not that merely encountering obstacles by any means *guarantees* we'll be able to become stronger. Which is why, though the wise may understand that obstacles represent opportunities for personal growth, genuinely "rejoicing" when they appear is difficult, to say the least. As I mentioned in Chapter 3, especially when we don't know *how* to transform an obstacle into a benefit, more often than not we decide we can't.

Such was the case with my patient Paul, a forty-one-year-old American history teacher at a local South Side Chicago junior high school, who came to see me following his first arrest for drunk driving. Pale and thin with stringy red hair and freckles, he'd told me three months before when I first met him that he regularly counseled his students about the dangers of substance abuse, organizing and delivering lectures about it several times a year. So when I'd asked him about his own drug use, I did so only out of habit, presuming he avoided it. "Actually," he admitted, "sometimes a little cocaine now and then."

I looked at him in surprise. "You counsel your kids not to use drugs, but then you use them yourself?"

"Just once in a while," he said.

"For how long?"

"I don't know . . ." He paused to consider. "Maybe . . . ten years? Twelve? Like I said, it's just once in a while. And nothing bad's happened yet," he added cheerfully.

"Yet," I emphasized.

"I know," he said. "I should probably stop. The problem is, Dr. Licker-man, I *like* it."

"That *is* a problem," I reflected.

"It's all good," he said.

I was struck by how indifferent he seemed to the risk he was taking. "Have you ever thought about what would happen if any of your students found out?"

His eyebrows rose. Then he looked down at the floor, an embarrassed, almost painful smile tugging at the corners of his mouth. Then, after a few moments, he looked back up. "Well," he said quietly. "That would be devastating."

Now, Paul told me, his worst fears had been realized, and he was panic-stricken. When the arresting officers had searched his car, they'd found a gram of cocaine he'd hidden in his glove compartment. Disastrously, the parent of one of his students had read about his arrest in the newspaper and reported it to his principal. Word soon got out and now a group of parents was demanding he be fired.

"What does your principal say?" I asked apprehensively.

"He thinks I should get into rehab."

"But not fired."

He shook his head. "He's actually being very supportive."

"So what do *you* think? About rehab, I mean." We'd discussed the issue several times in the past in relation to his alcohol use, but despite a pattern of elevated liver enzymes that suggested the presence of alcoholic hepatitis as well as a number of positive responses to the CAGE questions (a screen-ing instrument designed to identify alcoholism), he'd always refused.

He shook his head. "I can quit anytime. That's not the issue."

I nodded. "Your students."

"My students." He picked some lint off his pants with a trembling hand. "Dr. Lickerman, I don't mean to sound . . . overly dramatic . . . but this . . . this is the worst thing that's ever happened to me. I know it's ridiculous for me to say it now, but I wish to God I'd . . ." His voice trailed off as he shook his head in self-reproach. "Well," he said, shrugging. "I guess everything's obvious in hindsight."

"Actually, it often is," I said. "So don't be so sure you know how *this* is going to turn out either."

He smiled. "I appreciate the encouragement. But I'm pretty sure I do."

But I wouldn't be deterred. "The idea that this is the worst thing that's ever happened to you is just that, Paul—an idea. It's a story you're telling yourself. That's all." Our minds are story-telling machines, I told him, constantly making predictions about the significance of everything that happens to us. But so rapidly and unconsciously do they do it that we often fail to realize our predictions are only that—theories, not unalterable facts.

He shrugged. "I'm just telling you how it feels."

"And I'm telling you the future's still unwritten," I said gently. "It may *feel* like the worst thing that's ever happened to you, but it's still possible to *make* it the best."

His eyes widened slightly. "With all due respect, Dr. Lickerman, you don't know what you're talking about."

"We don't change because we want to," I said evenly. "We change because we're forced to. Change *requires* pain." Aversive stimuli, I told him, are now recognized to contribute to growth even at the neurological level. According to recent research, learning itself—in fact, *thinking* itself—causes inflammation that, when followed by a sufficient stimulus-free period (meaning rest), actually increases our resistance to a number of neurologic conditions, including migraines, seizures, and even dementia.[2] Though no evidence yet links this finding to *psychological* resilience, it does at least suggest we're actually built to *benefit* from some degree of pain.

"But Dr. Lickerman," Paul said with a tolerant smile, "I don't want to change at all."

"I understand," I said. "But I also understand that knowing what this has done to your students has absolutely crushed you."

He winced as if I'd pricked him with a needle. He swallowed and lowered his gaze to the floor. "More than you know."

"Then don't just make this the best thing that ever happened to *you*," I said. "Make it the best thing that ever happened to *them*."

Making Use of Adversity

From the Buddhist perspective, I told him, all of us have the capacity to make use of any circumstance, no matter how awful, to create value. This ability to "change poison into medicine," as it's known in Nichiren Buddhism, makes plausible the transformation of even the most horrific tragedy *into something that enables us to become happier*. Or at least happier in ways we wouldn't otherwise have been. Research suggests, for example, that even after the worst kind of loss most of us could imagine—the death of a child—benefit frequently occurs. In one study, for example, 81 percent of bereaved parents actually reported feeling stronger as a result of their loss, 61 percent more courageous, and 38 percent that their relationship with their surviving children improved.[3] Not to minimize the enormity of such a deprivation or to suggest that such benefits actually make up for it—just that such benefits are indeed possible.

Paul's head snapped back in astonishment. "I can't even imagine how...."

"Most of the things we think aren't possible are really just incredibly unlikely or unbelievably hard," I said. "Usually the reason we say a problem isn't solvable isn't because the solution doesn't exist; it's because the solution isn't what we want it to be. It either seems too hard or too time-consuming, or we aren't willing to risk sacrificing something we already have to pursue it. Or we think from today's perspective we see all possible solutions and that none of them will work." I shook my head. "We think because we can't see the exact path to success from where we stand today, the path doesn't exist at all, and we let our misguided confidence in our restricted vision squash our determination. But our determination is what *creates* the path—our determination to make *use* of adversity rather than escape it."

He was listening quietly now.

"I'm not saying what's happened to you isn't bad," I continued. "But that doesn't mean it can't lead to an even greater good. We always think we can see at one glance the entirety of our lives from beginning to end and know the ultimate significance of every event the moment it happens. But we can't. In fact, the idea that such an ultimate significance even *exists* is an illusion. The meaning of events changes constantly as a result of the events that follow it. Think about a football player who suffers a career-ending injury. The worst thing possible, right? Until the plane he would have taken with his teammates crashes on its way to a game, killing everyone aboard."

Earthly Desires Are Enlightenment

But we don't change poison into medicine by waiting for circumstances to flip the significance of events from bad to good. We change poison into medicine by taking action to flip the significance of events ourselves. And not just by *reframing* adversity ("at least it's just a stroke, not cancer"), but by actually *overcoming* it. Not by *rationalizing* failure ("I didn't want that job anyway"), but by turning it into a genuine victory.

Of course, for victory to *be* victory it has to *feel* like victory; no consolation prize will do. Yet what victory actually *is* may not be what we think or even what we're able, before actually accomplishing it, to imagine. It may mean, on the one hand, turning a failure into the cause of an even greater success, whether one we intended, like scoring above the mean upon retaking the National Boards, or one we didn't, like becoming a better doctor as a result. Or it may mean something far less noticeable but ultimately even more significant: changing the way we think.

In contrast to other forms of Buddhism that consider the elimination of earthly desires the key to happiness, Nichiren Buddhism teaches that earthly desires *are* enlightenment. In other words, any and every determination we might ever make has a dual purpose: not only to enable us to accomplish whatever goal we've set for ourselves, but also in the process to induce personal growth. For only as a direct result of struggling to *fulfill* our desires, of facing and overcoming the obstacles that arise in the process, are we able to acquire wisdom that increases our resilience and thus our ability to enjoy life (the accumulation of wisdom also eventually enabling us to abandon the dichotomy of "good experience" and "bad experience" altogether in favor of a perspective that considers *all* experience an opportunity to become happier).

Such wisdom may appear in the form of insights that lend new meaning to past events, as when a patient of Frankl's realized that in surviving his wife's death (which had caused him to become severely depressed) he'd spared *her* the experience of suffering over *his* death, which transformed his surviving her into a compassionate sacrifice, and thus caused his depression to end.[4] Or it may appear in the form of insights that free us from delusion, as when I learned I didn't need my girlfriend to love me to be happy.

According to Nichiren Buddhism, we don't feel pain in life because we're denied our attachments; we feel pain in life because we mistakenly believe we can't be happy without them. But because we're frequently unaware that we're too attached to things, pain itself is often necessary for the prevention of further pain, not only signaling as it frequently does the presence of such delusional attachments (much like physical pain signals bodily injury), but also providing the main impetus for abandoning them (as when I needed to experience the pain of losing a woman's love to be motivated to learn that I didn't need the love of a woman to be happy).

Not that this justifies anyone intentionally inflicting pain on someone else. Nor that pain in and of itself guarantees we'll be able to recognize whatever delusional attachments may be responsible for its cause. Many alcoholics, for example, drink themselves into ruin and death without ever realizing their misery was caused by their attachment to alcohol. Pain may indeed be necessary, but it's clearly not sufficient. To gain wisdom from adversity, we need something else.

Unfortunately, just what that something else is—exactly why insight strikes some people and not others, and why it strikes those it does *when* it does—remains a mystery. The most we can say is that people who succeed in turning pain and suffering from a wholly aversive experience into a catalyst for self-transformation seem to be able to do so only because they make such self-transformation their specific focus.[5]

For that decision to transform ourselves is all we really have; we can't, for example, know *what* experiences we require to shake loose from our mistaken beliefs about what we need to be happy, mistaken beliefs which, to borrow another metaphor, are as resistant to shattering as a brick wall is to our running through it. Nor do we know all the ways we might need to fail to ultimately succeed. The true path to success, the path we actually end up traveling whether in turning a failure into success or adversity into wisdom, is almost never what we envisioned at the outset. We may *think* we enjoy an unobstructed view all the way down its length from beginning to end, but we can never fully anticipate how obstacles will conspire to change it, as they almost always do. Rarely is adversity overcome as easily as we want or any goal worth achieving accomplished exactly as planned.

Which, ironically, turns our lack of ability to predict the true path to victory into a benefit: most things turn out to be far more difficult to accomplish than we anticipate, and if we could accurately forecast the actual degree of hardship that accomplishing something is likely to involve, we might very well refuse to try.

"That all sounds great, Dr. Lickerman," Paul said. "But I don't see a path here at all."

"That doesn't mean it doesn't exist."

"How do you know?"

"Paul," I said, "do you really think you're the first person who was ever caught lying about using drugs? Or shamed by it?"

He smiled almost bashfully. "Not the first," he admitted. "No."

"No matter how unique you think you are, no matter how unusual you think your situation is, when you think about how many people there are in the world—how many people there have been—it's hard to imagine that someone else at some time hasn't had your problem and found a way to solve it. Which means a path to solving it almost certainly exists. You just have to find it. Believing in your ability to transform poison into medicine when you don't know how, and often won't except in retrospect, is difficult, I admit. But that's the confidence you have to find. That's the confidence that represents your greatest defense against discouragement."

"So what are you suggesting?" Then he added, "Besides rehab, I mean."

Rehab, of course, was exactly what I was suggesting. Or at least where I thought he stood his best chance to solve his most serious problem. But I also believed what I was telling him: that the path to victory couldn't be planned or predicted, but only discovered; that we turn poison into medicine by making a determination to take the next step in front of us, by launching ourselves into whatever appears to be the most prudent action. Not that we can't or shouldn't have a plan—just that we shouldn't allow ourselves to become so attached to it that we refuse to pursue other avenues when we find them better. Like a blind man with only a vague notion of the way home and his courage to guide him, we stumble along by trial and error, guided by the notion that though we can't necessarily see it, the path to a victory of some kind does exist.

"I'm suggesting you summon a great resolve," I told him. "Once you begin to conceive of adversity as the raw material necessary for advancement and personal growth, so does it become. But besides that? Question your assumptions. Challenge your weaknesses. Good advice grates on the ear, so if you don't like what you're hearing, you should probably listen to it."

"I suppose that makes sense," he said, but his expression was uncertain.

"The way you *don't* change poison into medicine is by doing what most of us do when everything we can think of to solve a problem fails," I said. "Which is go back to things *we've already tried*. Because they still won't work. Which, of course, doesn't stop us from trying them several more times. And which, by the way, despite what Einstein said, isn't the definition of insanity; it's the definition of cowardice."

Paul remained silent for a moment. Then he shook his head. "Even if you're right, even if there were some way my students would forgive me, I'll still never be able to undo the damage I've already done."

An image of my own son, who was just two years old, abruptly came into my mind—an image of him one day watching some future role model of *his* fall the way Paul had fallen. And as I imagined what he might feel upon discovering that such a trusted and beloved mentor was in fact a hypocrite and how easily he might turn against any message delivered by such a messenger, I felt a small lump rise in my throat.

I shrugged. "How can you not *try*?"

The Stories We Tell Ourselves

Optimism, it turns out, isn't just defined as the tendency to expect things to turn out better than probability predicts, nor is pessimism defined only as the tendency to expect things to turn out more poorly. Both terms are also used to describe the way we think about the *causes of adversity*, pessimism in particular being defined as the tendency to think about them in a way that makes us feel powerless. A pessimistic *self-explanatory style*, then, describes the tendency to attribute the causes of adversity to forces that are internal ("This is all my fault"), universal ("This affects absolutely everything"), and immutable ("This isn't changeable").[6]

Not surprisingly, numerous studies show that possessing such a pessimistic self-explanatory style places us at an extreme disadvantage, mostly by preventing us from responding to adversity in ways that make it easier to surmount. Telling ourselves, for example, that we failed a test because we lack good test-taking skills—meaning that we lack inherent ability—may discourage us from preparing for a makeup test, leading us to fail it again. On the other hand, if we tell ourselves we failed a test because we didn't study enough—meaning we didn't make the effort, something over which we have significant control—we're more likely to redouble our efforts the second time around and pass it. In other words, if we spend our energy defending a rationale for why we can't do something, we'll almost certainly not be able to do it. As Richard Bach writes in his book *Illusions*, "Argue for your limitations, and sure enough, they're yours."[7]

People with a pessimistic self-explanatory style are also at an increased risk for developing posttraumatic stress[8] and depression[9] when adversity strikes—as well as for losing their motivation when they fail. In one study, psychologist Martin Seligman asked swimmers to swim their best stroke and then told them their times were slightly slower than they actually were. When they swam again, swimmers with an optimistic self-explanatory style swam at approximately the same speed, whereas swimmers with a pessimistic self-explanatory style swam more slowly.[10] When things are going well—when the team on which we're playing is winning, for example—no difference in motivation or performance exists between optimists and pessimists. But when things aren't going well—when the team on which we're playing is losing—pessimists often stop trying.[11]

Or, at least, some do. It turns out that not all pessimists are created equal. *Depressive* pessimists, research suggests, believe they lack the necessary ability to succeed and therefore that their efforts are irrelevant. *Defensive* pessimists, on the other hand, worry about negative outcomes as well but use their anxiety to motivate themselves into action. Interestingly, defensive pessimism—acknowledging the possibility of failure without allowing it to discourage us from making the efforts necessary to prevent it—may represent the most adaptive self-explanatory style of all: in one study of female basketball players, subjects identified as defensive pessimists outperformed even optimists.[12]

What explains such a counterintuitive result? One possibility is that a *blindly* optimistic self-explanatory style might lead to overconfidence and therefore carelessness, an idea supported by the finding in the study above that subjects with an optimistic self-explanatory style garnered more fouls than those with a pessimistic self-explanatory style. Another is that a blindly optimistic self-explanatory style might actually promote a *reduction* in effort as we might not try as hard if we believe our ability eliminates the need. Finally, a blindly optimistic self-explanatory style might cause us to overlook the true reasons for our performing poorly—for example, because we're poorly conditioned—and thus prevent us from improving at the same rate as our defensively pessimistic peers.[13]

Given these potential pitfalls, a more constructive approach might be instead to develop what psychologists call *explanatory flexibility*, a willingness to reformulate how we think about the causes of negative events, abandoning even optimistic narratives when information that contradicts them comes to light.[14] How, then, do we develop such flexibility—a *realistic* optimistic self-explanatory style—remaining balanced in the way we evaluate the causes of negative life events without surrendering our sense of power and control over them?

If we tend toward a *blindly* optimistic self-explanatory style, we need to become more aware of the inclination we have to blanket optimistic explanatory biases over all situations equally and acknowledge when the causes of negative events really are outside our control (with an eye toward facilitating acceptance, the value of which I discuss in Chapter 7). On the other hand, if we tend toward a *depressively* pessimistic self-explanatory style, we need to practice refuting self-defeating views. For such practice does indeed work. In one study designed to evaluate the effects of self-administered optimism training, researcher David Fresco and colleagues asked subjects to identify both the best and worst events they experienced over thirty days and to offer explanations for their causes. Half of the subjects were then asked to offer revised explanations. (Hoping to make the training as simple as possible, the researchers asked subjects to look not for more *optimistic* explanations but merely for *alternative* ones, presuming that further reflection would yield more optimistic thinking as a natural consequence.) Surprisingly, at first the subjects produced revised explanations that were even *more* pessimistic than the ones they offered initially. But by the end of the study, apparently with enough repetition, both their initial *and* revised explanations had become less pessimistic than those of the control group.[15]

But does changing our self-explanatory style actually make a difference in outcomes? The answer, in some contexts at least, is yes. In one study, training male basketball players to attribute positive results—for example, making a free throw—to their *ability* and negative results to their *lack of effort* was found to significantly improve their subsequent performance.[16] In another study, optimism training was found to increase the persistence with which novice golfers attempted to improve their game.[17] Thus, how we explain the causes of our problems (like failing to make a putt) almost certainly plays an important role in determining how we respond to them. Which is to say, the stories we tell ourselves about why bad things happen really do affect what happens next.

Negative Thoughts

The most interesting finding in the golfer study, though, wasn't that optimism training had a positive effect on persistence. It was that pessimism training delivered to a comparison group had an *adverse* effect on persistence that was even *larger*. Apparently, depressively pessimistic self-explanatory narratives are even more *harmful* than optimistic self-explanatory narratives are helpful.[18]

Perhaps this is at least partly because negative thoughts, even if not the first obstacles to appear after we make a determination to accomplish a goal, are nevertheless the most insidious. And because we commonly fail to recognize them for what they are, they become uniquely capable of retarding our progress. Yet arguing with our negative selves—*devils* as they're called in Nichiren Buddhism—is akin to employing willpower to resist temptation: it rarely works. Instead, when brought face to face with the devilish functions of our minds, we must be neither influenced nor frightened by them, but instead respond to them as we might respond to negative *people*: by putting ourselves somewhere they're not.

Because negative thoughts *are* tempting to believe, we can use the same strategies to deal with them that we use to deal with temptation in general: distraction and avoidance. Rather than expend energy *resisting* our negative thoughts, then, we can concentrate instead on *ignoring* them, our ultimate aim being to treat them the way psychologists train

patients with panic attacks to treat anxiety—which is to say, not by denying them, but by observing and accepting them, waiting patiently until
they do what unresisted thoughts generally will: pass quietly away.

"So the goal isn't to convince yourself you're not going to fail," I told
Paul. "The goal is to stop paying attention to the possibility."

He looked at me uncertainly. "How?"

"By manipulating your focus away from it."

"With more *optimistic* thoughts?" he asked dubiously.

I shook my head. "With more *attractive* thoughts. Thoughts that naturally draw your attention because they make you feel better. You can turn
either to entirely unrelated thoughts, things pleasant enough to occupy
your mind and prevent you from focusing on the negative thought you're
trying to avoid, or if your negative thought is too tempting, too powerful to ignore, you can pick a related but alternative thought that turns
your mind only slightly, just *past* your negative thought, so that even if
you're not able to ignore it entirely, it fails to entirely command you. So
instead of telling yourself you can't undo the damage that's already been
done," I suggested, "tell yourself it's just going to be far harder than you
ever imagined."

He laughed. "That *is* more attractive than the alternative, I'll grant
you that."

"Ignoring negative thoughts is a skill like any other," I said. "It can be
learned. It just takes practice."

On the other hand, when our pessimistic selves are raging completely
out of control and we want to silence them entirely, we need to find
actual proof that their pronouncements are wrong, something we can
only obtain by achieving the very success they're arguing that we can't.
Here we find another reason to divide large tasks into smaller ones: it
enables us to claim early victories, which can actually "immunize" us
against losing our motivation to continue if we subsequently fail.[19] By

winning early, whenever devils begin to whisper malevolently in our ears that we can't do something, we can refer them, and ourselves, to evidence that proves them wrong.

Finally, sometimes our impulse toward negativity is nothing more than a habit, a reflex born of past feelings of frustration or powerlessness that have long since vanished but whose footprint nevertheless remains. In contrast to negativity that arises from a lack of self-confidence, negativity like this, the kind with no real thought behind it, can best be extinguished not by avoidance and distraction but by their opposite: vigilant self-monitoring. Studies show the best way to break a bad habit is by noticing when we do it and consciously forcing ourselves to stop.[20] If we interrupt ourselves in the act of biting our nails enough times, for example, eventually our fingers will cease to rise to our teeth of their own accord. Similarly, when negative thoughts become negative statements that exit our mouths by reflex, if we notice them and interrupt them—even in midsentence—over time we'll become less inclined to speak them in the first place.

But because no shortage of adversity is ever likely to occur, to be successful in the long term such a thought-stopping strategy would require us to monitor ourselves continuously and indefinitely, a proposition far too exhausting for most of us. Sometimes, therefore, it can also be helpful to substitute a *different* response to whatever may be cuing the habit we want to extinguish.[21] Rather than just interrupting ourselves from biting our nails when nervous, for example, we might train ourselves to stroke our chin instead. Likewise, rather than only interrupting negative thoughts, we might train ourselves to consciously substitute positive ones. That way, we're not just trying to stamp out a bad habit, but also trying to program in a good one—one that with repetition over time may eventually become as automatic as the one we're trying to abolish.[22]

"All of which is to say that you may *think* you can't repair the damage you've done to your students," I said finally, "but that's only another story you're telling yourself—and one you need to ignore. Or if you can't ignore it, you need to ask yourself why you believe it. Is it just habitual pessimism, or is there some specific reason you think you have no power to influence what's going to happen?"

He looked at me helplessly and then shrugged. "I wish I could tell you."

The Anxiety of Uncertainty

I didn't hear back from Paul for three weeks, by which time I'd become convinced that my attempts to encourage him had not only failed but had also caused him to reject the very point of view I'd been hoping to make him see. But then, to my surprise, he left me a voicemail message saying that he'd actually started attending Alcoholics Anonymous meetings, found a sponsor, and even started working on the Twelve Steps. He didn't particularly like the people he was meeting—he felt he had nothing in common with them—but he hadn't had a drink or used cocaine since he'd last seen me. But now something had happened, he said, and he wanted to talk to me in person. Could he come in, he asked, later that week?

I called him back to arrange it, and two days later we sat back down together in my clinic. "I can't do this," was the first thing he said with a shake of his head.

"What? Why not?" I asked, purposely keeping my voice calm in an attempt to counteract what wasn't an entirely unexpected panic. I knew from previous experience with drug-addicted patients that a legitimate attempt at abstinence almost always induced anxiety. "What happened?"

He shook his head in amazement. He'd been out shopping on Michigan Avenue the previous weekend, he told me, browsing for shirts at Water Tower Place, when he'd looked up from a clothes rack and saw—unbelievably—one of his students standing several aisles over, staring at him, her expression frozen in surprise. They'd looked at one another for a few moments in silence, neither of them moving. "And then she just turned away."

I leaned back in my chair. "Shit."

"Yeah," he said.

I mused. "Well," I said, mustering up the most encouraging smile I could, "you didn't think this would be easy, did you?"

"I didn't think it would be this hard." He paused. "I'm actually thinking about leaving."

"Leaving?"

"Moving to another city. Getting another job somewhere else. My wife and I hate the winters here anyway."

I let out a long breath. "You could," I said carefully.

"I'm just not sure I'm strong enough to do this."

I drummed my fingers on my desk. "Here's the thing, Paul," I said. "You're exactly as strong—or not—as you tell yourself you are. You may not *want* to go through this, imagining, as I'm sure you are, all the horrible things you might have to face if you do, but that doesn't mean you *can't*. *Can't* is just another story we tell ourselves. A decision we make." A decision, I told him, that had an important consequence: it would change his focus from trying to *solve* his problem to trying to *escape* it. And once we begin trying to escape our problems, they become paradoxically even more daunting, the consequences of not solving them abruptly appearing even more awful, and our sense of helplessness even more overwhelming. And as a result, we almost suffer more from *believing* we can't solve our problems than from actually having to do the work of solving them.

One reason we often prefer to believe we can't solve a problem is that it creates *less* anxiety than the alternative: not knowing if we will. In one study, patients requiring colostomies (a rerouting of the passage of stool from the rectum to an opening in the abdomen) that were potentially reversible were actually *less* happy six months after their operations than patients whose colostomies were permanent.[23] Why? Because uncertainty prevented them from adapting to the change, keeping them focused on and attached to what they still stood to lose.

Uncertainty also blinds us to the truth that our lives will continue despite the losses we suffer—and not just continue, but in light of the set-point theory of happiness, in most cases return, more or less, to feeling like they did. "One reason you can't imagine right now how you might be able to put your life back together," I told Paul, "is that you're obsessed with the possibility that it's about to fall apart. But because it hasn't, you haven't devoted any resources to figuring out how you *would* put it back together if it did, which makes you feel that you couldn't."

The only antidote to uncertainty, I told Paul, is to attack the very obstacle we doubt we can overcome. As Nichiren Daishonin wrote, "Only by defeating a powerful enemy can one prove one's real strength."[24] We tend to feel strong, in other words, when we're actually *experiencing* our strength. But this happens only when we're using it to lift something heavy (meaning deal with an obstacle). For example, in one study of cancer patients actively undergoing treatment—taking active steps, that is, to solve their problem—subjects were found to be more optimistic and have higher levels of self-esteem than even a control group *without* cancer.[25]

We also tend to find a way to experience ourselves as strong when facing an obstacle we think we can't avoid. I remember a high school classmate who was once paralyzed by anxiety when her turn came to deliver a speech until our teacher told her she had no choice, at which point she calmed down and delivered her speech without difficulty. One reason for this may be that fully accepting and embracing the notion that no other path remains available to us but forward activates our fight-or-flight response, concentrating the mind, as it were, in preparation for what it perceives as a life-or-death struggle. Another reason may be that freely *choosing* a painful experience reduces the degree to which we experience it as painful,[26] an effect that seems to occur even when the choice we make is *to decide that we have no choice*. Committing to the inevitable, in other words, seems to prepare us to endure pain.

"So what's also likely contributing to your feeling that you can't do this," I said to Paul, "is allowing yourself to believe you don't have to. Once you decide that you *have* to do something, whatever energies and focus you'd been bringing to bear on trying to escape it tend to reorient themselves almost of their own accord toward overcoming it."

"But I do have a choice," Paul said.

"Technically, yes," I agreed. "You do. You could leave. But do you really want to tell those kids that it's okay to lie? And not just lie, but run away when you're caught?"

Abruptly, his expression collapsed. "No," he said.

"I understand you're ashamed, and that you want to resolve that shame by running away and hiding from everyone who knows what happened. But do you honestly think that cutting yourself off from those kids will do anything to the remorse you're feeling but make it worse?" He blinked several times as if I'd slapped him. "You're carrying the seed of this disaster inside you, Paul. You say you don't want to change, but I can't imagine you want this to happen again. So how do you think you prevent it? Wherever you go, there you are. Given enough time, the same behavior is likely to produce the same results." I shook my head. "Don't do it. Not to yourself. And not to some other group of kids who come to love you, too."

There was a long pause. "I just didn't think it would be this hard," he said finally.

"It's not that it's hard," I corrected. "It's that it's harder than you *expected*."

Expectation Influences Response

To this day, my wife and I vividly remember the anesthesiologist's statement: "You may experience a little *pressure*." She spoke the word gently, as if her tone reflected what my wife would feel, and we believed her. Epidural blocks, she explained, don't numb the sacral nerve roots that deliver sensation from the pelvic floor, so my wife would likely feel some discomfort as she entered the last stage of labor and our son began passing through her birth canal. But we were both reassured. A mild bit of pressure seemed no threat to our hope of having the same experience that my sister-in-law had with her first child: she'd needed to be told when to push in the final moments because she couldn't feel anything at all.

My wife's block, however, failed to completely numb her left side. Whereas my sister-in-law couldn't feel or move either of her legs, my wife could have stood on her left one alone. But, again, we were reassured as the Pitocin-induced contractions the monitor told us she was having remained for her a distant, almost imperceptible cramping.

After thirty-six hours of peaceful, almost boring, labor, however, she began to feel significant discomfort on her left side. Over the next hour, then, it built to an intensity that began to worry us. The anesthesiologist was called back into our room. She adjusted the position of the epidural catheter and dialed up the dose as high as she could. My wife's pain, however, continued to worsen. "There's nothing else I can do," the anesthesiologist said finally, apologetically.

The last five hours of my wife's labor were an agony. I stood at her bedside without leaving once the entire time, unable to do a single thing to help her, utterly traumatized by the experience myself.

Though she was certainly well-intentioned, our anesthesiologist had made a crucial error: she only described the *best* possible outcome of the epidural block, not the worst, and in doing so failed to prepare us for what actually happened. As a result, the entire experience was transformed. Though the physical sensations my wife felt would have been no different had she been better prepared for them, her *experience* of them would have been altered entirely. But because she hadn't been better prepared for them, her pain was turned from something inevitable but ultimately joyful into something almost wholly terrifying.

A growing body of research now shows that our expectations profoundly influence our responses to our experiences. In some cases, in fact, our expectations have a greater influence over our responses to an experience than does the quality of the experience itself. In one study, for example, subjects primed to expect a bland cartoon to be funny rated it funnier than subjects who weren't primed.[27] (On the other hand, this may not hold true for everyone. Another study showed that pessimists, being more likely to notice when their expectations diverge from their experiences, tend to be less influenced by their expectations than do optimists.[28])

The expectations we have of *unpleasant* experiences, however, seem especially influential. In a meta-analysis of twenty-one studies designed to test the effect of warning patients both about what would be done to them and how much it would hurt when they were scheduled to undergo unpleasant medical procedures, such warnings were found to significantly reduce the amount of discomfort patients reported during the procedure.[29] It seems when we're warned that an experience will be unpleasant, we find it easier to tolerate.

Discrepancies between our expectations and our experience not only affect how we experience events, but also how we *respond* to them. When we expect a task to be easy but then find ourselves unable to complete it, for example, we tend not to try as hard on subsequent tasks and therefore perform more poorly on them.[30] But if we expect a task to be difficult and find ourselves unable to complete it, we experience no impairment in our subsequent effort in the least.[31] Just like when we achieve a small victory early on, having an expectation that achieving a goal will be difficult "immunizes" us against the tendency to give up when we fail, thereby increasing the likelihood of our succeeding in the long run. Though ignorance of what's coming may encourage us to try things we might not otherwise try, it also risks our giving up prematurely when unanticipated obstacles arise.

"So however long you think your goal will take you to achieve," I advised Paul, "however much work you think it will require and however many times you think you'll get it wrong before you get it right or fail before you succeed—multiply that by a factor of ten or a hundred. Expect a level of difficulty so beyond what it's likely to be that the chances of it actually being harder than what you imagine are minuscule, the contrast making what you do have to go through seem easy. Though we may not be able to control how difficult a goal is to accomplish, we can control how difficult we *expect* it to be."

But relinquishing an expectation to which we're already attached is no easy task even *after* we learn it was unrealistic, for we attach to our expectations as we do to our beliefs, as if they were valued possessions rather than mere ideas. Moreover, sometimes we feel as if we *shouldn't* detach from them, especially when the obstacles that frustrate our expectations are annoying—when, for example, they're the result of laziness or incompetence. Thus, though we may want to change our expectations to better manage our response to disappointment, we may not be able to do so until they're proven inaccurate and we become sufficiently frustrated. Though that same frustration also puts us at risk for quitting, it also seems necessary to get us to set new expectations that keep us going.

Resetting Expectations

To reset expectations effectively, however, requires that we set them *concretely*. But predicting the unpredictable, if not quite an oxymoron, is at the very least hard. Asking others who've already done what we desire to do just how hard it was for them may represent the best approach, as long as we make sure to ask about the specific difficulties they faced that *they* didn't expect. Had my father, for example, asked someone who'd already learned to play the saxophone just how difficult it was, he might not have given up his attempts after only two days. ("I knew I wouldn't be able to make it sound good right away," he said, "but I didn't expect I wouldn't be able to make a sound at all!")

Taking the time to predict what specific obstacles we might face on the way to our goal also prevents us from becoming too attached to the means by which we accomplish it. This, then, allows us to concoct contingency plans whose existence can greatly enhance the confidence we have in our ability to succeed. Preparing ourselves this way is like taking out an insurance policy against discouragement: even as our first plan fails, we can already be turning to our second.

"So don't worry about your students not forgiving you," I concluded to Paul. "Expect them *not* to. Expect them to shun you. Then ask some of the people in AA how they earned back the trust of people *they* betrayed. Ask how long it took *them*."

"So you're saying you think it can be done."

"I do. You just have to expect it to be incredibly hard. And to realize also that even if you can't—even if they don't forgive you—now that you've fallen you're in an even better position than you were before to encourage them."

He looked at me quizzically. "How?"

"By showing them how to get back up."

Empathy and Forgiveness

Two months passed, and school started up again. Though Paul agreed he would call me at the end of his first week back, I'd heard nothing from him by the middle of the second week. So I called him and left a message. But after another week, I'd still heard nothing back, so I called him again. Then abruptly, several weeks after I'd all but given up on hearing back from him, he showed up in my clinic.

The first thing that struck me when I greeted him was how well he looked: he'd filled out a little and wore a bright smile I hadn't seen before. When I stepped into the exam room, he stood up to shake my hand.

"You're looking good," I said cautiously.

"I *am* good."

We both sat down. "I got worried when I didn't hear from you," I said. "What happened? What did you tell your students?"

His smile grew even wider. "I told them the truth." The truth, he said, that he'd been using cocaine on and off for at least the last ten years and abusing alcohol even longer; that he was ashamed for having lied to them, but that lying was what addicts did to maintain their addiction; and that he was an addict. His pattern of abuse had been to binge only occasionally, which had kept the rate at which his life deteriorated slow enough that it had seemed to him—and to them—not to be deteriorating at all. But deteriorate it had, he'd told them, and in a way more painful than he'd ever imagined it might.

What hurt him most, he'd told them, wasn't the shame he felt at being exposed as a fraud, but rather that they might learn a different lesson from his fall than the one he wanted to teach them. Which was the real reason he was speaking to them about his fall at all. He wanted them to know that he now understood firsthand the truth about drug abuse: that, in the end, it stole everything from you that mattered.

Of all the things his addiction had taken from him, he'd told them, the most precious thing had been their trust. It was a loss he was mourning more than he could say, one made all the worse by his knowledge that even if they wanted to trust him again, they couldn't. Trust wasn't a matter of choice but of evidence, and he'd provided them more than enough that he didn't deserve theirs.

So he wasn't asking to be restored to their good graces, he'd said. Instead, he was asking for their empathy, for them to imagine as tangibly as they could the pain he was now feeling—not so that they'd forgive him, he'd been careful to say, but so that they'd never be tempted to copy his mistake. He'd spent his entire career telling students like them about the destructive nature of drug abuse, he'd said. Now he'd become an example of it himself—an example he was determined that none of them would ever follow.

I stared at him in amazement. Then in hushed tones I asked, "What happened then?"

With a half-laugh, half-choke, he said, "They forgave me. They all . . . forgave me." First one, he said, and then another, and then another. They'd spent the entire hour talking about it, about the nature of forgiveness, and about their pledge to avoid drugs at any cost.

We sat in silence for a moment. "Paul," I said finally. "Congratulations."

He nodded, wiping at his eyes a little. "That's why I came today, to tell you that. And something else." He took a deep breath. "I lied to you when I said I'd quit using drugs over the summer. I was still using when school started. *Dr. Lickerman, I was high the day I told my students the truth.*"

I couldn't stop my eyes from widening.

"I just never imagined they'd forgive me. And then . . ."

The thought that he was *still* lying to them in the very act of confessing the truth, Paul continued—in the very act of being forgiven—became so suddenly unbearable that he almost broke down in front of them. But he didn't, he said. And he didn't quit his job either.

"So I'm making amends to them," he said, "by making amends to *you*. I'm here to tell you I'm sorry I lied to you and that I really am done now.

For the last six weeks. Because of those kids . . ." His voice caught suddenly, and he stopped.

I wondered briefly if this confession was a lie, too. But I dismissed the idea almost immediately. He had no reason to tell me what he had, other than for the purpose he stated, to make amends to me and, through me, to his students.

Over the ensuing months, then, no evidence that Paul had gone back to using drugs ever surfaced. He kept his job, his marriage thrived, and his health never deteriorated. He had indeed, it seemed, found a way to turn poison into medicine. Not in the way either of us had predicted, but rather by putting others before himself. By hoping not for his own future but for the future of his students. For in doing so, he'd received something that had been not only his greatest desire but also, it turned out, the key to his sobriety: their forgiveness.

5

Stand Alone

Few concepts are as confusing and generally misunderstood as the concept of karma. Like love and happiness, karma seems to mean something different to everyone, even though most would agree it has something to do with destiny and reincarnation. Many consider karma a force that determines what happens to us, undoubtedly explaining why people attribute various things like getting sick, meeting the love of one's life, getting into car accidents, and finding parking spots all to the the workings of karma.

But if karma is a force that rigidly predetermines events, then our futures have already been constructed down to the last detail and we exist merely as bystanders to our own lives. And though we may sometimes feel as if the world operates this way, even the most nihilistic of us have had experiences that refute this view, experiences in which we aimed at a goal, fought through obstacles, and achieved success through our own efforts. Though we'd be foolish to believe we can exert complete control over what happens to us, we'd be equally foolish to believe we have no influence over it whatsoever (even if only, to argue a ridiculous extreme, through the minute amount of gravitational force our bodies exert on all other bodies in the cosmos). This suggests that karma, if real, must be alterable.

This represents the Nichiren Buddhist view, that not only is karma alterable but alterable only by actions we ourselves take—this, because karma is created by actions we ourselves have taken. As Shakyamuni Buddha explained, "If a person commits an act of good or evil, he himself becomes the heir to that action." And as Nichiren Daishonin wrote, "If you want to understand the causes that existed in the past, look at the results as they are manifested in the present. And if you want to understand what results will be manifested in the future, look at the causes that exist in the present."[1] That is to say, all the effects in our lives (meaning what happens to us) are without exception determined by causes we ourselves have made, *causes* here defined as our thoughts, words, and deeds (listed in order of ascending impact). This isn't to suggest, however—and this is crucial—that we're to *blame* for what happens to us, or worse that we *deserve* what happens to us; instead, it's to underscore the notion that at every moment we have the power to *affect* what happens to us. That at every moment we remain capable of taking new action and therefore of altering the trajectory of our future.

Unfortunately, this law of cause and effect as it's imagined in Nichiren Buddhism can't be investigated scientifically (meaning we can't design an experiment to disprove it). On the other hand, the idea that we ourselves are the authors of all the problems we face needn't be true for us to recognize that the responsibility for *solving* them lies entirely with us. Because what really makes a problem ours isn't that we caused it, but that it *affects* us (whether by affecting *us* or by affecting someone else we care about). "If you're suffering," a fellow Buddhist once told me, "it's your karma." Which is to say, if a problem is making us suffer, that suffering is our problem to solve.

Which isn't to say that we should—or must—solve our problems alone. The company of others—who if not also threatened directly themselves by the same misfortune that threatens us at least care enough to lend us their support—is always welcome and often helpful. Research shows, for example, not only that actively venting to others about traumatic experiences creates a psychological distance that engenders a more objective perception of them,[2] but also that the encouragement of others, as many of us know from our own experience, can increase the likelihood that we'll achieve our goals.[3]

Other research, however, suggests that too much support from other people may actually *prevent* us from taking action toward those goals. Once when I was jogging along Lake Michigan, I came upon a large crowd standing over a middle-aged man who was lying unmoving on the ground. Two people were bent over him trying to shake him awake. I stopped and asked a woman at the edge of the crowd what had happened.

"He fell," she said.

"Did anyone see it?"

"I did," another woman answered. "He was walking along, and then he just crumpled."

I identified myself as a doctor, pushed my way through the crowd, and checked to see if he was breathing. He wasn't. "Has anyone called 911?" I asked. Incredibly, no one had.

Though the reason for this omission related partly to the power of *social proof*, which causes people to assume that the actions of others around them reflect appropriate behavior (so that if everyone else is doing nothing they presume doing nothing must be appropriate), in my view the more proximate cause was a phenomenon known as the *diffusion of responsibility*. The reason no one had called 911 wasn't because the idea hadn't occurred to anyone, but rather because it had occurred to almost *everyone*, each of whom then in turn presumed that someone *else* had done it. The larger the group before which a task is placed, it turns out, the less that each individual will feel personally responsible for accomplishing it, and the *less* likely, without an explicit assignment of responsibility, the task will be accomplished at all.[4] It's not that having others around us diminishes our concern; rather, it's that having others around us changes our belief about our need to take action.

What's fascinating about this phenomenon is that the presence of a "herd" around us doesn't just diminish our drive to help others. It also diminishes our drive to help ourselves. Studies show that when we think about supportive partners helping us we actually become *less* motivated, a phenomenon termed *self-regulatory outsourcing*, so named because depending on others for their support causes us to unconsciously "outsource" our efforts to them.[5] Self-regulatory outsourcing likely explains, for example, why we're content to hand over responsibility to our spouses for things like filling out tax forms and signing up our children for soccer: we all have a hard time wanting to do something ourselves when someone else is available and willing to do it for us.

But accepting full responsibility for accomplishing tasks ourselves forces us to draw upon internal reserves of strength we might not otherwise be able to find. Accepting full responsibility for managing her own pain was what enabled my wife, for example, to get through the final stages of labor when she was giving birth to our son. After the anesthesiologist told her nothing further could be done for her, she realized, she later told me, "Absolutely no one could help me. Not the anesthesiologist, not my gynecologist, not you. Everyone was there, but I was totally alone." So she literally talked herself through it. As each contraction gripped her she would mutter, "Okay, okay, here it comes again, here it comes again, just breathe. . . ." With no one else able to help her, she turned to the only person who could: herself.

The reason to accept responsibility for solving our problems, then, isn't just that our problems belong to us, and that if we don't, no one else will. It's also that a growing body of research now suggests that accepting responsibility for solving our problems makes us more resilient.

For one thing, just like embracing a mission, embracing responsibility, as my wife did, seems to increase our ability to tolerate pain. In another electric shock study, investigators Gerald Davison and Stuart Valens administered an initial series of escalating jolts to subjects to establish the voltage at which they found it too painful or unpleasant to continue. Then they led half of the subjects to believe they were able to tolerate subsequent shocks of even higher voltage as a result of their own efforts and the other half to believe that they were able to do so as a result of receiving a pain medication (in both cases, investigators made subjects believe their pain tolerance increased by surreptitiously cutting the voltage in half). On a final round of shocks, subjects who believed the power and responsibility for controlling the pain of the previous shocks had come from themselves rather than from a pill were able to tolerate significantly higher voltages than subjects who believed they'd been able to better tolerate the previous shocks only after being given a pill.[6]

Embracing a sense of personal responsibility is also associated with better psychological adjustment following trauma. In a study of burn patients, subjects who felt the most personally responsible for having caused their burns themselves were found to have the *lowest* risk for developing acute stress disorder and long-term posttraumatic stress.[7] (Some researchers have suggested that this is because blaming ourselves for our misfortune may give us a sense of control over future threats—our thinking being that if we caused today's misfortune we can also prevent tomorrow's—while blaming others, or fate, may reduce our confidence in our ability to keep ourselves safe.[8])

In the elderly, feeling a sense of responsibility has been found not only to improve daily functioning but also to increase lifespan. In a study of nursing home patients by researchers Ellen Langer and Judith Rodin, residents on one floor were given a plant for which they themselves were expected to care (the experimental group) while residents on another floor were given a plant for which their nurses would care (the control group). After three weeks, 93 percent of residents in the experimental group showed an overall improvement in socialization, alertness, and general function; in contrast, for 71 percent of residents in the control group functioning actually declined.[9] And in a follow-up study eighteen months later, half as many of the residents who'd received plants for which they were expected to care by themselves had died as the residents who'd been given plants for which their nurses cared.[10]

Finally, perhaps the most significant way in which embracing a sense of personal responsibility increases resilience is by motivating action (remember, resilience is also defined by our ability to persevere through obstacles). In fact, feeling responsible for achieving an outcome may motivate us even more powerfully than our *desire* to achieve it. After all, a sense of responsibility often makes us do things we *don't* want to do. Perhaps nowhere is this more evident than in people suffering from, of all things, obsessive-compulsive disorder. Struggling constantly with intrusive thoughts about possible harm coming to themselves or others, patients with obsessive-compulsive disorder are sometimes completely incapacitated by their need to engage in neutralizing behaviors like compulsive checking, washing, and covert ritualization. What's surprising, however, is that intrusive thoughts about possible harm have actually been shown to occur *in all of us*.[11] Why, then, isn't obsessive-compulsive disorder a universal condition? According to some research, the fascinating answer may be that some people with obsessive-compulsive disorder also feel *an exaggerated sense of responsibility for preventing the harm they imagine*. That's why even as they recognize the likelihood of the harm they envision is vanishingly small, they're driven to take action that they think will in some way mitigate it. The greater the degree of responsibility such people feel, accordingly, the more irresistibly they feel compelled to act.[12]

Thus, while many of us experience responsibility as a burden, in Nichiren Buddhism it's actually viewed as a benefit, as something we should actively seek out. For not only does embracing personal responsibility for solving a problem produce a willingness to do whatever may be necessary to solve it, including embracing the need for self-transformation as discussed in Chapter 3, it also draws out of us an ability to endure adversity that no one, including often ourselves, expected we had.

Not that possessing such a *stand-alone spirit*, as it's known in Nichiren Buddhism, means refusing help that only others can give. Rather, as with everything else we might need to achieve victory, it means taking personal responsibility for getting them to give it—or for getting it from somewhere else. It also means refusing to allow that support to weaken our determination to take complete responsibility for the outcome of whatever task lies before us. To stand alone, then, is also to refuse to abdicate personal responsibility for solving problems even when other people have the power to solve them for us.

Nor, finally, does standing alone *only* mean accepting full responsibility for weathering obstacles, achieving goals, and resisting the urge to let others do for us what we can do for ourselves. It also means, from the Nichiren Buddhist perspective, standing up for what's right, even if others mock us for it or even attempt to prevent us from doing it. For standing alone also means standing up—against injustice.

At fifty-five years old, Sam had been my patient for almost fifteen of the sixteen years I'd worked at the University of Chicago and had always been one of my personal favorites. An executive administrator at a down-town law firm, he always came in with an easy smile and a gentle voice that seemed to soothe everyone to whom he spoke. Which was why I was surprised when he called me one day to tell me he was feeling depressed. When I asked him if he knew the reason, he told me that his fourteen-year-old daughter was having some trouble and had become depressed herself. He was depressed, he said, because she was.

"Why is *she* depressed?" I asked him.

"It's a real story," he answered. He wondered, in fact, if I'd be willing to talk with her about it. I protested that I was neither a pediatrician nor a psychiatrist, but he brushed my objections aside. "She doesn't need a psychiatrist," he said. "She just needs a new perspective." Because Sam had always been in excellent health, we'd spent the majority of his visits talking about everything *but* his health, including a number of Buddhist principles he found interesting and had tried over the years to apply to his own life. "I just think it would help her to talk with you," he said.

"Okay," I agreed.

When I met them together in my clinic a week later, Sam's demeanor seemed improved, the smile on his face as wide as it had ever been—in anticipation, I presumed, of the help he expected I'd be able to provide his daughter.

"Dr. Lickerman, this is my daughter, Audrey."

"Nice to meet you, Audrey," I said, shaking her hand. She had on a pair of women's cream trousers, a red blouse, and red pumps that made her nearly as tall as her father. Her face was fully made up with eyeliner and lipstick—a young adult in the making—but her expression was sullen underneath.

"So your dad tells me you've been feeling depressed," I said after we'd sat down.

"Yeah," she said.

"Why?"

She sighed heavily. "I stole something."

I cocked my head in surprise. "What?"

"A leather jacket."

"Why?"

"It didn't belong to the person who had it."

"Who did it belong to?"

"Neiman Marcus."

"The department store?"

She nodded.

"I'm confused," I said.

One of her friends, Audrey explained, had stolen the jacket while out shopping one day. When Audrey found out about it, she insisted her friend take it back. But her friend had refused. So Audrey had stolen it from *her* and returned it to Neiman Marcus herself. When her friend found out what she'd done (from Audrey herself no less), she told their other friends, who promptly ostracized Audrey so completely that she no longer wanted to go to school.

I stared at Audrey in disbelief, wondering what strange and wonderful combination of genetics and upbringing had somehow led her to care more about doing what she thought was right than she did about her social standing, something about which she obviously cared a great deal. "Not many *adults* I know would have had the courage to do that," I said. "I'm not sure *I* would have."

"If I'd known it was going to turn me into a pariah," Audrey replied, "I wouldn't have done it either."

Moral Transformation

Despite the impression we often get from the media, most of the world's population does in fact have a moral conscience.[13] Not that our awareness of right and wrong necessarily stops us from doing wrong when it's to our benefit. And not that doing wrong will necessarily make us unhappy. The power of rationalization cannot be underestimated; also, we tend to forget the little wrongs we do soon after we do them. But recent research suggests that striving to do what's right carries a benefit not previously recognized: it may actually make us stronger.

In a study led by psychologist Kurt Gray, researchers first assessed the ability of participants to hold up a five-pound weight. Then they gave all participants a dollar. Half of the participants (the experimental group) were then given the opportunity to donate their dollar to charity (all of whom did), and half were not. When participants were again asked to hold up a five-pound weight, those who had donated their dollars were able to do so a full *seven seconds* longer than participants who hadn't.[14] Why? According to Gray, because doing good increases our sense of agency, or potency, a phenomenon he terms *moral transformation*. (Interestingly, this effect wasn't seen only with acts of charity but also with acts of villainy.[15])

If we want to understand why doing good or evil might make us stronger, however, we first need to become clear about what good and evil are. Though philosophers and religious authorities have debated this question for centuries, Nichiren Buddhism offers a relatively straightforward answer: good, or right, is that which increases the joy or decreases the suffering of conscious creatures and therefore a priori should always be done, and evil, or wrong, that which does the opposite and therefore should not. Said another way, good is that which protects conscious creatures from harm, and evil that which subjects them to it. Good is also that which is just and fair, evil that which is unjust and unfair.

Moral Dilemmas

Interestingly, research has begun to show that belief in good and evil as conceptualized in Nichiren Buddhism may be far more universal than previously thought. In an Internet study by psychologist Marc Hauser and colleagues, 5,000 subjects in 120 countries were presented three moral scenarios and one control scenario and asked both to render moral judgments and to justify them. One scenario, for example, described the following conundrum: Denise is riding a train when she hears the engineer suddenly shout that the brakes have failed. The driver then faints from the shock. On the track ahead stand five people who are unable to get off the track in time to avoid being hit by the train. Denise sees a sidetrack leading off to the right onto which she can steer the train, but one person stands on that track as well. She can turn the train, killing the one person, or do nothing and allow the five people to be killed instead. Was it morally permissible, Hauser and his colleagues wanted to know, for Denise to switch the train to the sidetrack?

Results showed that an astounding 89 percent of subjects agreed that Denise should steer the train onto the sidetrack; in fact, the subjects agreed about which actions were moral and which weren't in most of the scenarios, delineating in the process a set of moral principles that seem to be shared by members of all cultures—namely, that it's less morally permissible to *intentionally* harm someone than to *allow* them to be harmed, that it's less morally permissible to *invent* a way to cause harm than to cause harm with an existing threat, and that it's less morally permissible to cause harm directly than to cause it indirectly. Yet the vast majority of subjects couldn't name these reasons as their underlying justification for judging the actions in each scenario as they did.[16]

Which, in fact, other research suggests may be the norm. When we take moral action, we seem to rely not so much on moral *reasoning* as on moral *intuition* and then work backward to rationalize the judgments we've already made.[17] (Which isn't to say our moral intuition can't and shouldn't be influenced by reason, but rather that our moral intuition remains the primary driver of our moral decision making.) Where does our moral intuition come from? The answer isn't yet clear. We know only that its rudiments seem to be present far earlier than we previously thought: research shows that children as young as three years old—an age at which it's been demonstrated we have no ability to articulate or even understand the concepts of right, wrong, or justice—have a negative emotional reaction to being given fewer stickers than their peers when they make an equal contribution to cleaning up a roomful of toys.[18]

All of which raises the intriguing possibility that the Nichiren Buddhism conception of good as any action intended to prevent harm or provide help (that is, halt suffering or bring joy) may actually be rooted not in the authority of a god or a religion or a philosophy but in the psychological and perhaps even neurological processes of the human mind. Even if we scoff at the notion that such processes could serve as the valid foundation for an objective and binding morality and reject the Nichiren Buddhism conception of good and evil, that conception nevertheless was the one that caused the subjects in Gray's study to become stronger.[19]

What Constitutes Harm?

Yet though we all seem to agree, according to Hauser's study, that causing harm is wrong, in many cases we just as clearly disagree—often dramatically, violently, and tragically—about what harm *is*. In fact, the things people consider harmful vary not only from culture to culture, but also across one culture over time and from person to person *within* a culture. Consider, for example, how strongly people across the globe disagree about whether harm is caused by premarital sex. What's more, even when people do agree about what constitutes harm, they often disagree about which harms are worse than others. We can see this in the strong disagreement about whether aborting a fetus on balance causes more harm than forcing a woman to carry an unwanted child to term.

How then are we to figure out what's right and wrong when confronted with the kind of complex moral conundrums we encounter in the real world? A belief in moral relativism, meaning that right and wrong are determined by local culture and custom, would seem to ignore the fact that people can disagree about what defines harm without disagreeing that harm defines evil. And yet a belief in moral absolutism—that some particular actions are *always* right or *always* wrong in all situations and therefore that context is irrelevant—ignores the fact that often the choice we make to prevent one kind of harm also represents a choice to cause another. That is to say, our choices are rarely between right and wrong, but are almost always between wrong and *less wrong* (meaning harmful and less harmful). And unlike the definition of wrong itself, what's wrong and less wrong *does* change depending on the context. Killing someone, for example, would be considered wrong according to the Nichiren Buddhist definition, but killing someone may be "less wrong" if doing so is the only way to prevent the deaths of five others, or is done to end the life of a person suffering agonizing pain from a terminal disease.

Unfortunately, our ability to calculate all the various harms we both prevent and produce with any moral choice dwindles rapidly as we move away in both time and place from the situation in which we choose it. How can we ever know our action to prevent harm today won't cause more harm tomorrow, or that our action to prevent harm here won't produce harm there? The answer, of course, is that we can't. In fact, given our propensity to make moral decisions based on intuition as well as our inability to foresee all the consequences of our decisions when we make them, we might argue that the only thing of which we should be certain (besides that we should always seek to minimize suffering and maximize joy) is that our best moral judgment will always be, to some degree, flawed.

A Balancing Act

We can perhaps be helped by logic, which tells us, among other things, that we should assign greater weight to *proven* harms (like stealing) than to *unproven* harms (like cursing God's name). We could also argue that if we ever find ourselves convinced beyond any doubt that our action is absolutely right, good, and just, we should consider we're probably looking at our choice and the context in which we make it too simplistically. If we're not making our moral choices with some degree of difficulty and even regret, we're probably not thinking about them carefully enough. Finally, we could say that if we find ourselves unable to identify a person or group who won't in some way be harmed by our choice, or if we can but we don't care about the harm our choice will inflict upon them—if we don't genuinely lament having to pay the price of one harm to buy avoidance of another—we must indeed consider ourselves at risk for becoming a monster. What makes people monsters, in other words, isn't their belief that the ends justify the means. The ends must *always* justify the means. What makes people monsters is that they don't agonize over the means they feel forced to choose.

To those who might be tempted to cite our flawed judgment as a reason to avoid choosing at all, Nichiren Buddhism would counter that not choosing is even worse than choosing something "less wrong." For as Edmund Burke reminds us, all that's necessary for the triumph of evil is for good men to do nothing. In fact, from a Nichiren Buddhist perspective, allowing an injustice to occur when we have the power to prevent it is to become complicit in committing that injustice ourselves. Justice, in the Nichiren Buddhist worldview, exists only because human beings make the effort to stand against injustice.

Which all suggests a reason that action in the moral sphere, whether good or evil, makes us strong: it requires us to be. Or, at least, that's what we think people who take moral action *are*: research shows that we're cognitively biased to "typecast" people who take such action as resilient[20]—a bias, it turns out, that affects not only our perception of others but also of *ourselves*.[21] And when we perceive ourselves to be endowed with a particular quality, we have a tendency to conform to that perception.[22] All of which implies that performing or even attempting to perform moral action may increase our resilience because it causes us to *perceive* ourselves as more resilient. This then makes us act, and therefore feel, as if we were.[23]

"I wasn't trying to take a stand against anything," Audrey said when I suggested this to her. "I just didn't want her to grow up thinking stealing was okay. Which is stupid, given that it's probably just a phase she's going through."

"Taking a stand against an injustice is never stupid," I said. "What we do matters. The world is only as good as people bother to make it."

Audrey rolled her eyes. "It's not like she killed somebody. It was just a leather jacket."

"We don't only make the world a better place in proportion to the size of the injustice we stand against," I said. "We also make it better in proportion to the influence our stand has on other people. And the power of that influence has less to do with the size of the injustice we stood against than with the fact that we stood at all."

She considered this for a moment. "It's not like I'm Little Miss Perfect myself."

"Is that what your friend said when you told her you returned the jacket?"

She rolled her eyes again. "Something like that."

"Well, I'm sure you're not," I said. But that was no reason, I told her, to allow herself to be swayed by the specious argument (most often made by those who know they're behaving badly to those who would expose them) that because we may not be a paragon of virtue ourselves in every situation we therefore have no right to fight injustice in any. In fact, I argued, we have the responsibility to fight injustice *even if we're commit-ting another injustice in some other way ourselves.* If only perfect people had the moral right to fight injustice, justice would never exist. Fight-ing injustice when we ourselves have been unjust doesn't make us hypo-crites. It makes us flawed people trying to improve.

"Are you just trying to make me feel better," Audrey asked, "or do you really believe all this stuff?"

"Both," I said. "Have you talked to her about why you did it?"

"I haven't talked to her about anything. That's what being a pariah means. No one will talk to me."

The Power of Authority

If we stand against injustice because we care about making the world a better place, we can increase our resilience as much as when we commit ourselves to a personal mission. But to be able to carry out a commit-ment to doing what's right (and therefore be able to typecast ourselves as resilient), we have to be able to stand against whatever forces rise up to sabotage our attempts. And to do that, we have to recognize where those forces come from.

In 1963 psychologist Stanley Milgram wondered if the Nazis perpe-trated the mass extinction of 6 million Jews because all of those involved were genuinely united in their desire to commit genocide or because only a committed few had managed to leverage the impulse to obey author-ity in the many who weren't. Far from seeking to exculpate those who claimed in their defense that they were "only following orders," Milgram was interested in which force was stronger, the tendency to obey author-ity or the desire to act according to one's values.

To answer this question, he designed studies in which an experimenter instructed subjects to administer a sequence of increasingly intense electric shocks to a confederate "victim" whom the subjects could hear but not see. (The victims didn't actually receive shocks but rather simulated increasingly desperate sounds of pain each time the subject thought he or she had administered a shock.) The results were astonishing: even though the victims were instructed to become silent as the shocks escalated in intensity (to imply they'd fallen unconscious), 65 percent of subjects continued the experiment all the way up to the final massive 450-volt shock, demonstrating that a majority of people will obey an authority even when that authority's instructions conflict with their principles.[24]

What explains these results? According to Milgram, when we perceive someone as a legitimate authority, we tend to accept the *meaning* they assign to actions even when that meaning contradicts what we ourselves perceive.[25] In Milgram's experiments, the experimenter told the subjects that the purpose, or meaning, of the experiment was to test how punishment influenced learning, which appeared to transform the purpose, or meaning, of the shocks into something constructive. Further, when an authority tells us to do something, we tend to surrender our sense of agency, so that, in Milgram's words, "when we feel responsible *to* the authority, we simultaneously surrender our sense of responsibility *for* the content of our actions."[26]

But when an authority commands us, why do we rush to substitute his judgment, his agency, for our own? Perhaps, we might speculate, because we think the authority has specialized knowledge or experience we lack. Or perhaps because we have immediate knowledge of the imperfections that mar our own judgment and simultaneously remain ignorant of the imperfections that mar the judgment of others, and therefore imagine theirs to be superior. Or perhaps because our judgment is connected to our egos and therefore is subject to our insecurities. After all, if *we* thought of the answer, we could only be as certain of it as we are of ourselves. And as we know we have no special connection to the ultimate truth of anything, it's far easier to allow ourselves to be convinced that others, whose minds remain opaque to ours, do. Placing our trust in the judgment of others, in other words, may be a strategy we use to alleviate our anxiety over uncertainty.

Or perhaps the tendency to place trust in the judgment of others over our own runs even deeper. At least one good reason exists to think natural selection itself may have had a hand in predisposing us to believe and obey authority: without such a predisposition, children might not recognize the power of their parents to limit their reckless behavior and might then find themselves at a significantly increased risk for injury and death.

In any case, whether learned or programmed into us by natural selection, the tendency to obey authority seems to be one that most of us can't escape—even when we're made consciously aware that we're subject to it. Hoping in fact to prove the opposite, psychologist Georgia Shelton conducted a study in which she provided subjects summaries of Milgram's work, quizzed them to ensure they understood it, and then asked them to serve as experimenters in a similar "learning" experiment. She told them they'd be supervising a "teacher" who was to teach a task to a "learner" by using electric shocks to punish the learner's mistakes. She informed the subjects that the learners were aware of the true purpose of the experiment but didn't disclose that the teachers were as well. As the experiment progressed, the teachers expressed increasing levels of distress at having to shock the learners, ultimately pleading with the subjects to halt the experiment. (As in Milgram's studies, no real shocks were delivered, but the subjects thought the teachers believed they were and thus that their distress at harming the learners was real.) Despite the pleas of the teachers, however, twenty-two out of twenty-four subjects continued the experiment to the end, ordering the teachers to increase the voltage up to the final 450-volt shock. Apparently, even understanding intellectually that people tend to blindly obey authority figures failed to enable subjects to draw a parallel between their obedience to Dr. Shelton and the teachers' obedience to them.[27]

Thus, the presence of authority figures in our lives may curtail the degree of resilience we're able to generate, for with them as with no one else rests the power to interfere with our autonomy. Not that our parents will necessarily want to prevent us from returning found money, or that our employer will necessarily want to prevent us from blowing the whistle on illegal activity at our workplace. But they very well might. And as Shelton's study suggests, our power to resist their direction may be more limited than we think.

How, then, can we increase the likelihood we'll do what's right in any particular circumstance and, through such action, gain strength? Perhaps not by resisting the negative influence of authority, but, as we should do also with temptation and negative thinking, by *avoiding* it. In other words, when facing a moral dilemma, we might consider deliberately *not* asking anyone we view as an authority figure for advice.

This isn't as risky an idea as it might seem. No evidence exists that turning to an authority figure for advice (or to anyone else for that matter) increases the likelihood that we'll do the right thing. In fact, some reason exists to think the opposite: we're more likely to seek advice from people who have our best interests at heart (like our family and close friends) who are therefore likely to rationalize along with us the choices we *want* to make rather than the choices we ought to make. Further, any authority figures we might approach are arguably more likely to encourage us to make the choice that *they* prefer to see. Though certainly we might be lucky enough to approach someone for advice in a moment in which they're especially concerned about doing the right thing and helping others to do the same (and therefore reduce the likelihood we'll be able to rationalize doing the wrong thing), such moments are hardly predictable. Thus, rather than risk being swayed by someone who may at best possess a moral judgment no better than ours and at worst actively guide us away from the most moral choice, we might all do better to focus instead on learning to recognize and combat our own tendency to rationalize doing what we want instead of what's right.

Of course, the power of authority doesn't influence us all to the same degree (remember, a full 45 percent of Milgram's subjects seemed at least partially resistant to it). Some of us, in fact, actively scorn authority—scorn any force, essentially, that might attempt to hijack our judgment and instead actually find *strength* in the idea of having to stand up to others, delighting in any opportunity to point in the direction opposite to the direction the crowd is pointing. How, we might then ask, have such people managed to ignore their impulse to submit to authority or the magnetic influence of peer pressure? Perhaps at least partly by having learned to resist the second of the two major forces aligned against us in our efforts to make moral choices: the desire to please others.

Self-Esteem and the Need to Please

As with many breakups, the end of my relationship with my first girlfriend came in fits and starts rather than as an abrupt but mercifully irreversible amputation. Yet even after we both recognized the relationship was finally over, she continued to ask me for favors—to pick her up from the airport, to take notes for her in class, to help her change the oil in her car—and I, inexplicably, continued to grant them.

Then while chanting one morning I found myself ruminating about how she continued to expect me to perform these favors, my indignation only rising after I'd finished chanting and began showering. And as I rinsed the shampoo from my hair and the last of the soapy water went swirling down the drain, I made a sudden and angry determination to refuse her the next time she asked for one.

At that moment, the phone rang. After I'd finished drying off, one of my roommates told me that it had been her calling and that she'd asked if I would call her back before I left for school. As I walked toward the phone I told myself that when she asked me for the favor for which I knew she'd called, I'd say no. I called her up, and, sure enough, she asked me if I would record a television show for her on my VCR. Yet even as I went to speak the word, "No," I heard my mouth say, "*Yes.*"

I hung up—and laughed out loud. I was as powerless to refuse her as I was to lift my car with my bare hands. And yet learning this failed to discourage me. On the contrary, it excited me—because if I could recognize this fact, I thought, I could find a way to change it.

Immediately, I decided I would begin chanting with the determination to free myself from my inability to say no. And months later, while chanting, I had an insight: the reason I remained unable to refuse her favors was that, in my mind, I'd signed a Good Guy Contract with her (a term, ironically, I learned later from her). Until that moment of insight, I had no idea what a Good Guy Contract was, much less that it was the standard contract I consistently established with almost everyone I knew. But in that startling moment of clarity I understood not only what it was but why I kept signing it. My self-esteem, which I'd previously believed had been built on things solely internal, was in fact entirely dependent on something external: the goodwill of others. The Good Guy Contract was simple: I would agree to be nice to you, to advise you, to sacrifice for you, to care about you, and in return you would agree to believe that I was wise, compassionate, excellent in every way, and finally and most importantly, *you would like me.*

With my girlfriend, however, I hadn't only expected to be liked; I'd expected to be loved. And once I'd had a taste of that love, I became addicted to it, which was why, when she took it away from me, I became profoundly depressed. Not because, as I originally thought, I'd been left by someone I thought was the love of my life, but because I genuinely believed that without that love *I couldn't be happy*. Why, then, did I keep doing favors for her after we'd ended our relationship? Because I couldn't shake the Good Guy habit. Some part of me believed if I continued to fulfill my contractual obligations to her, she'd start fulfilling hers again to me.

I didn't know at the time, but at the moment I awoke to my propensity to sign Good Guy Contracts, I stopped doing it. I recognized this only in retrospect three months later, however, when my best friend came to me asking why I seemed to have stopped paying attention to many of our mutual friends. My first reaction was to become defensive and deny it. But then I stopped myself, realizing that he was absolutely right. I wondered why I had in fact become so dismissive of many of my friends until I realized that I'd somehow stopped needing their approval to sustain my self-esteem. Freed from the need for them to like me, I was able to recognize that these were people with whom I had little in common, so I'd subsequently—and unconsciously—lost interest in them. My insight, in other words, had done more than show me what I'd been: it had changed me into someone I wanted to be, someone who could love and value himself without needing to be loved by anyone else.

"Not that I'm saying there's anything wrong with wanting to be liked," I told Audrey. "Or that I no longer *care* if I'm liked. But in freeing myself from the *need* to be liked, in learning to derive my self-esteem from internal sources, I can more easily let go of the dissonance that occurs when I'm not." Nor, I was careful to add, was I saying that being nice to people was undesirable. But if our main reason for being nice to people is to make them like us, our behavior will tend more to *appear* compassionate than it actually *is*. For though giving people what they want may indeed make them happier in the short term, it rarely increases their ability to become happier in the long term (and in fact often inhibits it, as it would the happiness of a child who wants to watch television instead of doing her homework, or the happiness of a gambler who wants to bet his life savings on a single turn of a roulette wheel, or the happiness of an alcoholic who wants to drink, and so on). If our principal aim is to act in a genuinely compassionate manner, to achieve the greatest and most enduring increase possible in the happiness of others, we need to find a way to free ourselves from the need to please.

Which means that if the idea of disappointing people, angering them, or causing them to dislike us makes us feel anxious, if we have difficulty enduring even a minor amount of conflict, if we're obsessed with worrying how others feel toward us, or if our actions remain motivated predominantly by the way we think they'll cause others to view us—in short, if we have no power to disappoint people when we should—we may find ourselves incapable of accomplishing any significant good at all. Not only that, but we'll feel continuously exhausted from working so hard to keep others pleased, finding ourselves with little energy left over to manage our own stress.

Unfortunately, even though the desire to please tends to weaken as we grow older and mature, it persists in many undiminished, as I believe it would have in me had I not confronted the suffering I experienced as a result of breaking up with my girlfriend. Indeed, for many of us, achieving control over our need to please requires a concerted effort.

Luckily, however, insight isn't the only route to this kind of self-mastery. It can also be accomplished incrementally through repeated practice. For if each time we're faced with the need to disappoint someone, we view it as practice for developing our compassion (when, of course, disappointing them is the compassionate thing to do), we'll be free to fail without judging ourselves as failures, as well as to find the strength to say no without needing to become angry. When we do fail then, as invariably we will, we can simply resolve to do better next time, encouraging ourselves by recalling that setting appropriate boundaries doesn't usually incite disapproval but rather respect.

And as we practice pitting our moral intuition against our need to please again and again, gradually the process will change from an uncomfortable, energy-depleting grind into a *habit*. And though learning to challenge our need to please may not guarantee we'll always be able to resist it, it will make our surrender to it less automatic, and therefore less likely overall.

"I don't have a problem disappointing people," Audrey said with a shake of her head. "What I have a problem with is not having any friends."

I sighed heavily. "I don't think I have any brilliant advice for you there," I said. "Talk to your friend again. People respond to sincerity even when they don't intend to. Even if they don't show it. Come at her humbly. Tell her the real reason you did it."

"I did," she said dully.

"What did you say?"

"That I didn't want her to grow up thinking stealing was okay."

"But why do you care about that?"

"Because . . ." She waved her arm in the air, groping for the underlying reason. "Because I'm stupid, that's why. I don't know. . . ."

"Because you care about *her*," I said. "*That's* what you have to make her understand. The way to reach the hearts of others is through courageous action and sincere demonstration of compassion for their suffering. What you need to do is find a way to reach her heart."

Audrey remained silent for a moment. Then she shrugged awkwardly.

I looked over at Sam. "I wish I had better advice for you. . . ."

"No," he said, gathering up his things, "that was great. Thank you for taking the time to talk to us. We really appreciate it."

Audrey, however, was staring at the floor. "Thanks," she echoed quietly.

A month later, Sam came back to see me in my clinic. "How's your daughter doing?" I asked him as we sat down to talk.

"Much better. She followed your advice."

"Really?"

"Yeah," he said with a clipped laugh. "She's just the most amazing kid." She'd been unable to reach her friend by phone, he told me, so she'd actually walked to her house and refused to leave until her friend agreed to come out and talk to her. "I don't know exactly what she said, but I gather it was something along the lines you suggested. And now they're friends again."

"So her days as a social outcast are over?"

He nodded. I was—again—astounded by Audrey's courage. I asked Sam if he thought reframing Audrey's returning of the jacket to Neiman Marcus as compassionate had made any difference in helping her find the strength to engage her friend in dialogue.

"I think it made *all* the difference," he said. "And I'll tell you a funny story." Apparently, soon after her social standing had been restored, Audrey had witnessed a different friend of hers sticking up for a new girl in school who their group of friends had been teasing. "When Audrey asked her why she'd done it, you know what she said? *She didn't want their friends growing up thinking that being mean was okay.*" He shook his head. "Can you believe it?"

"That's . . . amazing," I said. I found myself thinking about how often people would *tell* others they should stand up, but how it rarely worked as well as *showing* them, something Milgram demonstrated himself when he introduced a variation in his experiment that called for an additional accomplice "subject" to refuse to administer shocks to his "learners" and saw the compliance of his actual subjects plummet to 10 percent.[28] For in the end what inspires others to rally to a cause is the commitment we bring to it ourselves, our courage, as Gandhi said, to "be the change we want to see." For only when we stand up ourselves do we inspire others to stand up beside us, whether we're a world leader like Gandhi or a fourteen-year-old high school girl.

6

Accept Pain

No matter how much strength our willingness to stand alone may grant us, life is always able to assault us with measures of pain, both physical and emotional, that make us feel weak. Indeed, rather than thinking of resilience as the capacity to endure adversity, we might think of it more accurately as the capacity to endure the pain adversity causes.

Pain is a fascinating phenomenon. The way the brain registers physical pain, for instance, is not only complex but counterintuitive. Though the pain of a stubbed toe or a headache may seem like a single, unified experience, it actually represents the sum of two different experiences created by two separate areas of the brain—one called the posterior insula, which registers the *sensation* of pain (its quality, intensity, and so on) and the other the anterior cingulate cortex, which registers pain's *unpleasant character*. We know this is how the brain experiences pain because of imaging studies and because patients who've had damage to the anterior cingulate cortex feel the sensation of pain but not its unpleasantness.[1] That is, they feel pain but aren't bothered by it (interestingly, in some people, morphine has the same effect[2]). When the anterior cingulate cortex isn't functioning, pain is still experienced but seems to lose its emotional impact and thus its motivating force.

This finding, that the sensation of pain and the unpleasantness of pain come from distinct neurological processes that occur in different locations within the brain, explains how a single pain stimulus can cause such subjectively different pain experiences. Even if the physical sensation of pain remains constant, our "affective reaction" to it—how much it makes us suffer—will vary tremendously depending on several factors.

Research shows, for example, that how we interpret the *meaning* of pain has a dramatic impact on our ability to tolerate it. In one study, subjects reported pain they believed represented tissue damage to be more intense than pain they believed didn't,[3] possibly explaining why women rate cancer pain as more unpleasant than labor pain even when their intensities are the same.[4] Not only that, but when we focus on the *benefit* of pain (when one exists), we're actually able to *reduce* its unpleasantness. Another study showed that women in labor who focused primarily on their impending delivery rated the unpleasantness of their pain half that felt by women who focused primarily on their pain.[5] This seems to be true even when pain represents both benefit *and* harm, as anesthesiologist Henry Beecher found during World War II when he observed that 75 percent of soldiers with severe battlefield injuries—broken bones and torn limbs—reported experiencing only minor pain (even going so far as to decline morphine) because of what their injuries signified: they were going home.[6]

Studies have further shown that expecting pain to be severe worsens our experience of it, and expecting it to be mild improves it.[7] Further, being psychologically braced for pain also lessens its unpleasantness. This is true regardless of its cause, whether it's from a medical procedure done for our benefit, or from torture[8] (even though pain caused with the intent to harm has been shown to hurt more than pain caused incidentally or accidentally[9]).

Another way we might be able to improve our ability to manage pain is by retelling ourselves stories of previous painful experiences from a different perspective: not with a focus on the intensity of the pain we felt but on the fact that we survived it. For if we survived a terrible episode of pain in the past, we can survive a similar episode of it in the present. (When making these comparisons, it may be important to match painful experiences by *type*. Thinking about how we were able to complete a marathon may be helpful when climbing a mountain but not, perhaps, when grieving over the death of a spouse, something we might be better able to endure by recalling instead how we made it through a painful divorce.) Unconscious comparisons of this kind may explain why many women report their second delivery is easier than their first: not because the second hurts less, but because knowing that they handled childbirth before reinforces their belief in their ability to handle it again. In the same way, then, that believing ourselves to be strong can increase our strength,[10] believing in our ability to handle pain can increase our pain tolerance.[11] Knowing how much pain to expect also reduces anxiety, and studies have shown that lower levels of anxiety are associated with reduced pain unpleasantness as well.[12]

In fact, it turns out that the more familiar we are with a painful task in general—meaning the more times we've experienced it—the less pain it seems to cause us. In a study of elite cyclists, exercise physiologist Jeroen Swart found that the more familiar his subjects were with a cycling course, the better they could tolerate the pain of traversing it.[13] Even more interesting, knowing at every point along the course how far they had to go to the finish line also enabled them to tolerate more pain, and therefore to summon up greater effort, than when they didn't. According to Swart, the brain is constantly calculating how much effort to make—how much pain it can tolerate—based on the expected duration of exercise that remains, how certain it is about that duration, and what it calculates as the likelihood of encountering unexpected events along the way.

Yet the way cyclists approach racing isn't just a *metaphor* for managing pain; it's a *model* for it. For whether competing in a sport, writing a book, or giving birth to a baby, we often seem to pace ourselves in the same way as Swart's cyclists, adjusting our effort, and therefore our pain tolerance, based on minute-by-minute calculations of our need, a need reckoned largely by knowing the point at which our pain will end.

A Pain Puzzle

"I'm not sure how that helps me," replied Dan, one of my chronic pain patients, after I told him about Swart's study at one of his return visits. A bank manager and father of two, Dan had first come to see me almost a year earlier complaining of a runny nose that had been going on for several months. I thought he'd developed either allergies or vasomotor rhinitis (a condition in which the vagus nerve overstimulates mucus production in the nose for unknown reasons) and prescribed flonase, a nasal steroid, which should have helped either. But it didn't work. Then he started having headaches. When I asked him about them, his answers initially had me thinking they were tension headaches—painful, but entirely benign—until I asked what made them worse. "Standing up," he answered.

That stopped me. Headaches that become worse on assuming an upright posture suggest low cerebrospinal fluid pressure. The reason the flonase I'd prescribed hadn't worked, I suddenly realized, might have been because the fluid coming from his nose wasn't mucus.

A few days later, a neurosurgeon confirmed my suspicion: he was indeed leaking cerebrospinal fluid. What had started it? He couldn't

say. "Sometimes it happens from a sneeze," he told me. "Or sexual inter-
course. Or sports activity." When a CT scan subsequently demonstrated
a possible separation of the root of his right temporal bone from his skull,
I recalled that Dan was an amateur bodybuilder. Had a bout of intense
exercise been the cause?

There was no way to know. Nor, it turned out, did it matter. Whatever
its origin, the leak needed to be repaired, which, four days later, it was.
The surgery went well, and he was discharged home within a week.

His headaches, however, continued. What's more, they were now
worse when he lay down and *better* when he sat up, the exact opposite
of his experience prior to surgery. When the neurosurgeon performed a
lumbar puncture to measure Dan's cerebrospinal fluid pressure again, he
found to his surprise it was now *high*. Though he had no idea why this
had happened, draining some of the fluid off and returning the pressure
to normal temporarily improved Dan's headaches, so he decided to bring
him back to the operating room to insert a ventriculoperitoneal shunt
that would drain cerebrospinal fluid continuously from his brain into his
abdomen to keep the pressure normal.

The shunt drained the fluid as intended and resolved his headaches,
but only for about two weeks, at which point they came back as intense as
they'd ever been. So I prescribed a pain medication—and then another,
and then yet another. But nothing I gave him helped.

Pain as Disease

The establishment of pain management as a medical subspecialty
began by some estimates in 1965 with the publication of Ronald Melzack and Patrick Wall's now-classic article "Pain Mechanisms: A New
Theory," which for the first time drew the medical community's attention to pain as an important problem in and of itself.[14] Before that, pain
had generally been seen only as a *consequence* of disease, one that would

generally resolve along with the underlying process that had caused it. But after the publication of Melzack and Wall's article and the formation of the International Association for the Study of Pain, the medical community at last began to recognize that pain can sometimes act as a disease itself. Today we know that up to 25 percent of adults suffer from moderate to severe chronic pain, and as many as 10 percent have so much chronic pain that it affects their ability to work and interact socially.[15] In such cases, pain is no longer signaling danger but rather indicates a nervous system gone haywire.

Which is what the pain specialist to whom I eventually referred Dan concluded had happened to him. As with many chronic pain patients, his central nervous system had become the problem, she believed, and for some reason was now causing him to experience normal levels of cerebrospinal fluid pressure as painful. She pointed me to a number of recent studies showing that chronic pain originating from a myriad of causes—phantom pains in amputated limbs, generalized body pains in fibromyalgia, joint pains in osteoarthritis, perhaps even headaches that won't stop—is associated with a chronic increase in the sensitivity of pain centers in the brain.[16]

Whether this increase is permanent, however, is unclear. What is clear is that chronic pain is notoriously difficult to treat. Anti-epileptic medications like gabapentin and carbamazepine have been found to be effective for some patients, but often only partially. Also, doctors are frequently reluctant to prescribe narcotics due to their side effects and questions about their long-term efficacy, as well as concerns about addiction and abuse.[17]

Yet in the face of the intensity of suffering with which chronic pain patients often present, pain specialists find themselves, appropriately, willing to take greater risks. Which is why the pain specialist to whom I'd referred Dan placed him on both anti-epileptics and narcotics (oxycodone and methadone), and even started intermittent intravenous injections of ketamine, an animal tranquilizer.

But his headaches had never entirely resolved. "It's true we don't know when—or if—your pain is going to end," I admitted to Dan. "But I've been thinking about another treatment besides pain medication for you. Even though it may not significantly reduce your pain, it might help you manage it better." I told him I thought he should start seeing a cognitive-behavioral therapist who helped patients deal with chronic pain psychologically. I said I had a good one in mind and thought he might find her helpful. Though skeptical, he was by this time also unable to work, on disability, and desperate for relief of any kind, so he readily agreed.

Distraction

When I saw Dan in my clinic two months later, I was surprised to learn he'd gone back to his job. When I asked how he was managing it, he told me the therapist to whom I'd referred him had said something that made him think he could. "You're going to be in pain whether you're working or not," she'd said, "so if you want to work, you should work."

"To be honest," he admitted to me with an embarrassed smile, "it never even occurred to me that I could."

His therapist brought up the idea after suggesting several cognitive techniques for increasing Dan's pain tolerance, starting with her recommendation that he try distracting himself with humor.[18] But when he'd tried watching some comedies as she suggested, he found they only helped a little and only while he was actually watching them. Besides, he'd protested to her, he didn't want to spend the rest of his life in front of a television screen. He loved his job and wanted to go back to it.

So she'd suggested he do just that, reassuring him that because his pain wasn't signaling any ongoing harm or tissue damage, going back to work would be safe. And if he loved his job as much as he said, it might even distract him from his pain. But for that to happen, she'd cautioned, he'd probably need to find his work more than just interesting.[19] The key to making distraction work, she said, wasn't just doing something that riveted attention, but doing something that *aroused emotion*.[20] For the mechanism by which distraction reduced pain, she'd said, seemed to involve not only having one's attention turned elsewhere but also being made to feel good as a result.[21]

But she'd also warned him that pain was essentially unrivaled in its ability to command our attention (as it needed to be given the survival advantage that attention to injury or potential injury clearly provided[22]). Relatively minor pain, like the kind associated with jogging, seemed reasonably amenable to distraction with humor or daydreaming or conversation (useful for getting into shape, certainly), but past a certain level of pain, distraction, in her experience, offered chronic pain patients only minor relief.

Also, given the severity of *his* pain, getting back to work to test the power of distraction would undoubtedly prove physically challenging. So she had something to suggest in addition, she'd told him, a type of cognitive behavioral therapy called *acceptance and commitment therapy* that had as its goal not the reduction of pain but the improvement of the ability to function in spite of it.

Acceptance and Commitment Therapy

Acceptance and commitment therapy proposes that by fully surrendering to pain, the sufferer can paradoxically prevent himself from being defeated by it. Such acceptance, his therapist had said, while having little power to decrease his pain, might have great power to decrease his suffering. For one thing, accepting his pain might enable him to stop making futile efforts to avoid it and perhaps to start doing things he wanted, like going back to work. Also, she suggested, clinging to the possibility that he might still avoid his pain could also be engendering fear—fear that he might *not* avoid his pain—which could actually be intensifying the unpleasantness of his pain. In sum, his therapist had said, several studies had shown that acceptance and commitment therapy could improve functioning in people suffering from chronic pain,[23] and if he was interested they could begin trying to make it work for him. Dan said he was.

Because studies had shown that simply becoming mindful of one's emotional response to pain decreases its unpleasantness and improves functioning,[24] and because meditation had been shown to reduce the unpleasantness of acute pain by almost 60 percent[25] (making meditation by some measures superior even to morphine[26]), she first began teaching him how to meditate. She instructed him to focus specifically on attending to his breathing and on acknowledging any and all negative internal reactions without judgment, thinking the latter would be especially useful in helping him learn to accept his pain. Interestingly, she told him, meditation had also been found to decrease the activation of several of the brain's pain centers, hinting at the possibility that the pain-sensitizing derangements found in the brains of chronic pain sufferers might actually be amenable to repair.[27] Further, other research showed that when chronic pain patients were trained to reduce the activity in their anterior cingulate cortex by receiving real-time visual feedback from inside a functional MRI scanner, they were able to reduce their pain by as much as 50 percent *without specifically intending pain reduction as their goal*, offering evidence that conscious control of nonconscious brain activity is not only possible but also might represent another way to control pain.[28]

In addition to recommending meditation, she emphasized how chronic pain differs from acute pain; that unlike acute pain, chronic pain doesn't represent harm. She stressed the need for him to abandon the short-term strategies he used to treat his pain, strategies that interfered with his ability to work (for example, remaining still or not going outside). She also started him on a program of gradual exposure to work-related activities that he'd previously avoided to minimize his pain, like taking public transportation and working long hours at a computer. Finally, she emphasized the importance of identifying his goals as clearly and concretely as he could and of consistently reaffirming his commitment to them.

Though ultimately Dan found meditation only minimally helpful in reducing his pain, the idea of acceptance, he said—the idea that he could do what he wanted in spite of his pain—proved "liberating" in the end. Liberating enough, at least, to enable him to get back to work.

Accepting Emotional Pain

Though the experience of physical pain and emotional pain are clearly different, functional imaging studies show that, with few exceptions, the regions of the brain that these types of pain activate are identical.[29] These include not only the regions responsible for giving pain its unpleasant character, but also those responsible for regulating its size, location, and intensity (perhaps partially explaining the startling finding that Tylenol, a centrally acting pain reliever, alleviates not only the pain of a smashed finger *but also the pain of hurt feelings.*[30]) No wonder, then, that physical and emotional pain produce the same reaction: a strong desire to avoid the things that cause them. "Suffer what there is to suffer. Enjoy what there is to enjoy. Regard both suffering and joy as facts of life," wrote Nichiren Daishonin.[31] Yet most of us clearly don't.

Unfortunately, the strategies we use to avoid emotional pain often cause more harm than does the experience of emotional pain itself: more harm results, for example, from excessive drinking or drug use than from the anxiety they're often used to anesthetize; more harm results from relationship sabotage than from the fear of intimacy that often drives it.[32]

Not only that, but attempting to suppress emotional pain may paradoxically *increase* it.[33] In contrast, being *accepting* of emotional pain, being willing to experience it without attempting to control it, has actually been found to decrease it. In one study of patients with generalized anxiety disorder, for example, subjects who were taught to accept their anxiety reported substantial reductions in worry, reductions that persisted even beyond the duration of the study.[34]

But such a decrease is only a happy byproduct, for the true purpose of acceptance isn't to diminish emotional pain but rather to become *more comfortable feeling it*. In fact, aiming to diminish emotional pain purposely via acceptance is functionally no different than trying to suppress it, and as a result such attempts typically backfire. For acceptance isn't about *feeling* better so much as it is about *doing* better—about preventing hunger from causing us to overeat, or anxiety from causing us to socially isolate ourselves, or chronic headaches from causing us to decrease our activity level. By accepting and even embracing such painful experiences, we prevent ourselves from engaging in the undesired behaviors to which they often lead.

In learning to recognize just when we're trying to avoid emotional pain—a feat that requires, surprisingly, significant amounts of practice—we become more capable of experiencing emotional pain without judgment. With practice, for example, we can move from thinking "anxiety is bad" to thinking "I'm feeling anxiety." Likewise, when painful *thoughts* arise—for example, that we're worthless—an exercise in which we repeat the words "I'm worthless" again and again until they stop triggering any meaning at all, becoming in essence nothing more than sounds, can help us recognize that our thoughts are just stories, not truths that *necessarily* reflect objective reality at all.[35] In this way, by learning to withhold judgment of our painful feelings and draining the meaning from our painful thoughts we're able to *reduce our desire to be rid of them*.

A number of other techniques can help with this as well. We can imagine our painful thoughts as letters sent to us by others—perhaps people whose judgment we find flawed and with whom we often disagree, thus predisposing us to accept any such negative ideas with a proverbial grain of salt. Or we can practice "thanking our minds" for painful thoughts as if we were thanking a small child for offering a quaint but ultimately nonsensical idea. Or we can imagine a painful feeling as a discreet package of a specific size and weight that we might need to hold for a little while but which eventually we'll be able to put down. Anything and everything that draws our attention to the fact that our thoughts and our feelings are not tyrants we have to obey but merely phenomena of our minds. This then helps us with the real goal of acceptance: preventing those phenomena from interfering with the achievement of our goals. For acceptance doesn't mean allowing our problems to go unchallenged; it means accepting the painful thoughts and feelings that invariably arise when problems occur so that they don't stop us from trying to *solve* them.

Research shows that acceptance works in a variety of contexts. Accepting rather than rejecting obsessional thoughts, for example, significantly reduces compulsions in people suffering from obsessive-compulsive disorder.[36] Accepting food cravings reduces eating and helps people lose weight.[37] Accepting nicotine cravings helps people quit smoking.[38] And accepting warning signs of an impending seizure even decreases the severity and frequency of epilepsy.[39]

Thus, though we might think we need to control our emotions when facing adversity—to feel brave when fighting cancer, for example, or stoic when losing a loved one—we might do better if instead we give ourselves permission to feel what we actually do. For if we fail to give ourselves that permission and instead aim to be something we aren't, we'll be more likely to experience suffering not only at the hands of our pain, but also at the hands of our failure to live up to our expectations. Approaching painful internal experiences with an attitude of acceptance, in contrast accepting that sometimes we're weak—paradoxically may be the key to our becoming strong.

Going back to work, however, cost Dan dearly. His pain had not only continued but actually worsened. He was coming to me now, he said, because the pain medications he was using were no longer providing him the relief he needed.

I told Dan we were running out of options. Frankly, I confessed, I wasn't sure what else to try. What I didn't tell him, however, yet what was perhaps an even more important truth, was that when he said the narcotics were no longer working for him, I became annoyed. He must have sensed it in my tone, though, because as I paused to consider what to do next, he said suddenly, "I really appreciate how you're sticking with me through all of this. It must be frustrating for you, too."

Embarrassed, I recalled another patient of mine, a woman named Celia, who also suffered from chronic pain, hers from back surgery that had gone horribly awry. The first time I met her, she described in clear yet unemotional detail not just the quality and severity of her pain but all the losses she'd suffered at its hands: days to weeks of time absent from work eventually leading to complete inability to work at all, periods she desperately wanted to but couldn't play with her children in her neighborhood playground, and the strain on her marriage that eventually shattered it. I'd told her in response that I'd do everything in my power to help her and promised not to abandon her. Her response to that was to choke up with tears, which she tried, heartrendingly, to hide.

Only several months later did she explain her reaction. When other providers before me had tried and failed to help her—through no fault of their own, she acknowledged—they'd lost all interest in her, gradually returning her phone calls sluggishly or not at all, resisting filling prescriptions for her, and even becoming irritated when she would report her pain had increased as it sometimes did for no discernible reason. They'd all seemed to care when they'd first met her, she said, but all failed to remain interested in her over the long run. She knew medicine's ability to help her was limited, but what she wanted more than anything besides pain relief, she told me, was someone who would stick with her, even if that was the full extent of what they could do.

Though I never said so, I understood why none of her previous physicians had: not out of indifference or lack of caring, but as a result of their inability to manage their own sense of futility. Perhaps as a result of a psychological coping mechanism, doctors as a group tend to ignore what they can't improve.

I also had felt inclined to ignore patients I couldn't help. And after proving no more adept at controlling her pain than the doctors who'd tried before me, I began to want to ignore her, too. But she'd warned me well. By calling attention to the way her previous doctors had abandoned her, she'd forced me to reflect on my impulse to mimic their behavior. And in making me acutely aware of my impulse to turn my back on her, I became far less likely to indulge it.

An impulse, though, I was now tempted to indulge with Dan. Yet largely as a result of my experience with Celia, I couldn't escape my understanding that my annoyance was really only a reaction to my own sense of helplessness. So, following Dan's example, I resolved to neither deny nor suppress my feelings but instead to fully accept them and move on. Which then enabled me to tell Dan what I'd once told Celia: that I would not abandon him.

Despite my skepticism about its likely long-term efficacy, I agreed to try him on a higher dose of methadone. Which, he let me know a week later, actually helped. Unfortunately, it also made him feel significantly more fatigued. His wife, Cheryl, also now began noticing long pauses in his breathing while he slept. Concerned about the possibility that he'd developed respiratory depression from such a large narcotic dose, I ordered a sleep study. Two weeks later the results came back: he had indeed developed central sleep apnea.

Dan now faced an agonizing decision: reduce the dose of narcotics to improve his sleep and thus his energy or continue his current dose but suffer not only extreme fatigue but also dangerous reductions in his oxygen levels at night.

In the end, it was no choice at all. Hoping his newfound skill at accepting pain would enable him to keep working, Dan decided to taper his narcotic dose back down to its previous level. At the same time I started him on a continuous positive airway pressure machine (CPAP) to treat his sleep apnea. Unfortunately, like most patients, he found CPAP nearly impossible to tolerate and asked me to stop it. But I encouraged him to try to adjust to it, arguing that it might enable him to return to the higher dose of methadone. Discouraged by the additional discomfort he was now being asked to tolerate, he nevertheless agreed to try.

Then he noticed something odd. When we added oxygen to his CPAP at night, he stopped awakening in the morning with headaches altogether. I found this intriguing: cluster headaches, a particularly painful type of vascular headache, are well known to improve with oxygen. Might his headaches, I wondered, be responding to oxygen, too?

We decided to have him experiment by wearing oxygen during the day when his headaches were so bad that he had to stay home from work and discovered that half the time it actually resolved them *entirely*. So he began using portable oxygen to abort his headaches on a regular basis. To our amazement, he soon found himself able to work with not only a lower narcotic dose but also better headache control than anytime since his original operation.

And then, months later at a follow-up visit, Dan surprised me again. "I've gone back to the gym," he told me, adding quickly, "Nothing strenuous. Just light weights and a little jogging."

"Doesn't it make your headaches worse?" I asked.

He nodded. "I only go on good days. And then I just deal with it," he added with a shrug.

That shrug made me smile. For though luck in the form of oxygen therapy had indeed brought him a degree of relief that neither of us had believed possible, I realized his ability to accept the pain it *hadn't* improved had impacted his life even more. And as I checked his blood pressure and noted the increased tone of his biceps, I realized that what actually gave acceptance its power was simply this: we all want to quit far sooner than we must. Which was why by learning to accept whatever pain we feel—as Dan had—we become capable of handling, and thus of accomplishing, far more than we ever believed we could.

7

Let Go

No matter how powerful our determination, no matter how well-prepared we are for obstacles both expected and not, no matter how much personal responsibility we take, and no matter how good we may be at accepting pain, the unpleasant truth is that some maladies in life can't be remedied and some goals can't be achieved. Which is why sometimes choosing to cease fighting and instead let go engenders resilience, too.

I've cared for many patients with cancer throughout my career, but one in particular stands out in my mind: a forty-year-old journalist who came to me with a glioblastoma multiforme, a malignant brain tumor with an almost uniformly fatal prognosis. The reason I remember him so vividly isn't just that he was nearly my age, or that, like me, he had a wife, a three-year-old toddler, and loved to write, but also because of something he told me at our second visit. "Hope," he said, "is the only thing standing between me and peace."

His thoughts continually vacillated tens, even hundreds, of times a day, he told me, between two extremes: on the one hand, toward a hope that he would somehow be cured, and on the other, toward a recognition that cure was, if not impossible, extremely improbable. Paradoxically, though, it was embracing the idea that he *wouldn't* be cured that he found the most comforting, and hoping for a cure that kept him awake at night awash in anxiety.

People usually consider hope among the most wondrous of gifts: it keeps us going when we want to quit and makes possible victories that seem unattainable. A uniquely human emotion—for only humans can envision the future well enough to feel anything about it—hope has a long and glorious history of bringing out the best in humankind. The key to hope's value, however, is that the thing about which we feel it must actually be possible. Luckily, because we tend to judge far more things impossible than actually are, in most cases hope serves us well. But in those cases in which the thing for which we hope is destined not to occur, hope does indeed stand between us and peace, blocking as it does our ability to feel the one thing that might bring us peace: acceptance of the inevitable.

The problem with continuing to hope for the unattainable is that it makes us continue to want it. And wanting something we can't have is awful: tethered to uncertainty, our minds ruminate obsessively, inventing improbable schemes for somehow finding a way to get that which we desire, both raging and trembling at the thought of being denied it. In such cases, hoping for the future we want does nothing but prevent us from letting go in our hearts of a future we can't have, thereby intensifying and prolonging our suffering.

Intellectually, my patient knew he wouldn't be cured, but his desire to live prevented him from abandoning hope for it; and his inability to abandon hope not only drove him toward things he knew would prove useless, like macrobiotic diets, vitamin supplements, and fasting, but more importantly kept his focus on what he knew would never be his: a normal lifespan.

He so very much wanted to stop pining for life, he told me several months after I'd first met him. He was a fighter and wanted to fight, he said, but only a fight he had a real chance to win.

"You don't know you can't win," I argued, my own desire for him to survive momentarily clouding my judgment, thinking, as I was, about his wife and daughter—especially his daughter—and my own wife and son.

"That's exactly the problem," he said. "Intellectually I know this ends. But I can't *feel* it. I can't stop hoping to survive."

A few weeks after that, however, because of the location of the tumor in his brain and its inexorable growth, he lost the ability to write. And though this was by far the most devastating blow his cancer had dealt him, it also turned out to be, ironically, its greatest gift.

"I've finally given up hope," he told me at our final visit, though by then his speech was so garbled his wife had to translate the sentence for me to understand it. My throat constricted and my eyes moistened when I heard this, though how much from sadness and how much from relief, I didn't know. He died less than a week later. Peacefully, his wife said.

The Inevitability of Loss

From the moment we're born into this world we face a troubling paradox: what makes life interesting and fun are the attachments we form, but those same attachments become the cause of our worst pain in life when we lose them. Even when merely *threatened* by the loss of an attachment, whether a person or a thing, we often suffer horribly. How then can we achieve any kind of lasting happiness when so many important things to which we become attached, including our own lives, will eventually be lost to us?

The answer lies at least partially in the acceptance of the inevitability of loss. For only by letting go in our hearts of something we've lost or are about to lose do we become able to free ourselves from the suffering that our inability to keep it brings us. If grief is what we feel when we lose something to which we're attached, letting go may be the most effective strategy at our disposal to resolve it.

Not that there aren't other strategies as well. We can, for instance, attempt to limit the *number* of things to which we're attached to reduce the likelihood of losing something upon which our happiness depends. But three problems exist with this approach: First, we're not necessarily in conscious control of our propensity to form attachments or of the strength with which we form them. Second, we remain vulnerable to losing *everything* to which we're attached, including those few things we think we can't lose and remain happy, whatever they may be. And third, reminding ourselves when we lose something to which we're only modestly attached that we haven't lost something *else* to which we're strongly attached, like our children or our health, typically proves unhelpful in blunting the pain of the loss we did experience.

So some attempt to attach to *nothing*. Though this is a strategy frequently promoted by other sects of Buddhism, Nichiren Buddhism considers it a foolhardy one. Desire is ingrained in all living things if for no other reason than to ensure survival. How, for example, could we live if we weren't attached to eating or breathing? Further, how can we create value if we refuse to attach to goals? And how would it serve our friends, our spouses, or our children to limit the degree to which we care about them simply to be able to diminish the force of the blow that losing them will one day bring?

A final strategy, then, lies in attaching to things while denying, even to ourselves, that losing them will cause us to suffer at all. Unfortunately, this frequently leads to behavior, like alcohol and drug abuse, that causes even more harm than does allowing oneself to feel the pain of loss.[1] Even worse, refusing to acknowledge or feel the pain of loss seems, incongruously, to perpetuate it, often turning what would otherwise have been an acute grief reaction into a chronic one.[2]

This is what I thought had happened to my patient Ravi, a sixty-five-year-old English professor of East Indian descent, who came to see me one day complaining of steadily diminishing strength. He'd begun to notice it a month prior to his sixty-fifth birthday. Ever since his fortieth birthday, he explained, every Sunday he'd been doing a number of push-ups equal to his age. But this time instead of advancing by one to yield sixty-five, he'd fallen back by four, finding himself barely able to complete sixty.

"Sixty is pretty good," I said. I had a hard time imagining his inability to do sixty-five push-ups meant anything serious was amiss.

"I should have been able to do sixty-five," he insisted with a worried expression.

A quick neurologic exam revealed his strength was normal and shifted my concern from his triceps to his anxiety. "Ravi, you're one of the few people I know over sixty who can even *do* push-ups," I said, hoping he might respond to simple reassurance. "This seems more like a consequence of aging than anything else."

He shook his head, closing his eyes. "I'm getting weaker more quickly than I should be." He emphasized also how tired he felt despite getting a full eight hours of sleep every night.

"Is fatigue stopping you from doing anything else besides exercise?"

"It's not that I *can't* do other things," he said. "It's that I don't *want* to." He was, in fact, having a hard time enjoying anything. He'd recently retired, he told me, and was struggling mightily with the loss of what he termed "approbation" from his former students. Additionally, he'd always considered himself the grand patriarch of his family of four children, but as they'd grown older and started families of their own, he'd found himself feeling more and more marginalized. He felt less capable, both physically and mentally, less depended upon, and less valuable, he confessed, than he ever had before.

"How's your appetite?"

He looked surprised at the question. "Not so good, actually."

I asked if he was having difficulty concentrating. He said he was. Was his mood low? Yes. How long had all this been going on? About a month, he said. Had he ever felt this way before? Never to this degree, he answered.

"Ravi, I think you're depressed," I told him. It explained his decreased motivation, I said, which in turn explained his inability to complete the push-ups. To reassure us both, however, that the cause of his depression wasn't physical, I ordered a complete blood count, thyroid tests, and a sedimentation rate.

When I told him the next day that all was normal, however, he seemed to become even more despondent and asked me to order more tests, skeptical that depression was the cause of his symptoms. "Depression is actually common in retirees," I said when I saw him back in my clinic a week later, "especially ones who place a high value on living a contributive life. Even when you choose it yourself, retirement still amounts to a loss."

His shoulders sagged and his head drooped. "You look forward to it for so long," he mused, "and then when it comes, part of you doesn't even want it." He shook his head. "I thought it would be a transition to freedom, but it feels more like a transition to decline."

"Transitions are hard in general," I said. "But just because you've lost one thing doesn't mean you can't gain something else." I suggested he think about how he could leverage his professorial skills to create value in a new way, in a new context. He responded by saying that he couldn't envision doing anything else with his professorial skills but what he'd always done—teaching.

"Give it time," I suggested. "It's hard to move on to something new when you're still mourning something you've lost."

"Mourning?" he said, startled. Then he paused to consider it. "Maybe I am."

"Losing something and letting go of it in your heart are two entirely different things."

He smiled wanly. "Any advice on how to do that second one?"

I gave a small shrug. "You have to choose it."

Finding Meaning in Loss

When we lose, or are about to lose, an important attachment—whether a loved one, a desired outcome, a material possession, a daily routine, a delusional belief, or our life itself—we seize it in our minds with all our might, raging against the forces that conspire to take it from us as if our refusal to accept losing it could somehow prevent or even reverse its disappearance. But remaining attached to what we no longer have will lead us nowhere. On the one hand, if the attachment we're refusing to surrender is to a solution that won't work—for example, if we're attached to suing someone for libel to reclaim our reputation—we may mistakenly conclude that a problem isn't solvable when in reality it's simply not solvable the way we want. Alternatively, if the attachment we're refusing to surrender is to a person we loved, we may find ourselves clinging to the pain of loss itself, which sometimes comes to represent the only thing keeping alive our sense of connection to our loved one.

But if we refuse to let go of our pain, we'll find ourselves less capable of both enduring adversity and mustering the determination to attack obstacles. For this reason, as much as we may yearn for our lost attachments, as much as we may ache once they're gone and wish desperately to have them back, when no hope for their recovery remains, *letting go* of them is what it means to be resilient. This was true with Dan and his headaches: though approaching them with an attitude of acceptance helped him to get back to work and even to begin working out, what made that acceptance possible was letting go of the need for his pain to end—letting go, in other words, of his attachment to a pain-free life. If the purpose of accepting painful *feelings* is to be able to continue fighting for desired goals, the purpose of accepting painful *losses* is to be able to *stop* fighting for goals that lie beyond our power to achieve.

Not that letting go of our attachments means ceasing to care about them, that they were never really important to us, or that we no longer miss them when they're gone. Rather, it means finding a way not only to accept that we can't get them back but also to believe our happiness doesn't depend on our being able to keep them. And though no one can predict exactly what experiences we need to have to reach this place—a place where we can peacefully accept the loss of even our most beloved attachments—most people eventually do find a way to reach it.[3]

Which doesn't mean that all paths are equally good or equally speedy. Attempting to resolve grief by finding the *reason* for a loss, for example—a type of meaning-seeking that psychologists call *sense-making*—though extremely common,[4] may be not only ineffective but also counterproductive. For one thing, research suggests that we find explanations for our losses in less than half of the cases in which we look for them. In one study of parents whose children had died from sudden infant death syndrome, for example, only 41 percent of those who sought an explanation for their loss reported ever finding one.[5] For another, even though people who seek such explanations and find them seem to be less sad, anxious, and angry than people who seek them but don't find them, they also seem to be no happier than people who *never* seek them in the first place.[6] And though we can't entirely rule out the possibility that the latter group refrains from seeking such explanations *because* they're more resilient than the former, studies suggest that attempting to make sense of loss might increase one's suffering without offering any benefit beyond that gained from avoiding the attempt altogether.[7]

Even more surprising is research showing that even when we do find an explanation for our misfortune, *we continue to search for additional ones*. In a study of survivors of incest, 80 percent of women who reported finding a satisfactory explanation for their victimization also reported continuing to ruminate about it.[8] Trying to make sense of misfortune, in other words, doesn't help us move on as much as we think—perhaps, we might speculate, because the causes of misfortune are often inscrutable, and therefore the only explanations we can offer ourselves are, by definition, incomplete or difficult to believe.

Unfortunately, our desire to make sense of misfortune is sometimes hard to resist. This is especially true when misfortune strikes unexpectedly or seems unfair—as when a child dies before a parent—for such misfortune represents evidence that challenges our view of the world as predictable and controllable, often creating an intense cognitive dissonance.[9] But instead of trying to resolve that dissonance by explaining the evidence away, we'd do better to revise our worldview. Certainly, we all want control over our lives, but in a universe in which all things are mutually interdependent—where all phenomena rise and fall only in relation to all other phenomena, a principle that Nichiren Buddhism calls *dependent origination*—none of us can be said to have complete control over anything, not even, as only a moment of reflection makes clear, ourselves. What we have instead, and often in abundance, is *influence*: not the power to *guarantee* the result we want in all circumstances, but the power to make those results more *probable*. I can, for instance, write a sentence that perfectly expresses an idea I want to convey, but I can't control the way readers react to it, nor how many of them will want to buy the book in which it's written.

Though influence may seem a poor substitute for control, recognizing that it's all we have can help us more easily resist the need to make sense of our losses and thus help us let go of them more easily. For if we recognize that what lies behind the apparent arbitrariness of events is actually the sum of innumerable influences, many of which we simply can't see, we already know the essential explanation for every loss we might ever suffer: the most powerful influence we were able to exert was simply rendered ineffective by other more powerful ones.

Given that sense-making exposes us to an increased risk for prolonged or even increased grief, to speed our recovery from loss we might instead consider employing a different type of meaning-seeking that psychologists call *benefit-finding*. Unlike sense-making, research shows that attempting to create *benefit* out of loss—attempting to turn poison into medicine—actually reduces grief.

In one prospective study of the effects of journaling on grief and distress in undergraduates, researchers Wendy Lichtenthal and Dean Cruess divided subjects into three groups, one that wrote about their deepest thoughts and feelings concerning a recent loss (the emotional disclosure group), another that wrote with a focus on finding an explanation for it (the sense-making group), and a third that wrote with a focus on any positive life changes that resulted from it (the benefit-finding group). Additionally, members of a fourth control group wrote about a neutral topic unrelated to their loss. Results measured three months later showed that grief declined in all three groups compared to the control group, but that the greatest decline occurred in the group that wrote about finding benefit. What's more, the benefit-finding group also showed the greatest decline in posttraumatic stress symptoms and symptoms of depression.[10]

The Value of Our Attachments

Yet as valuable as finding benefit in loss may be in helping us recover from it, it's often not enough. Depending on the type of loss we've suffered and how it occurs, four additional things may be necessary. First, we may need to arrive at a moment of conviction that the loss of our attachment was inevitable—for example, that we did everything possible to save a loved one—or in cases where our loss was sudden and unpredictable, that we believe we had no power to prevent it.[11] Second, we may need to prepare ourselves against inappropriate and distressing questions that often follow ("Was she wearing a seat belt?") as well as well-meaning but ultimately unhelpful advice. For advice that discourages the expression of feeling ("Tears won't bring him back"), that attempts to minimize the loss's impact ("You had many good years together"), or that encourages us to recover faster ("You should get out more") may provoke a prolonged focus on what we've lost and therefore retard our ability to let it go.[12] Third, if we lose something that subsequently alters our self-image—for example, our ability to exercise—we may either need to find another way to retain that self-image or to accept and embrace an entirely new one. But this we can do with the help of the fourth and most important thing: a recognition that our happiness is never entirely dependent on the things to which we are attached.[13]

But believing that our happiness isn't dependent on those things is extremely difficult. For even if we believe we could give up *some* of our attachments and still be happy, most of us believe that without certain ones—a spouse, a child, a limb, our sight—our happiness would collapse and never recover. So, held captive by the notion that we require certain attachments to be happy, we continue to cling to them long after they've been irretrievably lost and as a result suffer far longer than we otherwise would. We forget, or fail to realize, that genuine happiness doesn't come from having things but rather from a strong life force forged by adversity, a life force that enables us to enjoy *all* of life. We forget, in other words, the crucial difference between building our happiness *out of* our attachments and building our happiness out of a strong life force that enables us to *enjoy* our attachments. We fail to realize, ruled as we are by loss aversion, that even were we to lose everything in the world that matters to us at once, most of us would still retain the capacity to recover and eventually even flourish.

"It sure doesn't seem like it," Ravi said with a sad smile.

"Not to me, either," I said, and we both laughed.

The Faulty Premise of Regret

Then Ravi confessed that he'd also been ruminating about a number of his past mistakes, especially about his decision thirty years ago to divorce his wife. He felt intense guilt about breaking up his family, he said, and about what it did to his children. He wondered if he wouldn't be feeling so down if he wasn't also feeling so guilty.

"It's hard not to feel regret about *something* you did, or didn't do, when you lose something to which you're strongly attached," I admitted. But that regret, I argued, is caused by a belief in a faulty premise: that had we only chosen a different path from the one we did, our life wouldn't just have turned out different but *better*. We idealize the road not taken, imagining only the good things that would have resulted from our taking it, conveniently leaving out the bad things that would invariably have followed as well, including all the unrelated bumps and bruises that would happen in the day-to-day course of any alternative life.[14]

Which means any confidence we have that some other choice would have brought us to a present filled with less suffering than our current one is typically unjustified, even when the choice we did make has brought us great suffering indeed. For how could we ever know that if we'd made that other choice that we wouldn't be suffering now even more? We may pine for the life we've left unlived, but that life almost certainly wouldn't have existed the way we imagine it. Though it might have been better, it also might have been worse.

"I'm not arguing that the choices we make don't matter," I told Ravi. "Just that they don't matter as much as we think. Despite how fervently we may argue to the contrary, happiness isn't as much a function of what our lives look like on the outside as it is a function of how we feel about them on the inside. So rather than allow ourselves to wallow in suffering over what might have been, we should try to remind ourselves that the grass only ever *seems* greener, and that there's inevitably something to enjoy and something to suffer over in *every* circumstance. So rather than focus on what might have been, we should focus on making what *is* just as good, if not better."

But letting go of an alternative past is sometimes more easily said than done. Research shows that trying to "undo" past events—ruminating about what we could have done differently, especially to prevent a loss—is extremely common. In one study, 58 percent of subjects who'd lost a spouse or a child in a motor vehicle accident reported at some point trying to undo it, and half of them said they had such thoughts up to seven years later.[15] Just as some of us often feel driven to understand how a loss occurred, some of us also feel driven to imagine how it might *not* have occurred. Yet such imaginings are just about as useful: as with trying but failing to understand why a loss occurred, the undoing of traumatic events is also associated with more intense and prolonged suffering.[16]

"'Things without all remedy should be without regard: what's done, is done,'" Ravi quoted. Then he sighed. "If only letting go of past mistakes were that easy."

"Well, if you can't let go of them," I said, "you can at least try to change what they *mean*."

Rewriting the Past

In seventh grade, a cabal of classmates made me the target of anti-Semitic persecution so traumatizing that my parents were forced to carry two mortgages for six months until they could sell the house we were living in so that we could move back to the suburb from which we came. I exited that school year mistrustful, fearful, and socially isolated. In the years that followed, I would occasionally look back and wonder how else the experience had affected me, figuring vaguely that what didn't kill me had made me stronger, but never really delving too deeply into the fear that still remained in the pit of my stomach whenever I was thrust into the midst of a group of people I didn't know.

Nearly a decade later, then, when I was introduced to Nichiren Buddhism, I was told that practicing it would enable me to change the past, present, and future. Present and future I understood—but past? How, I wondered, could anyone change something that had already happened?

But then one day while chanting and thinking about my seventh-grade experience, I had an insight: I'd been victimized in part because I'd failed to stand up for myself. Whenever I'd perceived I was in danger of being attacked, my strategy had been to ingratiate myself with my would-be attacker in any way I could. I'd allow myself to be teased, disdained, embarrassed, or humiliated as long as I believed it would prevent me from being hurt. Not once did I ever fight back.

In a flash, I realized that this pattern of behavior stretched back through my failed relationship with my first girlfriend, extended further into my past to include my experience in seventh grade, and landed somewhere in the most remote recesses of my earliest childhood. Making myself into a victim had been a strategy I'd used throughout my life, I realized, for many reasons: to get attention, to convince others to protect me when I felt threatened, and to appear invisible to malevolent peers.

I didn't recognize it until sometime later, but the moment I consciously apprehended that I had a tendency to represent myself as helpless, I stopped doing it. And as my change in attitude gradually began to affect my interactions with others, the relationships I'd created that required I play that role eventually dissolved.

And though this was a breakthrough for which I was profoundly grateful, an even bigger realization struck soon after: the way I felt about my seventh-grade experience had changed as well. It was no longer a sensitive wound I took pains to avoid rubbing but was now a well-healed scar I could hardly see. I had indeed changed the past: not by changing what had happened but by changing its *significance*. By retrospectively awakening to a behavior pattern that had contributed to a trauma in my past, I'd changed my behavior in the present, and in so doing had not only transformed that trauma's significance, but also freed myself from the pain associated with my memories of it.[17]

"So if an event from your past remains painful to think about," I told Ravi, "you should understand that pain as an indication you have unfinished business, not with whomever or whatever else was involved in the event, but with yourself."

Maybe someone hurt us. Maybe we hurt someone else. Maybe we made a choice out of weakness or fear or anger. But we needn't waste time in recriminations or in wishing we could go back in time to change what happened. We can turn that hurt or regret into a catalyst for personal growth, into motivation for examining the reasons we made the choice in the first place and for asking ourselves how we might change to avoid making the same mistake again. For we achieve victory over past mistakes when we learn how to make a choice we *won't* regret when facing a similar circumstance in the future. Certainly, *anticipatory* regret may be adaptive, often motivating us to do things we don't want to do but should—like pay a condolence call or study for an exam. But regret over past actions, I said to Ravi, is nothing but a poison that prevents us from enjoying the life that's resulted from the things we did do, which is the only life available for us to enjoy at all.

"What you're saying makes great sense, Alex," he said. "But I'm still having a hard time not beating myself up about some of the things I've done."

"Then the other thing you need to do," I said, "is work on being more compassionate toward yourself."

Self-Compassion

I told Ravi about another patient of mine named Terry, whom I thought also judged himself too harshly, constantly criticizing himself for being, in his words, "embarrassingly needy." He thought it related to an early childhood trauma: when he was six, his three-year-old sister had been killed in a car accident. He didn't specifically remember her death, he said, but he did remember being left alone with a maid for a year after it and feeling a painful sense of abandonment as a result.

His neediness had recently resurfaced, Terry told me, when his son became seriously ill. Unfortunately, as in the past, Terry again became what he thought was *too* needy, finding that his urgent desire for comfort was driving away the very people to whom he turned for support. So he felt resentful. And as a result of that, he spent a lot of his time not only feeling needy but also beating himself up for feeling it.

In response to this I'd suggested that if he couldn't get the comfort he needed from others, he could get it instead from *himself*. I suggested he try something called *compassionate mind training*, which had as its goal the changing of "an internalized dominating-attacking style into a caring, compassionate way of being with one's distress."[18] Compassionate mind training teaches that automatic reactions—our emotions—are not our fault; that we have no direct control over our feelings and therefore can't be blamed for them.[19] It also teaches people to reduce their submissive acceptance of self-attacks, not by attempting to refute them but instead by asking themselves why such attacks occur. Finally, it teaches people to have empathy for their own distress by accessing feelings of warmth they have for others and then transferring them onto themselves.

I'd cautioned him, however, that the greatest barrier to self-comfort wasn't the actual degree of difficulty involved in creating it, but rather that we often think we *don't deserve it*. Even when we haven't been exposed to and internalized early parental criticism ("Why are you so stupid?"), we're frequently our own worst critic. And while the tendency to hold ourselves to a higher standard is beneficial in many ways, it also carries with it a cost: a decreased ability to turn to *ourselves* for words of comfort when we're hurting.

Of course, I'd told Terry, the positive impact that comforting words have on us may have less to do with the words themselves than with the fact that they come from someone we think cares about us. For even when words ring hollow, even just sensing another person's *desire* to comfort us often makes us feel better. Which suggests that to self-comfort effectively we need to be able to generate such feelings of loving-kindness toward ourselves.

The Nature of the Self

Luckily, I'd told Terry, our minds are constructed in a way that positions us to do just that: despite the persistent feeling we all have of being a unified self, we are in fact the sum of multiple selves. This is more than just a metaphor. Some patients who've had their cerebral hemispheres surgically separated in an effort to control debilitating epilepsy have been found to develop a condition known as *alien hand syndrome* in which one of their hands will sometimes act of its "own" volition—for example, by unbuttoning a shirt the patient has just buttoned.[20] In Nichiren Buddhism as well, people are considered to harbor dual selves, a *smaller self* and a *larger self*, the smaller self sometimes referring to the ego whose concerns are selfish while at other times to the seemingly endless capacity we have to believe wholeheartedly the various delusions that populate our thinking. The larger self, in contrast, is considered to be our best self, our wisest self, and our most selfless self—in short, our most enlightened self.

Yet conceiving of ourselves this way doesn't only help us see the self we should be trying to be; it also raises the possibility that one part of us

could actually comfort the other *as if the two were entirely separate people.*
For in imagining our larger self as our own loving parent, we might then
be able to say to ourselves the same things we might say to a suffering
friend or loved one. Or if that fails to evoke feelings of loving-kindness
toward ourselves, we can speak the same words to someone *else* we think
likely to mirror them back to us, finding the path to self-comfort through
indirect means instead.

Of course, if we're full of self-disgust, we may find the summoning
up of compassionate feelings for ourselves quite challenging. But self-
comfort is a skill that can be learned, even by people who specifically
don't feel they deserve to learn it—and in learning it we can reduce
feelings of depression, anxiety, inferiority, and shame.[21] In one study
of recently divorced adults, researchers found that subjects who demonstrated higher levels of compassion for themselves had less divorce-
related distress not only immediately following their divorce but also
up to nine months later.[22] Further, high levels of compassion for oneself
have also been found to correlate with decreased levels of anxiety in situations where people tend to evaluate their performance critically—for
example, on dates, during job interviews, and when engaged in public
speaking.[23]

To Terry's surprise, simply being introduced to the idea that he *could*
comfort himself seemed to grant him the power to do it. After our conversation, he sat down one morning, grasped hold of an image of his
larger self as supremely forgiving, compassionate, and wise, and turned
it on the part of himself that was afraid for his son and needed to be
told everything would be okay. Out loud, he spoke gently and lovingly to
himself, acknowledged that what was happening to his son was terrible,
that he hadn't failed as a parent, and that his own suffering was indeed
awful. He even went so far as to stroke his left arm with his right. He said
he felt silly doing it, but that it worked. He not only felt better, but also

was able to rid himself of the resentment he felt toward other people in his life for not comforting him in the way he wanted.

"So if he could do it, then so can you," I told Ravi. "Forgive yourself for whatever past mistakes you've made. Empathize with yourself for all the losses you've suffered. Your job, your physical prowess, your professional status, your role as patriarch of your family." I paused. "It's a lot to lose all at once."

"It is," he acknowledged quietly.

Stages of Change

Ravi told me he liked the idea of becoming more compassionate toward himself but that he had a hard time understanding how it would help him let go of things to which he was still attached in his heart. In response, I had one final suggestion for him to try: the *transtheoretical stages of change model*.

Originally developed to help people stop smoking, recent research, I told him, had suggested that the transtheoretical stages of change model could be adapted to help people who were dealing with loss.[24] It recognized five distinct stages through which people pass on their way to making difficult behavioral changes or adjusting to new circumstances. The first it termed *precontemplation*, a stage in which conscious recognition of the need to change (to quit smoking, for example) or, in the context of bereavement, to accept a loss, hasn't yet occurred. In this stage we know that we've suffered a loss but not that we haven't yet let go of it or that we need to do work to do so. We often say we feel "numb" in this stage, but what we really mean is that we feel overwhelmed by emotions we can't easily identify or articulate.

We know we've entered the second stage, *contemplation*, when the emotional tumult of precontemplation starts to abate. At that point, we typically come to realize that we're still attached to what we've lost and

that we have to take some kind of action to let go of it, even as we typically remain ambivalent about doing so. What ultimately resolves this
ambivalence and moves us from this stage into the next is when the idea
that letting go is important changes into the *belief* that we actually need
to. What leads to this change, however, seems to be different for everyone
and to be largely unpredictable.

In the third stage, *preparation*, we finally recognize we have to move
forward and begin to muster the determination to do so. We may be
helped in this by preparing to do things that symbolize our intent: by
imagining rituals of completion (for example, to whom we might give
away our deceased spouse's clothing), or by designing alternative routines
that accommodate a life without the thing we've lost (for example, fitting
swimming into our daily schedule when arthritic knees stop us from running). Because moving from contemplation to preparation means tran-
sitioning from ambivalence to determination, painful emotions often
resurface in this stage. We often feel confused, afraid, and overwhelmed
by the prospect of continuing on with our lives.

Yet in the fourth stage, *action*, we do just that. Here, we consciously
choose to bid our attachment a final good-bye with a promise not to
forget it, but also with a firm decision to live without it. Our decision
may reflect itself in concrete action—perhaps in finding a new job, a new
hobby, a new exercise routine, or in remarrying—but it need not.

The final stage, *maintenance*, acknowledges that feelings of grief may
resurface at any time. To navigate this stage successfully is to allow them
to do so without judgment, recognizing, especially with unexpected and
traumatic losses, that a return to grief is common, and that longing for
what we've lost is acceptable as long as we don't allow our lives to halt as
a result.

The value of the transtheoretical model in the context of bereavement, I told Ravi, was twofold. In helping him mark his progress, it

would not only encourage him when he was further along in the process of grieving, but also suggest effective ways for him to nudge himself forward if he got stuck. For what would make a strategy effective
for resolving grief would depend on the stage in which he found himself. If one's spouse dies and one becomes stuck *contemplating* the need
to move on, moving forward would mean *preparing* to move on, not
leaping immediately into *action* and actually moving on. Which might
mean, for example, looking at an Internet dating site but not asking out
someone at a party. While jumping over a stage isn't, strictly speaking,
impossible, it is in general more difficult than taking the time to "ripen"
ourselves gradually from one stage to the next. The length of time we
occupy a stage may be short—seconds, even—but when it comes to letting go, the fastest way to action and then maintenance seems to be
through precontemplation, contemplation, and preparation.

Ravi asked me what stage I thought he was in. "Precontemplation," I
answered. "Which is why I think you should begin *contemplating* ways to
leverage your old skills to create value in a new way."

"Hmm," he mused. "Maybe I will." He thanked me for all my suggestions, including my final one that he start an antidepressant medication.
"At least for a little while," I said. "Let's just see how you do with it." And
with that, we made plans for him to follow up with me again in six weeks.

Happily, when I next saw him back in my clinic, he told me was feeling much better. With uncharacteristic excitement, he said that he'd
come upon the idea of editing a book of twentieth-century short stories. When he'd started to work on it, not only had his mood improved
and his energy returned, but he also found himself reconnecting with
two of his sons, both of whom were English professors themselves and
who wanted to edit the book with him. To his delight, their interest
in working with him also helped him to forgive himself for divorcing
their mother. Finally, in talking with them one day, he'd learned that the

reason his family had previously grown distant from him, leading him to feel marginalized, was that his depression had actually been present long before he'd decided to retire and had actually caused *him* to distance himself from *them*.

"But I've forgiven myself for that, too," he said.

8

Appreciate
the Good

When we lose an attachment, even though reminding ourselves
that we haven't lost something *else* may not improve our pain,
it can actually still make us feel better. For as we all know from
our own experience, we needn't *stop* feeling one emotion to *start* feeling
another. Which is to say, our moods aren't controlled by a single dial that
can be turned only to one emotion at a time. Rather, we can feel multiple,
even diametrically opposed, emotions at once—even about the same
thing. For few emotions possesses the power to stop us from feeling others. It only seems that they do because *events* often stop and start different
emotions simultaneously. Thus, fear stops and relief begins after we learn
our child is going to make a full recovery from cancer not because relief
halts fear but because a single event exerts opposite effects on two separate emotions at the same time. Which explains how gratitude for what
we still have *can* come to our aid when we suffer a loss: not by diminishing our pain but by rousing a feeling of joy that competes with it.

Studies suggest that positive emotions in general play a key role in increasing resilience.[1] They diminish physiologic stress by reducing heart rate and blood pressure,[2] as well as broaden the scope, creativity, and flexibility of our thinking, which increases our ability to cope with adversity psychologically.[3] In fact, according to psychologist Barbara Fredrickson's *broaden-and-build theory*, the resources we accrue through experiencing positive emotion (the ability to take a long-range view of short-term problems, for example) tend to "outlast the transient emotional states that lead to their acquisition."[4] In other words, finding a way to make ourselves feel good in the present also improves our ability to survive and thrive in the future.[5] Nichiren Buddhism holds a similar view, expounding the concept of *life-condition*—conceived as the "temperature" of our inner life state—which both internal and external forces cause to vary from moment to moment. Our life-condition determines how we experience everything from events that occur in our lives to events that occur in our bodies. The higher it rises, according to Nichiren Buddhism, the greater our joy, and therefore the less suffering that negative events are able to cause us.[6]

And few internal forces are as effective as gratitude at making our life-condition rise. Gratitude not only brings joy but also improves our sense of satisfaction with life to an even greater extent than either pleasure, meaning, or engagement.[7] In fact, the strength of gratitude's ability to make us feel good about life is second only to that of love.[8] And as an added bonus, gratitude also increases the frequency with which we feel other positive emotions, like warmth, altruism, and tenderness.[9]

Yet gratitude doesn't increase resilience only in the manner of other positive emotions, by making us feel good. It also does so by making us feel *less bad*, lowering our levels of anxiety, anger, depression, self-consciousness, and emotional vulnerability.[10] As a result, gratitude can be leveraged to improve our sleep (making a list of things for which we're grateful

before going to bed both increases positive thoughts and decreases negative thoughts, both of which independently decrease worry and stress),[11]
as well as to decrease our anxiety about death (which decreases, apparently, when we're made to feel that our lives have been well-lived by making a list of things that happened in it for which we're grateful[12]).

In short, gratitude represents a powerful tool to help us construct and
maintain an undefeated mind. It improves our well-being and buffers us
against a wide range of maladies, including major depression, generalized
anxiety disorder, phobias, nicotine dependence, drug abuse, posttraumatic stress disorder, and even bulimia.[13] The only problem with gratitude is this: it's hard to make ourselves feel it.

Finding Gratitude

The first time I met Anne, a statuesque forty-seven-year-old woman
who worked as a management consultant, she told me, rapping the side
of her head playfully, that she felt she was living a charmed life. She loved
her work, she said, had a loving relationship with her husband and two
children, and had never been sick, as she put it, "a day in my life."

That is, until she returned to see me one day complaining of a minor
tremor in her left hand. It occurred only at rest, she said, which, along
with the cogwheel rigidity in her arms that I found on physical exam, led
me to diagnose her with Parkinson's disease.

I offered to send her to a neurologist to confirm my diagnosis, but told
her that I was pretty sure she had it. She declined, accepting the diagnosis without much concern given that her symptoms were mild—until
she went home and read about it on the Internet. "This is terrible!" she
exclaimed when I called her on the phone after she'd left me a panicked
voicemail message. Like most people, she'd thought Parkinson's disease
was largely a disorder of movement. She'd had no idea it could also cause

fatigue, depression, anxiety, and dementia, to name just a few of the things for which she discovered she was now at risk. I did my best to reassure her, explaining that the likelihood that any of those things would happen to her was actually low, which calmed her down considerably. But unfortunately I had even more upsetting news to give her: a routine mammogram had found a suspicious lesion in her left breast that needed to be biopsied.

Anne now found her distress at having Parkinson's disease eclipsed by the fear that she might have breast cancer, the experience she'd had of watching her mother die of it replaying in her mind over and over. She spent the better part of a week in mortal terror waiting just to have the biopsy and then several more days waiting for the results.

When I called her up to tell her they were negative, she began to cry. "I'm just so grateful," she said as we both rejoiced. She may have been struck by one bullet, she told me, but as far as she was concerned she'd dodged another that would have been far worse.

Over the next few years, then, she actually did quite well. And with each negative mammogram, she would reiterate how appreciative she was that she didn't have cancer, a perspective she said that made her Parkinson's disease continue to seem like a minor inconvenience.

That is, until her symptoms started to progress. It began subtly: first her tremor became more pronounced; then she started having difficulty getting up from a seated position. Then one day she walked into my clinic using a cane. "I've started falling," she explained. After one such fall, she'd fractured her elbow. I told her it was time for her to see a neurologist.

The one to whom I sent her specialized in Parkinson's disease and promptly increased the doses of several of her medications. And though they quickly improved both her balance and her tremor, the higher doses also made her drowsy and compromised her ability to concentrate—so much so that she began to worry she was no longer going to be able to work. By then she'd also started to develop masked facies—a flattening of the facial expression that occurs commonly in Parkinson's disease—and I could tell the gratitude she felt for having escaped breast cancer was no longer doing much to sustain her.

"To be honest," she admitted when I remarked on it, "these days I'm having a hard time feeling grateful about anything."

Maintaining Gratitude

Though research shows that comparing a negative event to a worse alternative ("I may have Parkinson's disease, but at least I don't have breast cancer")[14] as well as comparing *our* experience to the experience of someone less fortunate ("At least I only had a lumpectomy, not like that other girl who had her entire breast removed")[15] will, in fact, make us feel better, it also shows the effect doesn't tend to last. The problem, unfortunately, is that we habituate not only to experiences but also to *thoughts*. That is, the more we think about something, the less our thinking about it arouses emotion.[16] This may not matter if we're trying to mitigate the negative impact of an event whose consequences are relatively self-limited and from which we're able to recover quickly—for example, failing an exam—but for events whose negative impact persists, such comparisons quickly lose their power to improve our mood.

Not only that, but when the negative impact of an event actually *intensifies* over time—as with worsening symptoms of Parkinson's disease—we have to work harder and harder to find something worse with which we can compare it. And even when we *can* think of something worse, in order to awaken our sense of gratitude, we need to feel as if we nearly *did* experience that worse thing, or at the very least as if we *could* have. Research suggests that the closer we come to attaining a desired outcome, the easier it is to imagine achieving it, and therefore the more difficult it is to accept that we didn't, which is why missing winning the lottery by one digit is harder to accept than missing it by eight.[17] Conversely, the *less* likely we are to experience an *undesired* event, the harder it is to believe we might have, and therefore the less gratitude we're able to feel that we didn't.

Unfortunately, our ability to make ourselves feel better by summoning up gratitude for the good things we *have* experienced, as opposed to summoning up gratitude for the bad ones we haven't, is also limited by our tendency to habituate. Habituation eventually turns all of our possessions—our marriages, our health, our arms, and so on—into parts that feel indistinguishable from the whole of us, parts that we therefore rarely, if ever, imagine we could lose. Which in turn makes them harder to appreciate. Our ability to enjoy and appreciate a new car, for example, is never greater than immediately after we first buy it, simply because it doesn't yet feel as if it's a part of us. But the further away in time we get from our purchase, the more we habituate to it and therefore the more we begin to focus on other things. Eventually, we hardly think about our car at all, and our ability to appreciate it correspondingly decreases.[18]

This all suggests that simply pausing to remind ourselves that we still actually have our cars, our health, our marriage, or our arms should be enough to make us feel grateful. And sometimes, in fact, it is. But sometimes it isn't. Results from research measuring the long-term effects of making lists of things for which we're grateful have actually been mixed.[19] Though some studies show that making gratitude lists on a daily basis can decrease worry, improve body image, and increase well-being, others have shown it has little effect if any.[20]

Which made psychologist Minkyung Koo wonder if the key to overcoming the narcotizing effects of habituation isn't thinking about *having* the things we do, as the majority of the studies on gratitude had asked their participants to do, but rather thinking about *not* having them. "Having a wonderful spouse, watching one's team win the World Series, or getting an article accepted in a top journal are all positive events, and reflecting on them may well bring a smile," Koo writes, "but that smile is likely to be slighter and more fleeting with each passing day, because as wonderful as those events may be, they quickly become familiar."[21] So, inspired by the classic Frank Capra movie *It's a Wonderful Life*, in which everyman George Bailey learns to appreciate the good parts of his life when an angel shows him what the world would have been like if he'd never been born, Koo and her colleagues decided to see if mentally *subtracting* positive parts of their lives would make people feel more appreciative than merely bringing those positive parts to mind. In other words, Koo and her colleagues wondered, might there be a way to "unadapt" to positive events?

To find out, they first asked a control group to describe an event for which they felt grateful and measured how much positive emotion it induced. Then they asked an experimental group to write about how an event for which they felt grateful might *not* have happened and measured how much positive emotion that induced. When they compared the difference, the results were unequivocal: participants in the experimental group experienced significantly higher levels of positive emotion than patients in the control group.[22] Undoing positive events, Koo and her colleagues concluded, does increase our sense of appreciation more than simply bringing those events to mind.

The challenge involved in leveraging the undoing of positive events to create gratitude and therefore resilience, however, lies in doing it consistently. Even when we're feeling the pain of a loss acutely, getting ourselves to sit down and actually write about ways in which something else good in our lives might never have happened, or even just to think about it, may require—like making the short trip down from our living room to our basement to exercise on our treadmill—more energy than we have.

"Sounds like a good idea to me," Anne said.

Encouraged, I told her further that if imagining ways in which good things that had happened to her might not have occurred was too challenging, she might find it easier to imagine instead how she might lose something to which she was attached in the *future*. For even when merely *threatened* with the loss of an attachment, we tend to appreciate it more.

Research shows, for example, that people who've been confronted with serious illness often develop an increased appreciation for life.[23] Which caused psychologist Araceli Frias to wonder: could people be induced to feel greater appreciation for life by simply *imagining* their deaths? For if imagining how a past positive event might not have happened can increase our feelings of gratitude, might imagining a future loss of something we valued do the same thing? To find the answer, he ran an experiment in which he divided 116 undergraduates into three groups. The first he asked to imagine a scenario in which they died in a fire ("You wake up in the middle of the night in a friend's apartment on the twentieth floor of an old, downtown building to the sounds of screams and the choking smell of smoke, trapped and unable to breathe"); the second he asked to imagine dying in purely abstract terms ("What thoughts and feelings do you experience when you think about your own death?"); and the third he asked to imagine waking up to begin a typical day ("Making breakfast, doing laundry, cleaning"). When he then assessed their resultant levels of gratitude, he found subjects he'd asked to imagine dying in a specific and vivid way felt significantly more grateful than either subjects who imagined dying in abstract terms or subjects who imagined only a typical day.[24]

Though Frias only examined the effect of imagining one's death, Koo's study suggests that a similar increase in gratitude might result from imagining other kinds of future losses.[25] The key, according to Frias, is to imagine the loss vividly enough to make the possibility that we might lose it feel real. The ability to summon up gratitude, then, may depend mostly on the strength of our imaginations—on our ability to picture an alternative life in enough detail that we can *feel* the absence of something we haven't yet actually lost.

"Like an actress summoning up real emotion to play her role as convincingly as possible," I told Anne, "you have to convince yourself that something you love—some elemental part of your life—might soon be gone." We can best do this, I said, by vividly imagining *specific* ways an attachment might be taken from us, playing out scenarios in our mind in which some entirely believable event snatches our attachment away.

"Try writing out a list of things you love about your life," I told Anne, "and carve out some time every morning, even if just a few minutes, to imagine how you really could—or better yet, one day *will*—lose them." By repeating this practice on a regular basis, I told her, she could transform it into a habit. And as a believable fear of loss doesn't seem to be something to which we habituate, it might become a habit that would continue to fill her with gratitude as long as she continued to do it.

I suggested also that she'd be more likely to have an emotional reaction to her imaginings if she envisioned the absence of her attachments as *visually* as possible.[26] So if she wanted to imagine her life without her husband, for example, she would imagine *seeing* the empty space his absence would leave in her life, *seeing* the same bed in which she now slept but without him lying next to her, *seeing* the same table at which she now ate dinner but without him sitting across from her, and so on. And when she thought about how she would have to alter her daily routines in his absence, she would again imagine doing so with images—images of going to movies alone, taking vacations alone, attending parent-teacher conferences alone, and so on.

"That actually sounds a little scary."

I nodded. The one problem with imagining the loss of our most beloved attachments as a way to generate gratitude, I acknowledged, is that the better we are at it, the more likely we are not to feel gratitude but anxiety. Given that she was sick, I suggested that vividly imagining her death might be something to avoid, and instead that she pick something she *wasn't* likely to lose anytime soon. I also thought she might consider sending her husband and children on a vacation without her. "After all," I said, "there's nothing quite like *trying* life without an attachment to help us appreciate that we still have it."

Gratitude for Obstacles

To my chagrin, when I saw Anne back in my clinic three months later, her symptoms had progressed. She was now having a difficult time speaking at a normal pace, initiating movements, and buttoning and unbuttoning her clothes. And yet her demeanor seemed calm, almost serene. When I asked her if this was indeed the way she felt, she told me it was. When I asked her why, she told me it was because of something her seven-year-old son had said to her husband.

She no longer felt comfortable interfacing directly with clients because of her decreasing ability to express emotion through facial expression, she said, so she'd decided to reinvent herself professionally by shifting her duties from consulting for clients to supervising other consultants within her firm. As a result, she no longer had to travel to work on-site with clients in other cities and now spent her entire workweek in Chicago. Several weeks after she'd made this change, her son had taken her husband aside one morning and said, "Don't take this the wrong way, but I'm kind of glad Mom got sick." Shocked, her husband had asked why. "We get to see a lot more of her now."

"Ouch," I said.

"Yeah." Rather than hurt her, however, it made her realize just how unbalanced her life had become. "I really thought I could work full-time, be a wife and a mother and a daughter and a board member, exercise regularly, read, go to movies, host parties, and still find time to relax! But that he would be happy that I have Parkinson's disease because it's forced me to spend more time with him—" She shook her head. "Well, that tells me just how far off the mark I was."

"Out of the mouths of babes . . ."

She nodded. "He really changed my thinking. All I was asking myself before was, *Why me?* But now I'm thinking, *Why* not *me? I'm so special that I should expect only good things are going to happen to me?* When I start to think that way, it just makes me resentful."

So instead she became determined to use my suggestions to become more grateful for what she still had, beginning with the realization that she now found as much, if not more, job satisfaction in mentoring other people in her firm as she had from directly working with clients. She told me, for example, how she would encourage subordinates who were dissatisfied with their lives to perform a thought experiment, instructing them to create a workable plan for getting rid of every part of their lives they didn't like. Then she would ask them to inventory all the good things they'd lose in making the change as well and how—or *if*—they might re-create those good things in some other way. With a few exceptions, most realized ridding themselves of what they considered to be negative wasn't worth also having to give up what they considered to be positive. She told me that in conjunction with the way her family life had improved, these kinds of interactions had actually enabled her to feel appreciation for the Parkinson's disease itself.

"I'd certainly rather I didn't have it," she emphasized, "but that doesn't mean there can't be some good that comes of it."

"No, it doesn't," I agreed. Her ability to recognize that something as dreadful as Parkinson's disease had also brought her benefit reflected a truly sublime state of mind, I remarked.

Though the real trick, I told her, wasn't just learning to appreciate obstacles in retrospect; it was learning to appreciate them *before* we knew what benefits they might bring. It only required confidence, I said—confidence enough in our ability to wrestle value out of adversity that at the very first moment we encounter an obstacle we feel gratitude for the opportunity it represents instead of fear of the suffering it might bring. That level of confidence, I said, embodies the ideal to which we should all aspire.

And indeed, studies suggest the belief that we can always turn poison into medicine in *some* way isn't as naively optimistic as it might seem: even when encountering obstacles from which it seems no good could possibly come (for example, being diagnosed with a life-threatening illness), studies show good often *does* come (for example, in the form of increased empathy for others, altered priorities and life goals, and improved interpersonal relationships).[27] The good may not *outweigh* the bad, but any good is something for which we can be grateful—and, in fact, for which we should strive to be.

"Funny you should say that," Anne replied. After her breast cancer scare, she told me, she'd taken stock of her life and created a "mental file cabinet" of past ordeals upon which she could meditate whenever she felt incapable of handling a challenge, whether one related to her Parkinson's disease or something else. Now whenever she felt discouraged or daunted, she'd summon up vivid memories of how horrible and helpless she felt when those past problems first confronted her and soon would usually then find herself awash in confidence that having survived *them* she could survive anything.

"Yes!" I said. "That's exactly how you do it!" Transforming poison into medicine meant not only obtaining a conspicuous benefit, like gaining more time with one's family, I said, but also obtaining the inconspicuous benefit of *increased confidence in one's ability to turn poison into medicine*. For a belief in the ability to turn poison into medicine is something we can only develop by actually turning poison into medicine. Thus, the victories we've achieved in life represent more than just our past accomplishments; they represent evidence of our ability to win, which, when we call upon it, will buttress us against the despair we often feel when facing obstacles that lie ahead of us. And the more we believe in our ability to win, the more we become capable of feeling grateful for obstacles themselves.

"That's how my son was saying he felt about my Parkinson's," Anne said. I nodded. "And how it sounds like he helped you feel about it yourself." Her eyes became moist. "I just appreciate him so much," she said quietly.

I told Anne that I was most grateful for my relationships with people, too—the positive ones for the enjoyment they provided and the negative ones for their power to teach me something about myself.

She looked at me skeptically. "Not that the negative ones are so easy," I added. We were just talking now, like two friends reminiscing over a shared experience. I told her about an incident I once had with a fellow Buddhist who, no matter what we were discussing, seemed determined to find my ideas objectionable, often voicing criticisms I found illogical and extreme. Talking with him was so frustrating and unpleasant that I frequently refused to answer my phone when he called. And when I couldn't avoid him, I would become entirely passive, often refusing to respond to his assertions at all.

When another Buddhist asked me one day what I thought I had to learn from him, I scoffed at the notion that I might have anything to learn from him at all—until one day while chanting I realized suddenly that in reflexively dismissing what he said I'd been dismissing his humanity. Dismayed that I'd begun to see a fellow human being as nothing more than an irritant, I decided from that point forward I would stop avoiding him and instead gently but firmly refute any statements he made that I found outrageous.

I expected our relationship to become even more contentious, but instead to my surprise our conversations actually became friendlier. But this wasn't because *he'd* changed, I realized one day, but rather because *I* had. He still made the same outlandish comments, but they no longer made me cringe. When I asked myself why, I realized my problem with his statements had never actually been about the statements themselves but about the feelings of inadequacy they stirred up in me. To my great surprise, I realized I hadn't felt that my point of view deserved to be defended. And not just with him, I saw, but also with others. And when I saw also that this had somehow changed as a result of my determination to embrace his humanity, that I had indeed changed the poison of a contentious relationship into the medicine of an increased belief in the validity of my perspective, I became flooded with appreciation. "Not so much for *him*," I told Anne, "but for his *life*—for the influence it had exerted on mine."

"I'm not so good with people who annoy me either," Anne said with a smile.

I nodded. "The more you try to avoid them, the more annoyed you get when you can't. Then you start thinking the thing that's annoying you is a much bigger deal than it is. And then you start stereotyping people into black-and-white caricatures, thinking about them as *entirely* self-centered, *entirely* insensitive, *entirely* undisciplined. You totally lose sight of everything in them that's good. Which isn't good."

But because of my Buddhist friend, I now thought to search for things about other people that I could appreciate and subsequently call to mind whenever I found myself overly focused on their flaws. I found this especially useful to do with people I saw every day or with whom I was especially close, who were unfortunately the people most likely to annoy me.

"Funny, but I've always found the opposite," Anne said. "It's always been harder for me to appreciate people I *don't* care about."

When I smiled in response to this, she said, "You know what I like *best* about gratitude? It helps me see how many things I spend my time caring about that are actually trivial."

Which, she continued to assert even as her disease progressed and she had to give up working altogether, was just about everything. "When so much is taken from you," she told me from the wheelchair she eventually required, "you figure out what's really important."

Even when she finally grew too debilitated to leave her home without assistance, she still found things for which to be grateful: her children's health and continued success in school, her husband's unwavering devotion to caring for her—and the occasional visits from the former employees she'd mentored before she quit working, who would come to express *their* gratitude for *her*; for how her advice and concern for them had helped them grow both professionally and personally.

"It's like having students come to see their old teacher," she told me one day. "I'm so happy I had the chance to affect them in a positive way. I may be bitter about this disease, but I sure am grateful about that."

9

Encourage Others

I f experiencing gratitude makes us strong by making us feel good, then experiencing love, which contributes even more to life satisfaction,[1] should make us even stronger. What's surprising about love's power to make us feel good, though, is that it has nothing to do with whether we get anything in return for it: feeling love for a perfect stranger, it turns out, elevates our mood almost as much as does feeling love for someone close to us.[2]

Which suggests that the reason love makes us feel good has less to do with romantic attraction or even personal connection than it does with the way it causes us to regard those for whom we feel it. That is to say, not just with empathy (according to *Oxford Dictionaries Online*, "understanding and sharing the feelings of another") or sympathy ("pitying someone else's misfortune"), but with compassion—meaning with the same concern for their happiness as we have for our own.

In Nichiren Buddhism, the term *jihi* is used to denote the profound mercy, or compassion, a Buddha is said to feel toward all living beings. Egoless and unconditional, jihi requires neither credit for its concern nor reward for its good deeds, the joy of feeling jihi itself representing a greater recompense than anything we might receive from the person toward whom we feel it. Though romantic love may provide the spark that gives birth to jihi, jihi and romantic love are not the same. If we feel jihi toward someone with whom we're also *in* love and at some point fall out of love with them, though our romantic feelings for them may disappear, the jihi we feel for them will not. If our children cease to speak to us, do we stop caring about their happiness—in effect, stop loving them? No. The love we bear our children, in fact, may represent the closest thing to jihi an unenlightened mind can feel. In one sense, then, to feel jihi is to feel the compassion we have for those we love above all others for everyone.

Measuring Compassion

Compassion, in general, makes its focus only on the potential people have for good. Which isn't to say that it requires us to believe all people *are* good. Just that the capacity to *be* good can never be destroyed by a thousand evil acts and must therefore always be sought beneath the morass of selfishness and greed under which it's often hidden. Even when the people for whom we feel compassion are suffering horribly, perhaps even railing against us and treating us even more shabbily than others who don't care about them, to feel compassion is to refuse to be discouraged or turned away by their obstinacy.

On the other hand, though compassion can indeed make us strong, if we fail to temper it with wisdom it can also make us dangerous. Without wisdom we may mistakenly conclude that to behave compassionately toward others means only and always giving them what they want. And though, as mentioned in Chapter 5, giving others what they want often *does* make them happy, it usually only does so transiently—and, what's more, may actually deny them important opportunities for personal growth and therefore even greater happiness in the long run. Further, people often want what *isn't* good for them. Thus, if our aim is to help others become happy, we must always apply our own judgment to the actions we're asked to take on their behalf.

Also, though we may be tempted to measure the depth of our compassion by what we're willing to give up for those toward whom we feel it, we shouldn't conclude that *only* action involving sacrifice qualifies as compassionate. For no one person's happiness is more important than any other's. Indeed, a compassionately wise person cares about his own happiness as much as the happiness of others—no more *and no less*. This isn't to say that sacrifices aren't sometimes appropriate, but rather that we have to be wise in deciding which sacrifices to make. Sometimes we may care about another person's happiness but find them too dangerous to remain near, as with an alcoholic determined not only to drink her life into ruin but to take her spouse and children down with her. In such cases, the most compassionate thing to do may be to detach with love, removing ourselves from her environment without ceasing to care about her in our heart.

Nor does being compassionate require us to adopt a passive demeanor and express only gentle kindness at all times. Though compassion can certainly be gentle, it must also sometimes be harsh, forceful, and even angry. We can't judge the quality or intent of an action only by its superficial appearance. With the intent to increase another person's happiness as our constant aim, we may sometimes find ourselves taking action that paradoxically seems on the surface to lack the very compassion that drives it, as when a parent reprimands a child to teach him not to hit other children.

Nor, finally, does compassion even require us to *like* those for whom we strive to feel it. Being compassionate may mean thinking benevolently about people despite their flaws, but it doesn't mean acting as if those flaws don't exist. Nor does it mean we can't prefer one person to another. We neither have to pretend that some people don't annoy us nor open ourselves up to establishing personal relationships with those who do annoy us for their happiness to matter to us.

Our Conceptions of Others

On the other hand, to be able to feel compassion for others clearly requires more than an understanding of its definition. Once when my son was just eighteen months old and I'd taken him out in his stroller for a walk, I was approached by a homeless woman asking for money. I'd noticed her before in the neighborhood many times, including in the alley behind our condominium where I'd seen her buying drugs. For that reason, I pretended that I hadn't heard her and continued on as if the wind had blown a newspaper against my leg and I'd kicked it away without any thought.

I regretted my action almost immediately. Not that I thought giving her money was the compassionate thing to do given the strong likelihood that she would have used it to buy more drugs. But I'd done more than disregarded her request: I'd disregarded her humanity. Not because I'd refused her, but because I'd ignored her. I'd failed even to look at her, sending the unmistakable message that she wasn't even worth the breath I would have had to expel to make a reply. Even telling her no without providing any explanation would have been better. I cringed as I thought about someone treating my son with the same indifference, the same callousness, with which I'd treated her.

Abruptly, I recalled once changing in my school's locker room before gym class when some of my seventh-grade classmates began to bully a boy named Pino, whom they discovered had developed breasts over the summer break (a condition known as gynecomastia that sometimes occurs in boys at puberty and usually disappears spontaneously). I failed to rise to his defense, too afraid to have their malevolent attention redirected toward me, but felt awful for him, wondering how people could be so effortlessly cruel.

Now as I hurried away from the homeless woman, I realized that my classmates had bullied Pino for the same reason I refused to respond to her: because we're all to some degree predisposed to conceive of other people as *functions* or *labels* rather than as human beings. Dubbed the "spirit of abstraction" by the French philosopher Gabriel Marcel,[3] this unfortunate tendency explains, among other things, how in pre–Civil War America a large segment of the South was able to compress the humanity of the entire African American race into a single word— *slave*—enabling slave owners to treat their fellow human beings as property. It also explains how Adolf Hitler was able to convince the German people to turn a segment of their population—the Jews—into something so despicable that they felt no compunction about murdering 6 million of them. And it explains how around the same time America turned the entire Japanese people into "Japs," a term that reduced them from human beings with hopes, loves, families, and fears into the enemy on whom it was therefore eventually permissible to drop two atomic bombs. The spirit of abstraction also explains today why we snap at telemarketers who call us at home during dinner, customer service representatives who insist on following a "no receipt, no return policy," and fellow drivers on the road when they refuse to let us merge into traffic (a practice of abstraction of which I'm particularly and frequently guilty).

For even if we don't greet others with cruelty, we often greet them with indifference. When we see a mail carrier dropping off our mail, how often do we allow her to expand in our minds to her full dimensions as a person, perhaps even wonder about her mother, her kids, her health problems, or her dreams? How often do we even think about our spouses outside of the function they play in our lives, regarding them as human beings in their own right whose desires and needs exist apart from our own? How often do we think this way about our children, confronting our tendency to picture them merely as extensions of ourselves? When I ask myself questions like these, wondering how frequently I view the people who populate my everyday life as human beings rather than as abstractions, I've been chagrined to discover the answer is "not often."

This, in fact, is the main reason I continue to chant: because increasing our compassion for others is hard. And because evidence suggests that at least one form of meditation does just that.

Loving-Kindness

Loving-kindness meditation consists simply of making conscious attempts to generate feelings of compassion for others, a practice that research now shows improves our ability to feel compassion in general. In one study, researcher Stefan Hoffman and colleagues asked participants to close their eyes and imagine two people with whom they had close personal relationships standing beside them, sending them feelings of love. After four minutes, the researchers then asked the participants to open their eyes and to redirect the feelings of love they'd "received" toward a photograph of a stranger. In comparison to members of a control group (who were asked to imagine the appearance of two acquaintances standing beside them for whom they had only neutral feelings and then, after four minutes, to focus on the appearance of a stranger's photograph), participants in the experimental group reported significantly greater positive feelings toward the photographs of the strangers, suggesting that the loving feelings we have for people with whom we're close can indeed be leveraged to generate loving feelings for people with whom we aren't.[4]

In Nichiren Buddhism, however, practitioners are taught to go one step further and chant for the happiness of people they actively *dislike*.

The idea is that what prevents us from recognizing the humanity in others is our own delusional beliefs about which characteristics do and don't make people worthy of our concern. Nichiren Buddhism argues that only by systematically identifying such beliefs—most easily done in the context of our relationships with people about whom we have the hardest time caring—can we develop compassion not only for our loved ones, our friends, and our acquaintances, but also for all of humanity. In other words, only by challenging our selfish impulses can we change, bit by bit, into our most compassionate selves—and thus our most resilient selves. And though no study has yet been done to prove chanting has this delusion-shattering power, this is the effect it seems to have had on me as well as on other Nichiren Buddhists I've known.

Some, for example, have realized that people who disagree with them still deserve to be happy. Others have realized that another person's gain isn't always their loss. And still others have managed to embrace one of the most controversial ideas of all: that people we deem purposely malevolent are in fact only grievously deluded. Deluded, that is, in believing that someone else's suffering has in some way become necessary for their happiness. From the woman who believes she needs to betray her friend's confidence to protect her social standing to the man who believes he needs to murder a rival to protect his gang's turf—all may offer other, more superficial reasons for making their choices, but in every instance such choices are made in the pursuit of happiness. And though it may be true that we need to become angry to fight against injustice, that doesn't mean we can't also feel compassion for the people who commit it.

Of course, we'd rather label those who commit such crimes as evil than conceive of them merely as tragically deluded. But if we don't hate a three-year-old who points his father's gun at his brother and accidentally shoots and kills him, why would we hate adults who lie, cheat, steal, or even murder? We may think they should know better, but wisdom isn't an inevitable consequence of aging. Why then shouldn't we feel compassion for an adult as we would for a three-year-old? Why not, in fact, as if they had once been *our* three-year-old? For were they not at one point someone else's?

Judging Others . . . or Understanding Them

If we can internalize two premises, then—that we all want to be happy more than anything but that many of us are profoundly confused about how to do so—we may be able to interest ourselves more in *understanding* people, in figuring out the reasons they do the things they do, than in judging them. For if we can approach people first and foremost not with judgment but with curiosity we'll have taken an important step on the journey to compassion and thus to an undefeated mind.

Not that making curiosity our first reaction to foolish or irrational behavior is easy. Once, for example, I had a patient named Clark who came to see me complaining of chest pain. At first the pain had come on only with exertion, but in the two weeks before he'd come to see me it had begun to bother him at rest. It radiated to his jaw and was associated with some mild nausea and sweating. He'd been a pack-a-day smoker for thirty-five years, and he had hypertension and diabetes as well as a family history of premature heart disease.

Alarmed, I told him this was without a doubt unstable angina caused by blockages in one or more of his coronary arteries and that he needed to be admitted to the hospital for an immediate cardiac catheterization. When he asked me what that entailed, I explained that a cardiologist would insert a catheter into an artery in his groin and thread it up his aorta until the tip of it was positioned in front of his coronary arteries. Then the cardiologist would squirt intravenous contrast into them to see where and how extensive the blockages were. He would then perform an angioplasty, place a stent, or, if the extent of disease was severe enough, pull out without any intervention at all and turn him over to a cardio-thoracic surgeon who would perform a bypass operation. It all depended on what was found. Afterward, he would have to lie flat on his back for six hours with a sandbag on his groin to ensure the puncture site clotted properly. I told him that few circumstances existed in medicine in which the choice confronting a patient was as black-and-white as this one: if he didn't have this procedure he would almost certainly suffer a heart attack at some point and possibly die.

To my stunned surprise, however, he refused. Did he understand, I repeated, that he could die? Yes, he said, he did. Though my inclination was to launch into a recitation of all the reasons I thought he was being irrational, I stopped myself, realizing my impulse to label him as such was only a lazy way of dismissing some hidden concern he'd not yet articulated. So instead I asked him why, given what I'd told him, he was refusing the procedure.

He looked at me sheepishly. Then, after a pause, he finally blurted out, "I don't want anyone looking at my groin."

Wide-eyed, I asked, "Why?"

"I'd rather not say."

I thought for a moment. "I respect your right to make this decision, ill-advised as I think it is," I said carefully. "But I really do care about what happens to you, so I'd like to know why it's so important that no one sees your groin."

He sighed. "I only have one testicle."

I knew this, of course. He'd been born *monorchid*, one testicle simply having failed to develop. "You're embarrassed?"

His expression grew pained. He nodded. "You must think I'm being ridiculous, worried about my manhood at my age."

"Not at all," I replied. "We're not in charge of how we feel about a lot of things." I paused. "All I can think to tell you is that your manhood

doesn't have anything to do your anatomy. It has to do with your character. With doing what you don't want to do when what you don't want to
do is what's right or what's best," I added pointedly.

Clark didn't agree to having the catheterization that day. But he did a
day later. And a good thing, too: he had a 90 percent blockage of his left
main coronary artery and underwent a bypass operation the day after that.

Understanding promotes compassion, even if we already care about
the person for whom we're trying to feel it. For only when I learned how
trapped Clark felt between his fear of dying of a heart attack and his fear
of embarrassment was I able to ignore my first reaction and approach
him with compassion. Because my first reaction—lasting only a moment
to be sure, but my first nonetheless—was to leave him to his fate.

Compassion Fatigue

Even when we do manage to summon up feelings of compassion for
others, *maintaining* those feelings can be exhausting, often requiring that
we simultaneously restrain our annoyance, frustration, and even rage.
Which is why, as my patient Brenda discovered, sometimes not even the
most heartbreaking of circumstances can prevent compassion fatigue.

Brenda and Nathan had been married thirty-five years before he was
diagnosed with amyotrophic lateral sclerosis (commonly known as Lou
Gehrig's disease). At first he hardly seemed affected by it, its presence
evinced by only an occasionally dropped coffee cup, but within half a
year he found himself unable to stand, lift his arms above his shoulders,
or even talk clearly. Stunned by the speed with which his ability to care
for himself deteriorated, Brenda nevertheless quietly assumed responsibility for attending to whatever needs he couldn't.

When I saw her for her own annual checkup, though, she appeared
haggard and worn. When I asked her how she was doing, she admitted

not well. Caring for her husband, she said, had taken over her entire life. He now required her help to dress, bathe, eat, and even go to the bathroom. Frankly, she said, she was struggling just to care. Not just *for* him, she added, brushing tears out of her eyes, but *about* him.

I suggested she needed to get help with him at home. "Caregivers routinely make their first priority the caretaking of someone else," I said, "but so much so they often forget to take care of themselves. But if you don't take care of yourself, if you don't give yourself time and space to recover from caretaking, you'll start to feel resentful that you're having to provide care at all."

"I already do," Brenda told me quietly.

I told her I doubted she no longer cared about her husband, but suggested instead she was simply overwhelmed. I shared with her my observation that caregivers commonly project their frustration onto the people for whom they care even though their frustration is usually more with the experience of caregiving itself, or with themselves for being unwilling, or feeling unable, to care for their own needs while providing it. I stressed that caring for oneself, far from being selfish, is *necessary* to sustain the ability to care for others.

"I don't have time to take care of myself," she protested.

"Which is why," I reiterated, "you need help. Most family members caring for sick loved ones only think to get help long after they've passed the point at which they actually need it. But to be able to continue to feel compassion for your husband, first and foremost you need to manage your own stress."

With a sigh of relief, as if she'd only been waiting for someone else's permission to recognize just how worn out she was, she agreed to hire both a home health nurse and a homemaker. If she were able to spend just a few hours a day away from home, we thought, she'd feel much more capable of continuing to care for him.

"What a difference," Brenda told me after just one week. She'd been freed from resentment, she said in a voice choked with emotion, and now thought she had the strength she needed to carry on.

But not enough strength, sadly, to prevent her from returning to see me six months later, grieving, exhausted, and guilt-ridden after he finally died. When I asked her what she felt guilty about in particular, she said that she thought she should have felt a greater sense of dread in anticipating her husband's death. But looking back she realized she hadn't felt anything close to it. What kind of wife, she wanted to know, doesn't fear the impending death of her husband?

I tried to console Brenda by pointing out that the likely reason she'd felt little anxiety in anticipation of Nathan's death wasn't because she didn't care about him but rather the opposite: her determination to take care of him had been so focused it allowed no room for weakness, her concern for his well-being making her stronger than she knew she could be. It had been a concern, I argued, that could only have arisen from a deep and abiding love. As proof I offered the observation that though her commitment to the care of her husband had prevented her from feeling anxiety prior to his death, it clearly wasn't protecting her from grieving after it.

Over the ensuing weeks, however, rather than gradually extricating herself from her grief she fell more deeply into it, and eventually started reporting significant insomnia, loss of appetite, poor concentration, lack of energy, and a depressed mood. I diagnosed her with depression and placed her on an antidepressant. I also recommended therapy. At a six-week follow-up visit, however, she reported that neither was helping. When I suggested she find a support group for bereaved spouses, she refused, arguing that getting advice about how to grieve from other widows was the last thing she wanted and that hearing their stories would only depress her more. So, in desperation, I suggested she volunteer. As a home hospice worker.

Helping Others to Help Ourselves

Research now shows what many of us know from experience to be true: taking action to alleviate the suffering of others helps us better manage our own. In one study by researchers Carolyn Schwartz and Meir Sendor, patients with multiple sclerosis who were asked to call other patients with multiple sclerosis each month for a year to offer their support in any way they could reported significantly higher levels of adaptability, confidence, tolerance, and self-esteem than the patients they were calling.[5] Something about trying to help others, they said, made them feel better able to manage problems themselves.

Why might this be? One possibility, suggest Schwartz and Sendor, is that focusing on the problems of others alters the way we see ourselves in relation to our own.[6] Thinking about a problem *we* have in the context of someone *else's* life, divorced from how it impacts *us*, may open up avenues of creative thinking and produce ideas about managing it that would otherwise have remained obscured by our emotional reluctance to apply that same creative thinking to ourselves. Further, the better we feel, according to the broaden-and-build theory of positive emotion, the more resourceful, and therefore the more resilient, we become. And helping others has clearly and repeatedly been shown to possess an almost-unequaled ability to make us feel good: according to Schwartz and Sendor, the patients *making* the calls were found to experience more than a *sevenfold* increase in well-being than the patients receiving them.

Not only that, but providing support to others also makes us feel *less bad*. In a study of 180 women and 25 men grieving the loss of their spouses, providing instrumental, if only minor, support to others by giving rides, running errands, doing housework, and so on was found to accelerate recovery from depression in subjects experiencing intense grief.[7] Interestingly, being on the *receiving* end of such support was not.[8]

In other words, when grieving a loss, helping others may be one of the best ways to help ourselves.

Importantly, however, providing help to others seems to increase our well-being only when we provide it of our own free will. If we feel *compelled* to help, whether by another person or by internally self-generated pressures such as shame or pride, helping others *won't* actually increase our well-being.[9] Our sense of well-being may indeed increase in proportion to the help we provide, but only if our desire to provide it is autonomous.[10] Any action we take to help others, in other words, must feel as if it was our idea.

What creates such an autonomous desire to help others? Ironically, often the very same thing that helping others produces: *good feelings*. In one study, male undergraduates given cookies to briefly improve their moods were found to be subsequently more likely than controls to agree when asked to help with a sham experiment.[11] In another study, subjects who found leftover money in a pay phone—again presumably producing brief elevations in their moods—were subsequently found to be far more likely than controls to help a stranger pick up dropped papers.[12] Other research also suggests that the *lower* our mood the *less* likely we are to feel like helping others, even when we think we should.[13]

Which brings us to an ironic truth: we're the least likely to help others when helping others is the most likely to help us—that is, when we feel defeated by problems or devastated by tragedy. At such times, finding the emotional energy and autonomous desire to focus on someone else's problems seems not only impossible but also illogical. After all, don't we need that energy for ourselves?

Though this seems sensible at first glance, such an attitude actually results more from the smallness of thought that accompanies discouragement than from a sober assessment of the best way to recover one's happiest, most capable self. For just as exercise can actually *provide* us with energy by forcing us to summon it when we're feeling tired,[14] helping others can provide us with enthusiasm, encouragement, and even joy by forcing us to summon them when we're feeling discouraged. "If one lights a fire for others," wrote Nichiren Daishonin, "one will brighten one's own way."[15]

The Causes of Altruism

Luckily, however, good feelings aren't the only thing that promotes altruism. Studies have also suggested that altruism may actually be born of suffering. Though self-reported results must always be viewed with some skepticism, in a sample of 100 Holocaust survivors, 82 percent said they helped other prisoners in concentration camps, sharing food and clothing and providing emotional support.[16] Experiencing suffering oneself, especially if intentionally provoked by a malevolent actor, can promote a desire for revenge, but it can also promote empathy for the suffering of others. What's more, helping others seems to enhance the sense that our lives are meaningful, which can serve as a potential antidote to our own suffering.[17] In fact, finding our altruistic behavior increasing after the "poison" of a tragedy may be just the "medicine" we need to fully recover and move on.

Making a Habit of Compassionate Thinking

How then can we turn helping others into a tool for increasing our sense of well-being, and thus our resilience, when we feel least like doing so? Part of the answer lies in consciously making room for it. If our lives are so busy, so filled with errands and responsibilities and passions that we feel we have no emotional capacity or time to take compassionate action when confronted with the opportunity to do so, we need to consider reordering our life priorities.

But the rest of the answer, I told Brenda, was to leverage the power of habit; to challenge ourselves to think about our worst moments not just as our worst moments but also as *cues* that signal us to think about helping others endure theirs; to turn compassionate thinking, in other words, into a *habit* whose trigger is nothing other than our own feelings of despondency. For just as feeling compassion without taking action can make us feel good, taking altruistic action can make us feel good even when we don't feel compassion. Supporting someone else while we're suffering ourselves may be the last thing we want to do, but like swallowing bad-tasting medicine, it's often the best thing for us.

"So don't think about all the reasons you don't want to become a hospice volunteer," I said finally. "Just do it."

"I guess . . . I guess I could try that," Brenda replied.

A month later, then, to my surprise and delight, she did. Encouraged by what she read about hospice on the Internet, she called a local organization and was soon put in touch with and began visiting a woman with terminal lung cancer named Rachel. Heavily sedated by narcotics, Rachel was mostly bed-bound and needed help with the most basic activities of daily living, much in the same way, Brenda told me, as Nathan had. And as she watched Rachel and her husband, Charles, struggle with the same issues and progress through the same stages she had with Nathan, she felt both devastated and comforted to see that she wasn't alone in her suffering, as well as grateful to have the opportunity to exchange encouragements with them. Being able to forget her own suffering for a little while was indeed a relief, she said.

But when Rachel finally died, Charles became inconsolable, causing Brenda to fly into a panic. Though she found the desire to ease his pain that rose up in her strangely relieving of her *own* pain, she had no idea how to help him. She recognized in Charles her own refusal to accept support, to want to swim in grief as if it were an enjoyable hot bath. How, she wondered, could she combat that? She tried giving him advice, thinking he might view her as wise in the ways of grief. But he seemed as resistant to taking hers as she'd been to taking mine.

Walking in Another's Shoes

Several years ago, a friend of mine told me he was thinking about getting a divorce. He'd been unhappy in his marriage for some time, he said. His wife was irrationally jealous and sometimes behaved in ways that were shockingly inappropriate, offensive, and stress-inducing.

Or so he told me. Though he painted a clear picture of her personality and character, I couldn't personally verify any of it because I'd never met her. Which didn't stop me from immediately deciding that he needed to run as far away from her as fast as he possibly could.

But I didn't say that. Not because I was uninterested in helping him, but because I wasn't convinced that I was wise enough to give him good advice. For even if his wife was all the terrible things he'd described, what reason did I have to believe that my ideas would necessarily lead him to the best possible outcome? Did I really think I knew enough about his situation to know better what he should do than he did himself?

In other circumstances with other people—for example, with certain of my patients—my answer to this question has been a resounding yes. Some people really do operate with an alarmingly distorted thought process, or a thought process that consistently distorts around certain issues or relationships, and that impairs their ability to make good decisions.

And yet, even with such people, we should always proceed with caution. We may be right that we have better judgment than do those who come to us for advice, but we can never understand the totality of another person's life the way he does. Thus, even if we have superior judgment, we're doomed to having inadequate access to the data on which we must base it. We may therefore have strong opinions about the personal choices of others, but we should hold them lightly and consider carefully when—or even whether—to share them.

I remember the outrage felt by much of the country when O. J. Simpson was acquitted. I was outraged, too, as convinced as the rest of the country that he was guilty. Yet, unlike the jurors in the case, I'd heard little of the specific evidence the prosecution had presented. Nor had I received explicit instructions from the judge on how to consider what I'd heard. Nor was I one of the people actually responsible for deciding whether to find him, a fellow human being, guilty of murder. So it was easy for me to have a strong opinion, to be outraged like so many others at the apparent injustice of his acquittal: my opinion carried no real significance; it sent no one to prison or to the gas chamber. And though my gut still tells me O. J. was guilty, I refuse to judge the jury that decided he wasn't. I didn't hear what they heard. I didn't have to decide anything.

Nor had I been present during the years of interactions that my friend had experienced with his wife that now caused him to want a divorce. Yet there came a pause in our conversation in which I felt he wanted to hear my judgment about what he should do. And though the temptation to tell him my opinion rose up like a strong urge to cough, I refused to indulge it. Instead, I offered him my empathy. "What an awful situation for you both to be in," I said. "Just even to be seriously contemplating divorce must be terrible for you." He agreed with a heavy sigh it was. I told him I had confidence he would figure out what was best for him and that I'd support whatever decision he made.

His reaction was immediate: his expression softened, his posture relaxed, and his frustration visibly retreated. He nodded, thanked me for having listened, and left. (Months later, they reconciled.)

The Power of Encouragement

We may think our advice represents the most valuable thing we have to offer those who suffer, but it pales in comparison to the power of our encouragement. Encouragement, at its heart, represents an attempt to make others feel that they have the strength, wisdom, courage, and ability to solve their problems themselves; it aims not to provide specific solutions but to make others believe they can find those solutions on their own. With encouragement we express our belief in the indefatigable power of the human spirit to make what appears to be impossible possible, all in the hopes of awakening the same belief in those we're trying to encourage.

But encouraging others is difficult. For one thing, people themselves don't usually know what will encourage them. For another, they often don't even notice the statements we make that we think will help them the most. Usually it's something else we say, something we may not later even remember saying, that gives them the hope to go on. Something we just as easily might never have said.

Yet most of us will at some point in our lives have a friend or a loved one tell us something has happened to them that's so awful we won't know how to respond at all. Perhaps it's a diagnosis of cancer. Or the death of a beloved parent or child. Or a spouse asking for a divorce. Upon hearing some stories, we can only recoil at the immensity of the storyteller's suffering, often finding ourselves reduced to grasping at platitudes that sound entirely inadequate or trying to suggest, inanely, that things aren't as bad as they seem.

But people who feel as if they're drowning in pain tend not to want to hear platitudes, and often we're left feeling as inadequate as our words sound. Yet when words fail, it doesn't mean we have. For we have one other thing to which we can still turn: the power of touch.

The Power of Touch

When I was a fourth-year medical student, I did a monthlong rotation in the emergency room. One night a woman came in whom the attending physician decided needed some lab work. When I let her know we needed to draw her blood, she began to tremble. "I'm scared of needles," she whispered.

She squeezed her eyes shut as the phlebotomist set up next to her gurney to draw her blood. "It'll be over before you know it," I tried to encourage her, but she didn't even acknowledge I'd spoken.

The phlebotomist glanced at me once, probably more concerned that the patient was going to jump or prove to be a hard stick than with her fear, and then said to her, "You're going to feel a little poke."

The patient tensed, tears appearing at the corners of her closed eyes. Desperate to comfort her and not knowing what else to do, I reached out and took her hand, feeling awkward and foolish as I did so. Yet she clamped down on my fingers so hard they soon started to hurt until I shifted my grip to better allow for the force of her squeezing. When the needle went in, she squeezed my hand even harder. I felt strangely and warmly connected to her, urgently wishing the phlebotomist would finish as quickly as possible.

When it was over, the patient continued to lie there with her eyes shut, my hand still in hers. I watched as she forced her breathing to slow and then opened her eyes. She dabbed at her tears with her free hand and then looked directly at me. "Thank you," she said in a relieved voice. Then she gave my hand a final squeeze—this one mercifully gentle—and let it go. My hand started throbbing a little, but I hardly noticed.

Perhaps because in the end we all have to face the trials life has in store for us by ourselves—experiencing pain, fear, doubt, and loss in the confines of our own minds and bodies—when obstacles appear we long for evidence that we're not alone, that others care about how we feel and what happens to us. There just seems to be something intrinsically encouraging and comforting about the physical presence of others when we're in pain or afraid. Words may come out wrong or ring hollow in our ears, but a touch intended to encourage—on a hand, or a shoulder, or with an embrace—rarely fails to make us feel better, even if only a little. It may require courage—the courage to invade another person's personal space without being invited. But how lucky for us all that we seem to be built in such a way that something as simple and easy to provide as a kind and loving touch can sometimes bolster our spirits so much.

Showing We Care

I try to remember the lesson that patient taught me as often as I can. It helps me not to feel inadequate when I'm unable to find words of encouragement in the face of someone else's pain, and reminds me that what words of encouragement I *can* find aren't necessarily as important as the message my attempts at making them communicates: I care. When I—who pride myself on always being able to find not just the right words but magic words, words that illuminate, enlighten, and comfort—can find nothing appropriate to say, I remind myself that encouragement comes not just from eloquence but also from a willingness to share the problems of others as my own. From finding some way—any way—to help others believe that those problems can actually be solved.

Which was why, I told Brenda, I thought Charles would almost certainly respond better to encouragement than advice. And not just anyone's encouragement, I said, but to hers in particular.

"Why mine?" she asked.

"Because no one has the power to encourage us like someone who's been through the same thing we have."

The Last Way to
Turn Poison into Medicine

Even if we can't produce a victory from failure, even if we don't grow personally as a result of adversity, we can always—always—use our experiences to encourage others. Especially when others are facing obstacles similar to those we ourselves once faced and survived.

Had I passed Part I of the National Boards the first time, for example, I wouldn't have had an experience with which I could encourage other students who themselves had failed. My failure, and subsequent victory over it, thus became a poison that I continue to turn into medicine each time I pull it out to encourage someone else. In this way, my victory has continued to expand, to rise to even greater heights.

As Brenda's overcoming the loss of her husband could do, too, I encouraged her. Because she herself had experienced what Charles was experiencing now, *her* encouragement, coming as it did from someone who had demonstrated that overcoming the loss of a spouse was possible, would likely have a far greater impact than the encouragement of others who hadn't. So when she empathized with Charles, when she told him that things would eventually get better, when she commiserated with him about life after such a loss and told him how she'd approached the same problems he was facing himself, and when she gave his hand a small squeeze, he would more likely greet her attempts to encourage him not with doubt or even scorn but with the one thing that gives all words of encouragement their special power: trust.

"It's like you're both running the same race but you're farther ahead and calling back to him a description of the terrain he's about to see himself," I said. "Just run with him a while."

When I saw her back in my clinic six months later, she told me she'd done exactly that. He'd been getting over the loss of Rachel with agonizing slowness, she said, as she had over her loss of Nathan before him. Until, she added with a hint of pride, she'd made the same suggestion to Charles that I had to her: that he join her as a hospice volunteer.

My eyes widened in surprise. "How'd he respond to that?"

She said he'd taken a while to warm to the idea. But eventually he'd agreed, and they'd started visiting one of her terminal patients together (she'd been involved with three more families since his, she told me). Several weeks into it, then, as they were leaving their patient's home together, he turned to her suddenly and said quietly, "Thank you for saving my life."

10

Muster Your Courage

Few things have as much power to make us suffer as fear. More than merely an obstacle to strength, fear is nearly its antithesis, for nothing weakens us quite as much. And though for this reason we often yearn for a life without fear, it remains, like all emotions, something from which we can never entirely free ourselves. Then again, neither would we want to: for also like all emotions, fear is neither good nor bad in itself but becomes one or the other depending on the context in which it occurs and the action it causes us to take (or avoid). For example, fear can both increase our likelihood of survival, as when it motivates us to flee a burning building, and decrease our likelihood of success, as when it prevents us from attempting to learn a new skill.

The Benefits of Fear

The ideal, then, would be to feel fear only when it benefits us. Unfortunately, most of us haven't yet mastered this art. In fact, most of us feel fear of the nonbeneficial variety quite frequently. And because it's often impossible to tell the difference between what we should fear and what we shouldn't, evolution has built into us the tendency to react to all fear as we do pain: by avoiding the things that cause it.

Further, because fear feels bad, when we can't escape the things that cause it, we often try to stop the feeling itself. But trying to suppress fear rarely works. In fact, as described in Chapter 6, it often leads to greater harm than that caused by fear alone.[1] In contrast, *accepting* fear often paradoxically *reduces* its intensity.[2] Accepting fear also (and arguably more importantly) reduces fear's *influence,*[3] thereby providing a path for us to find courage, the ability to take action in *spite* of fear. Aiming to be courageous rather than fearless, then, may be not only safer but also more realistic.

Distracting Ourselves

Which doesn't mean, of course, that finding courage is easy. Like everything else worth finding, it requires effort—and a viable strategy. Instead of accepting fear, for example, we might try to *distract* ourselves from it. So when afraid of being turned down for a date, we might focus instead on the anticipated pleasure of a fine meal. Or when afraid of finding out that we failed a test, we might focus instead on the vacation we have planned for the week after. Or when waiting for the results of a biopsy, we might focus instead on doing something fun, a strategy that helped a patient of mine whom I once diagnosed with lung cancer.

A workup for metastases had revealed a small mass in his liver that had the radiographic appearance of a benign liver cyst. But in the setting of a newly diagnosed cancer, we couldn't be sure it wasn't a metastatic lesion, so we decided to biopsy it. Due to scheduling issues, however, we couldn't get the biopsy done for a week.

Two days into the seven, he called me in a panic over the possibility that the lesion was indeed cancer, a fact that he knew would change his prognosis from good to dismal if true. I offered him a prescription for

Valium, which he accepted gratefully, and then suggested he try to manage his anxiety with distraction. "Denial gets a bad rap it doesn't entirely deserve," I told him. I pointed out he'd already taken the action necessary to secure the best chance of a good outcome when he'd decided to have the biopsy, so no further amount of thinking about his cancer would increase his chances of survival.

To make effective use of denial, I suggested he focus on turning his mind *toward* something gripping rather than *away* from something anxiety-producing. Which meant, I said, taking some kind of action. So that's what he decided to do: over the next five days, he saw three movies, read two books, and visited his favorite niece. And indeed, he said later, he hardly thought about his cancer for the rest of the week at all and as a result his anxiety became far more manageable. (The lesion was later found to be a benign liver adenoma, and he had his lung cancer removed a week afterward. Three years later, he remains disease free.)

Though research shows that 80 percent of people suffering from anxiety aren't receiving professional help for it,[4] it also suggests that most of them don't actually need it: anxiety self-management techniques in many instances work just as well.[5] (Which isn't to say people who suffer from anxiety that they *can't* manage on their own should defer getting professional help.) Simple interventions like diaphragmatic breathing, imagining relaxing scenes, and meditating mindfully while walking have all been shown to reduce stress by approximately 45 percent in some of the most stressed people on the planet—third-year medical students—when practiced on a regular basis.[6]

We might also manage fear by realizing that in the long term we don't actually *remember* most of what happens to us. Thus, when facing obstacles, pausing to remind ourselves that we won't likely even recall having faced them—implying that we'll have found a way to surmount them or to live with them—may also offer us a path to facing them with courage.

Finally, research suggests, astoundingly, that anxiety can be diminished by reducing the amount of inflammation in the brain. Anxiety has long been known to increase the production of inflammatory cytokines,[7] and epidemiological studies have linked low blood levels of compounds like omega-3 polyunsaturated fatty acids, which have anti-inflammatory effects, with an increased risk of social anxiety disorder.[8] But the strongest evidence that reducing inflammation in the brain can reduce anxiety comes from a randomized controlled trial in which approximately 2.5 grams of eicosapentaenoic acid (EPA) combined with 0.03 grams of docosahexaenoic acid (DHA)—both found commonly in fish oil—were given to medical students and found to reduce not only their inflammatory cytokine levels by 14 percent, but also their anxiety levels by 20 percent.[9]

Panic Attacks

A full-blown panic attack, on the other hand, is as different from anxiety as a cup of water is from the ocean. Adrenaline surges through one's body, readying it for a flight-or-fight response, producing a cascade of physical effects: sweating, palpitations, dizziness, and tremulousness. An impending sense of doom makes concentration and even rational thought nearly impossible. In fact, people who suffer from panic attacks on a regular basis will often say that having them makes them feel as if they're about to die.

That's how the only panic attack I ever experienced felt, too. It happened when I was a first-year medical student taking my first biochemistry midterm exam. I remember opening the test, reading the first question, and thinking I had no idea what it was even asking. So I turned the page to the second question—only to find myself equally at a loss. I read all seven questions in turn, each time thinking that I'd be able to answer the next one, until I reached the last one and realized I couldn't answer any of them.

This had never happened to me before. I realized that, for the first time in my life, I was about to fail an exam. I broke into a sweat and my heart started pounding. I looked around the room in a panic, hyperventilating, feeling dizzy.

My best friend, who was sitting next to me, noticed my distress and whispered, "What's wrong?"

"I can't answer any of the questions," I whispered back.

"Try," he insisted.

I felt as if I were in mortal danger and struggled against an impulse to leap up and run out of the room.

"Calm down," he told me. But his words had no effect.

Despite its various causes, panic is always seeded by a thought (though one often not remembered). It may be the thought that the chest pain we're feeling is now radiating down our left arm, or that airplanes sometimes crash, or that we can't answer any of the questions on a biochemistry exam. But when such thoughts lead to the belief that we've become trapped in an acutely dangerous situation *from which we have no escape*, they begin to trigger many of the physical symptoms characteristic of panic. These symptoms then often lead to a belief that something is seriously wrong with us, something that might actually kill us. This fear serves only to intensify the physical symptoms, which in turn reinforces and intensifies our fear and conviction that we're in grave danger, which then cycles into full-blown panic.

Alternatively, we might find ourselves focusing not on the physical symptoms but on the life consequences that we think will follow from our inability to extricate ourselves from a panic-inducing predicament. I wasn't worried that I was in physical danger when I panicked during my exam. Rather, I was thinking that if I failed the test, I'd fail the course, and that if I failed the course, I'd fail out of medical school, and that if I failed out of medical school, I wouldn't become a doctor, and that if I failed to become a doctor—*then what would I do with my life?* Irrational as it was, that last thought—the abrupt belief that I had no future—immediately tethered itself to the high probability that I was about to fail a test and held me in its grip without mercy. It engulfed my entire thought process, filled me with dread, and ignited my panic.

To abort a severe panic attack often requires medication. But short of that, several nonpharmacologic techniques can be useful in situations that provoke acute anxiety. First, patients who suffer from recurrent panic attacks often report that simply carrying antianxiety medication with them often obviates their need to use it. Though they know a pill won't remove them from a situation that induces them to panic, they also know it *will* relieve the awful feelings that such situations stir up. Knowing they have the power to exercise control over their feelings then becomes the thing that helps them control their feelings.

A second technique to quell acute anxiety involves rating the severity of the anxiety as we feel it moment by moment. Few things bounce us out of an experience more quickly than pausing to examine our own reactions to it, which takes us from *having* an experience to *watching* ourselves have an experience.[10] (Think of the effect of being asked by your partner in the middle of making love, "So, on a scale of one to ten, how's this going for you?") Also, we're likely to recognize we're feeling anxious earlier in the course of escalating anxiety when self-monitoring for it, which then positions us to react to it before it becomes unmanageable.[11]

A third technique involves looking for and correcting thought errors that cause us to panic. Most of us, for example, think anecdotally rather than statistically.[12] That is, we tend to arrive at our beliefs about the frequency with which things occur not from statistical analysis but from the ease with which we can recall examples of their happening. So if we've recently heard a story of an airplane crash in the news, we'll believe the likelihood that the airplane in which we're flying might crash to be greater than it actually is. Or if a friend tells us about a complication he suffered following surgery, we'll believe the likelihood of that complication happening after our surgery to be greater than statistics suggest. In learning how to use statistical thinking to more accurately estimate the *true* likelihood of a disaster occurring—in learning to believe in the power of statistical thinking—we're far more likely to be able to prevent ourselves from panicking over things whose likelihood is actually low.

Finally, we can habituate ourselves to the things we fear by deliberately and repeatedly exposing ourselves to them. For just as pleasures become less enjoyable the more often we repeat them, fearful stimuli become less frightening the more often we encounter them.[13] If we're afraid of riding in elevators, for example, we might begin by looking at pictures of an elevator until doing so ceases to induce anxiety. Then we might stand several feet away from a closed elevator. Then we might stand directly in front of one. Then we might stand directly in front of one with the doors open. Then we might stand inside one with the doors open with a companion. Then we might take a short ride in one with a companion. Then a longer ride. Then a ride alone. In fact, this kind of desensitization works to control not only simple phobias, but also more complex fears like social anxiety (which is why forcing ourselves to ask people out on dates, for example, gradually reduces our fear of doing so).[14]

In the end, I did fail my biochemistry test. But I didn't flunk out of medical school. I applied myself, retook the test, and scored well, ultimately passing the class by a comfortable margin. The experience taught me several valuable lessons, though, the most important one being this: our minds cannot be trusted. With little justification, they begin to worry about the worst possible outcome when we're confronted with even minor threats.

One final technique that can help us counteract this tendency involves, paradoxically, imagining the worst possible outcome as well as we can. For in asking ourselves detailed questions about how a disaster might play out in the future, we'll often begin to imagine ways we might manage it and thus fear it less in the present. Also, when anticipating a disaster, we tend to imagine our future only in terms of the consequences to which we think the disaster will lead,[15] failing to consider all the good things that will inevitably occur as well.[16] Additionally, we fail to realize that disasters don't, in general, affect us as much or for as long as we predict they will.[17] Further, after playing out the worst possible outcome as well as we can, if we then envision *other* events we think will occupy our thoughts in the future besides thoughts about a potentially impending disaster, research suggests we'll start to believe our future won't be quite as bad as we think.[18]

Fear of Death

Of all the things we fear, however, perhaps none has the same power to sap our strength and make useless our fear-combating strategies as our fear of death, the one fear that arguably underlies all others. Knowledge of our mortality is a wound so painful that most of us employ, consciously or unconsciously, every cognitive trick we can to deny it. As with any skill, however, some are better at dealing with the inevitability of death than others, yielding a wide range of reactions to the notion of personal annihilation. Many people, for example, find it impossible to believe that they will one day entirely cease to exist, that their particular personhood will never recur, and as a result remain blissfully untouched by the fear of death. At the opposite end of the spectrum, some few others live in constant terror that any day might be their last, their ability to live ruined by their certain knowledge that they will one day die.

And some others vacillate back and forth between the two extremes. Like many people, I also had no emotional belief in my mortality for most of my life—until I was forced to confront it directly. While attending a brunch one Sunday in January 2007, I developed a mild stomachache and a general feeling of malaise. Initially, the pain appeared in the center of my abdomen just above my navel, but gradually over the course of the day it inched its way down into my right lower quadrant, causing me to wonder briefly if I'd developed appendicitis. But by evening the pain had actually begun to improve so I dismissed the possibility; I'd never heard of a case of appendicitis resolving on its own without surgery. But mindful of the adage that the physician who treats himself has a fool for a patient, the next day I asked one of my physician colleagues to examine me. When he did, he found a fullness he didn't like in my right lower quadrant and ordered a CT scan. To our mutual surprise, it showed that I had, in fact, developed acute appendicitis. Later that afternoon, I saw a surgeon who put me on antibiotics and scheduled an elective laparoscopic appendectomy, which he performed two days later. The surgery went well, and I was back at home that night with a bloated stomach but minimal discomfort.

At 3 AM, however, I awoke with projectile vomiting, and after a particularly violent episode, briefly lost consciousness. Panic stricken, my wife called 911, and an ambulance took me back to the hospital, where I was found to be anemic. My surgeon diagnosed an intra-abdominal bleed and began following my red blood cell count every few hours, hoping the bleeding would stop on its own. By late afternoon, however, it became clear that it wouldn't, so I was taken back to the operating room where the surgeon found and evacuated approximately one-and-a-half liters of blood from my abdomen. All told, I'd lost half of my blood volume over the course of sixteen hours.

Over the next few days, however, my blood count stabilized and my strength returned, so I was sent home four days after I'd been admitted, slightly less bloated than I'd been after the first surgery but now containing four units of a stranger's blood. Three weeks later, my wife and I left on a four-hour flight to Mexico for a vacation in Cabo San Lucas we'd planned before I became ill, spent three days on the beach, and then flew back home.

Then, two days after returning, I developed diarrhea. Because I'd only had bottled water while in Mexico, I thought I'd contracted a viral gastroenteritis that would resolve on its own within a few days. While driving home a few days later, however, I developed the abrupt onset of right-sided chest pain. I called my physician, who asked me to return immediately to the hospital to have a chest CT, which showed I'd thrown a large blood clot—a pulmonary embolism—into one of my lungs. I was taken immediately to the emergency room and placed on intravenous blood thinners to prevent another clot from traveling to my lung and possibly killing me. Luckily, this time my hospital stay was uneventful, and I was ultimately discharged on an oral anticoagulant called Coumadin.

A week later, however, the diarrhea still hadn't resolved, so a stool culture was sent for *clostridium difficile*, a bacterial organism well known to cause infectious colitis in patients following the administration of certain antibiotics. It came back positive, undoubtedly as a result of the antibiotics I'd been given prior to my first surgery, so I was started on Vancomycin. Then I developed an allergic reaction to the Vancomycin, so I was switched to Flagyl. Within a week the diarrhea resolved.

A week later, however, the nausea returned. It was absolutely crippling—as was the anxiety that accompanied it. What could possibly be wrong now? I longed for the blissful ignorance of a nonmedical mind that had no knowledge of all the terrible diseases I now thought I might have. I called my physician colleague, who suggested, after listening to my symptoms, that the nausea might be due to anxiety. I told him that idea hadn't occurred to me, that I'd supposed the anxiety was present as a *result* of the nausea, not as its *cause*, but that I was open to the possibility he was right. The next day I had a conversation with a psychiatrist who diagnosed me with mild posttraumatic stress.

Belief in Our Mortality

I find myself continually surprised by the number of people who tell me they're not afraid to die. Most are usually quick to point out they *are* afraid to die *painfully*, but not of the idea of no longer being alive. Though I can imagine people do indeed exist who, because of their young age or religious beliefs, genuinely feel this way, I've always wondered if that answer hints at a denial so deeply seated it cannot be faced by most.

Certainly, this has been the case with me. I love being here and don't want to leave. I've spoken openly of my fear of death to anyone who's ever asked, but I've rarely experienced moments in which I actually *felt* afraid. Whenever I've tried wrapping my mind around the concept of my own demise, tried truly envisioning the world continuing on without me, the essence of what I am utterly gone forever, I've unearthed a fear so overwhelming it's turned my mind aside as if my imagination and the idea of my own end were two magnets of identical polarity, unwilling to meet no matter how hard I tried to make them.

The true significance of my denial wasn't made clear to me, however, until I was diagnosed with posttraumatic stress disorder. The anxiety that began to envelop me at that point was of an entirely different order than I'd ever experienced. It began to interfere with my ability to function, which made plain to me that what my brush with death—twice— had taken from me was *my ability to believe I would never die*. Knowing *intellectually* that death awaits us is quite clearly a different thing from *believing* it, much in the same way knowing intellectually gravity will make you fall is a different experience from actually swooning at the edge of a parapet at the top of a tall building. Ultimately, being ill brought me to the realization, contrary to what I'd always believed in my heart, that there was nothing special about me at all. Like everyone else, I was only a piece of meat that would eventually spoil.

I felt like one of my longtime patients, Rita, who for as long as I'd known her had been consumed by a fear of death so great she'd become like a child in her need for constant reassurance that she would be all right. For Rita, every sore throat was cancer, every bout of chest pain was a heart attack, and an inability to fall asleep meant she was dying. She'd been on almost every antidepressant and antianxiety medication known but continued to experience a fear so intense that at one point she became unable to leave her home. Her anxiety, in short, made her inconsolable and her life a joyless nightmare.

Which I now understood in a way I hadn't before. Now, like her, my fear of death would rise up at the smallest provocation: whether I'd feel a minor twinge in my chest, develop a rash on my arms, or my hand would shake, I would become paralyzed with fear. Even though I recognized intellectually that my reactions were overblown, every new symptom I felt caused my doctor's brain to leap to horrifying conclusions simply because I now knew in a way I hadn't before that bad things could actually happen to me.

I'd always considered the shattering of delusion to be a good thing, something that had always brought me *more* happiness rather than less. And yet here seemed to be an example that contradicted that rule, for I was now suffering to a degree equaled only by the degree to which I suffered when my first girlfriend ended our relationship. Frankly, I was happier when I was living in denial.

Luckily, however, my anxiety eventually resolved with nothing more than the passage of time. Aided by the unexpected return of my ability to delude myself into believing I was somehow special and that through a combination of good luck and careful behavior I could sidestep death for many decades to come, my thoughts about dying, and therefore my worry, disappeared like a tortoise's head back into its shell.

Yet I found this result deeply unsatisfying. Even minor injuries or transient symptoms that I would have ignored before still stirred up feelings of exaggerated worry. And though my emotional awareness of my mortality seemed to have gone back into hiding, I remained acutely aware of how vulnerable I was to its recurring.

I also wanted something to offer Rita, who'd been struggling with anxiety since 1996 when she'd suffered a heart attack. Initially, her cardiologist had prescribed Ativan, but it hadn't helped, so he'd referred her to me. Amazed by just how violently her fear of death had been stirred up and by how awful her life had become as a result, I increased her Ativan dose, added Neurontin, and referred her to a psychiatrist. He in turn added Prozac and started her in psychotherapy.

But neither the medications nor the therapy seemed to help. So her psychiatrist began rotating her through a series of drug regimens, all of us hoping that with each new drug he introduced Rita would at last begin to show some signs of improvement. But she never did. Every time I saw her and asked how she was doing, her answer was the same: "I'm afraid all the time. I can't go on like this."

I tried to help her with every nonpharmacologic strategy I knew. When my expressions of empathy for her suffering seemed to do little but exacerbate it, I switched tactics and began pushing her to stop dwelling on what was making her afraid and to stop suppressing whatever fear broke through. I also suggested she try "grading" her fear moment by moment to bounce herself out of the experience of feeling it, but after attempting that a few times she said it was too difficult to do alone and that it yielded little benefit anyway. When I suggested she get involved in activities she found engaging as a way to distract herself, she replied that no such activities existed. I even went so far as to express my impatience with her fearful whining ("Am I going to live?"), not as a way to manage my frustration (which was considerable) but as a strategy designed to stop what I sensed might have been enabling behavior on my part. But, not surprisingly, that also failed to help.

By then her husband had begun threatening to divorce her. This of course only increased her anxiety and eventually caused her to develop severe agoraphobia. Soon, she refused to leave her apartment at all, even to see me. The idea of being alone, she told me tearfully over the phone, terrified her even more than dying (that staying at home served only to increase her isolation wasn't lost on her, but that awareness did nothing to provide her the courage to leave). Not knowing what else to do, I said I would call her once a day until she was able to come see me in my clinic, thinking that if I couldn't speak to her I couldn't help her. But no conversation we ever had and nothing I ever suggested—including the practice of Nichiren Buddhism, which she tried for a few months but then abandoned—ever had any noticeable effect.

I called her every day for a year. Then she had a stroke.

The Idea of Death

So powerful is our connection to life that when it comes under attack we become capable of focusing on nothing but defending it. But because life *can't* be defended against death, in the end we're left only able to ruminate about our mortality, or to deny we're going to die at all, either by ignoring the fact completely or by placing our faith in one of the many unsupported notions—including the Buddhist notion of reincarnation—of an afterlife. And though the strategy of denial works in general, never before in the history of humankind has it been more likely to fail when used against the fear of death: advancing medical technology has reduced the likelihood that death will catch us unawares to a fraction of what it once was. Thus, few of us are spared having to confront our fear of it.

Yet in his book *Staring at the Sun,* Irvin Yalom holds out hope for a third possibility: that by willfully and directly *confronting* our fear of death we can increase our determination to live well; that a finely honed awareness of death can help us avoid wasting time on pursuits for which we're ill-suited or in which we have no real interest but in which we participate out of a sense of obligation or guilt; and that keeping our life's end firmly in mind can help us focus on those things that the wise know are most likely to bring happiness: our relationships and helping others. In other words, Yalom argues, though death itself may destroy us, the *idea* of death may save us.[19]

He may be right. Many people who've peered into the chasm of death have indeed returned from the edge of that chasm changed, with a new set of values and behaviors that seem to make them and those around them happier and more fulfilled. Then again, others have been thrust toward the same precipice only to come back bearing terrible scars: post-traumatic stress disorder, anxiety, and depression.

What accounts for these varying results? Perhaps the same factors that predict personal growth in response to other, less severe kinds of trauma. In one study of parents raising children with attention deficit/hyperactivity disorder (ADHD), subjects with the most "emotional intelligence" who possessed an optimistic self-explanatory style and perceived problems as challenges rather than as threats were the most likely to exhibit personal growth in response to the stress of parenting.[20] And in another study, this one of Chinese women with breast cancer, subjects who believed that something good could come from their cancer—in other words, that poison could be changed into medicine—were also more likely to exhibit personal growth following their diagnosis.[21]

On the other hand, the challenges involved in raising children with ADHD *can* be overcome. Breast cancer *can* be cured. What good are emotional intelligence and an optimistic self-explanatory style against a problem that *can't* be solved, like death?

Medicine for Others

The answer, according to Yalom, may lie in marshaling our emotional intelligence and optimistic self-explanatory style to turn the poison of our mortality into medicine—not for *ourselves* but for *others*. Several years ago, a graduating medical school class invited me to be a guest at their graduation dinner. A resident with whom I'd worked previously had also been invited and was scheduled to speak. When the time came for her to make her remarks, she began by telling a story of a former mentor of hers who'd once said to her, "Someone is always watching you." She joked how at first she'd found that statement a bit "random" but then tied it neatly to the theme of her talk: we are all role models for one another and how we behave moment by moment sometimes powerfully influences the behavior of the people around us, especially other people who actively look to us for knowledge. "So as you go forward with your training," she told them, "remember to also look back at how you're leading the people behind you."

What she was describing, I realized suddenly, was Yalom's concept of *rippling*. As he writes, "Rippling refers to the fact that each of us creates—often without our conscious intent or knowledge—concentric circles of influence that may affect others for years, even generations. That is, the effect we have on other people is in turn passed on to others, much as the ripples in a pond go on and on until they're no longer visible but continuing at a nano level."[22] He then draws an important contrast between the hope to preserve our personal identity after we're gone—a futile attempt doomed to failure—and "leaving behind something from [our] life experience."[23]

We all carry with us a concrete yet paradoxically ineffable sense of self, a feeling of a coherent identity that we define as "us"—a core self that resides somewhere within our skulls amid a chorus of peripheral selves all locked within the same small space. It remains this core sense of self to which we're all desperately attached and in great fear of having annihilated by death. It is, unfortunately, this very thing we're all destined to lose.

But great value might be gained, Yalom seems to be suggesting, from asking ourselves what else we might consider to be uniquely "us" besides this internal sense of self. For example, might all the wisdom we accumulate over time that displays itself in our behavior also represent our "self," in one way even more accurately than our subjectively experienced sense of it? Are we not, after all, most clearly defined in the minds of others—even in our own—by what we *do*? Doesn't our *behavior* most accurately reflect our most deeply held beliefs, beliefs that make us far more unrepeatable than our own internal sense of uniqueness?

Our behavior toward others, in fact, doesn't just make them the objects of our intentions; it makes them recipients of lessons we teach them, whether or not they—or even we—know it. Why has the world, as Steven Pinker argues in his book *The Better Angels of Our Nature*, become demonstrably less violent over the millennia?[24] Only because the moral progress of individuals has gradually rippled across people and generations.

We may have a long way to go before we can say we've achieved a truly just and peaceful society anywhere on Earth, but that only means the parts of ourselves that we leave behind matter even more. None of us should think that by focusing only on raising our children or being kind to those in our immediate vicinity we're affecting only our children or those in our immediate vicinity. We may rarely get feedback from the people around us about how meaningfully we've influenced their lives for the better, and even less often how they then may have gone on, as a direct result of our influence, to influence the lives of still others. But there's little doubt this effect is real and frequently significant. The small kind word we leave with a stranger who we'll never see again may not just spread out like ripples on a pond but may strike with the force of a tidal wave. We just never know. Sometimes the message our behavior imparts goes out to someone who's particularly receptive at that moment to being influenced by it. And through the conduit they represent to all the others with whom they interact, and with whom *they* then interact and so on, we all have the potential to contribute to shaping the future of our world. As a fellow Buddhist once said to me, "The movement for world peace goes on with or without you. The question is, what kind of contribution do you want to make to it?"

This was what my former resident was trying to tell that graduating medical school class, I thought: that in affecting others we leave pieces of ourselves behind. And as she finished and stepped down from the podium, her husband, who'd been sitting next to me, leaned over and said with a smile, "That mentor who told her someone is always watching? That was you."

Our Sense of Self

Unfortunately, while it may be true in one sense that we live on after death through the influence that our actions continue to have on others, introducing Rita to that idea did nothing to calm her anxiety. Even though she made a full recovery from her stroke, being forced to confront her mortality yet again only served to anchor her even more firmly to her personal sense of self.

Not that I could blame her. When I'd become sick and my death anxiety had risen to its peak, I hadn't been motivated to live a fuller life either;

I'd been paralyzed. And though I'd endorsed the value of rippling to her, the truth was that my belief in its importance, though genuine, had done nothing to comfort me either. In fact, my fear of death, though for most of my life far less intense than hers, had never been satisfactorily ameliorated by anything and had in truth been one of the principal reasons I'd started practicing Nichiren Buddhism.

Initially I'd been drawn to the practice because it claimed enlightenment to be a real thing, that there really was a truth to know that would in some way explain the ultimate nature of reality and my relation to it and that, once grasped, would help me construct a life-condition of indestructible happiness. But what convinced me to give the practice a try was my thought that such a life-condition might also free me from my fear of death.

I thought this because I'd once caught a glimpse of what I believed such a life-condition would feel like. I'd come home for the summer after my sophomore year in college and had been sitting in my bedroom watching and listening to the trees swaying in an afternoon breeze through an open window when I found myself suddenly and inexplicably filled with the strongest sense of connection to my surroundings I'd ever known. At the same time, I began to overflow with the most powerful feeling of goodwill and loving assent toward everyone and everything I'd ever experienced. I seemed somehow larger than myself, as if what I'd always considered to be "me" was in reality nothing more than a personality within a personality—like the protagonist in A. E. Van Vogt's short story "Asylum," who discovers to his amazement that he isn't a man with an IQ of 110 at all but instead a facet of an alien mind that possesses an IQ of 1200, "an actor who'd been completely absorbed in his role, but who was now alone in his dressing room after the play was over removing the grease paint, his mood of the play fading, fading, fading . . ."[25] Wondrously, at that moment I felt as accepting of the idea of my death as

I was about the idea of the sun setting at the end of the day. And then as many others who've described similar experiences have reported, within minutes the feeling faded away.

Though the memory of that experience wasn't enough to prevent me from cowering in fear when I became sick two decades later, recent research suggests that for others it just might be. In a recent pilot study, researcher Charles Grob and colleagues gave the hallucinogen psilocybin, found in over 200 species of mushrooms, to twelve patients with advanced-stage cancer to induce awakening experiences similar to mine and found that it reduced their anxiety by almost 30 percent as measured by psychometric testing, an effect that lasted as long as six months following ingestion.[26] And though an independent drug effect hasn't yet been ruled out as the cause, in another study, 94 percent of subjects who were also given psilocybin and had a "complete" mystical experience as measured by psychometric testing rated it as the single most significant event that had ever happened to them. Retrospectively almost all identified it as the definitive cause of their persistently increased sense of well-being.[27]

The point of this research isn't that such drugs might represent a pathway to enlightenment, for to live with an *enduring* awareness of the interconnectedness of all life probably requires some kind of regular practice as well as the ability to interact with the world free from hallucinogenic distortions of perception. Rather, the point is that even transient mystical experiences may have a lasting impact on fear. Something about disconnecting from one's sense of self even briefly, about glimpsing oneself as belonging to a greater whole, seems profoundly and persistently comforting to most people who experience it.

But whether that comfort comes from merely *having* a mystical experience or from the belief in the persistence of life beyond death that such mystical experiences often create isn't clear. Many people who've reported such experiences, whether drug-induced or otherwise, say they have indeed concluded from them that life continues in some form after death and that they're no longer afraid of it as a direct consequence, while many who haven't developed such a belief (like me) often report their fear of death continues.

Reality or a Brain State?

But even if it *is* such beliefs that reduce our fear of death, how trustworthy can they be? Though our brains are clearly capable of having awakening experiences, no definitive evidence exists that the perceptions we develop as a result necessarily reflect reality. Such perceptions may in fact only arise from what amounts to a supremely desirable brain state, a brain state that has nothing to do with reality at all. We simply don't know.

Not that any of these musings mattered to Rita. She'd already tried Nichiren Buddhism to no avail. And because I wasn't prepared to suggest, or administer, a treatment as investigational as psilocybin, I realized I probably wasn't going to be able to help her with her anxiety at all. Glumly, I resolved to do my best to help her with what other issues I could.

Yet when she came to see me next, I found to my surprise and delight that for the first time since we'd met, her anxiety actually seemed to have receded. Gone were the usual melodramatic pronouncements about how likely she was to die soon or how her husband couldn't stand being around her. After addressing what amounted to a few minor complaints, I remarked at the end of our visit that she seemed much less anxious than usual and asked her if she knew why.

She answered that her son had lost his job and moved in with her and her husband. When I asked her why her son's misfortune had made her less anxious, she assured me she wasn't happy he was jobless; she was happy she was able to spend time with him. Somewhat skeptical that this represented the real reason for her newfound calm, I nevertheless marveled at the power of joy to suppress fear. And though I worried she'd achieved only a temporary respite from her suffering, I felt grateful she was afforded one at all.

And then, one week later, ironic disaster struck: while crossing the street near her home Rita was hit by a car. The emergency room physician who saw her told me she'd come in unconscious with a broken leg and a collapsed lung. She was placed on a ventilator and admitted to intensive care.

When I came up to visit her the next day, however, she'd already come off the ventilator and was awake and alert—and engaged in an animated conversation with a man sitting in a chair by her bed.

"Dr. Lickerman!" she exclaimed when I knocked on her door. "Come in! This is my son Jeremy. Jeremy, this is Dr. Lickerman."

We exchanged greetings. "We were just talking about getting her out of the ICU," Jeremy said. "Any idea how soon that might be?"

I shook my head. "We'll have to ask her ICU doctors. I'm here more for a social visit. I just wanted to make sure she was okay."

"I'm fine," Rita said with a wave of her hand. "Don't worry about me. I'll be out of here in no time."

I stared at her in shock. Where were her declarations of fear about looming invasive medical procedures, about suffering a fatal complication, about dying alone in a sterile hospital bed? I scanned her face for any sign of anxiety hiding beneath her cheerful demeanor but found none. And though I expected her to be scanning my face in return, seeking the same reassurance from me she always had, she wasn't in fact looking at me at all. She was looking at her son.

The *self-fulfilling prophecy theory* of social interaction argues that the way we expect other people to behave alters *our* behavior in such a way that causes *them* to fulfill our expectations. This was demonstrated in a study by researcher Mark Snyder and colleagues when they randomly assigned fifty-one male undergraduates to look at one of eight photographs of female undergraduates (four of which had been rated as attractive and four of which had been rated as unattractive by other men previously) and asked them for their initial impressions. Once they'd confirmed the findings of previous research that showed men expected attractive women to be warmer than unattractive women, they asked the men to engage in telephone conversations (so they couldn't see to whom they were talking) with the women whose photographs they'd seen. Unbeknownst to the men, however, none of the women with whom they talked were the women in the photographs. When blinded observers then evaluated tape recordings of the conversations, they found that the men who spoke with women they thought were attractive (and who they therefore expected to be warm) were warmer in conversation than the men who spoke with women they thought were unattractive (who they therefore expected not to be warm), confirming that the expectations the men had of the women affected their *own* behavior. Even more interesting, though, was that the women who the men thought were attractive were *also* rated by the blinded observers as warmer in conversation than the women who the men thought were unattractive. Thus, the expectations that the men had for the women drove the way the men behaved toward the women, which in turn drove the way the women behaved toward the men.[28]

Further, other research suggests that when we make our behavior conform to another person's expectations, we tend to internalize those expectations, which makes us more likely to repeat that behavior in the future.[29] Not only that, but we also tend to attribute our subsequent behavior not to previous expectations others have had of us *but to our own disposition*, especially if multiple people confirm our self-perception in multiple contexts.[30] Thus, if our parents, our teachers, and our friends all treat us as if we're helpless, helpless is what we'll believe ourselves to be and thus what we'll likely become.

How we behave, in other words, turns out to be influenced as much by who we're with as by who we are. How many of us, for example, feel and behave one way with our family but another with our friends, and even another with our employer? We may all be composed of multiple selves, but just which of them we are at any one moment is as much determined by the people around us as by the selves inside us.

Which of course is simply another way of saying that different people elicit different reactions from us. Yet because most of us spend the majority of our time in the company of others, what others elicit from us becomes what we spend most of our time being. Not that the people we *want* to be is of no consequence. But when it's at odds with what another person's presence triggers us to be, the person we want to be is sometimes subsumed. How often, for example, do we want to be loving and kind toward our spouse only to be left feeling cold and bitter by his lack of gratitude? Or fun-loving and silly with our children only to be left irritated and mean-spirited by their temper tantrums?

The people with whom we surround ourselves exert far more influence over us than we often realize, not by their conscious intent but by being who they are themselves. Yet because who they are themselves is just as strongly influenced by who *we* are, *we gain influence over who we are by influencing who they are.* In one sense, then, when two people interact, they're actually creating a third person: the person they are *together*, a melding of the recursive influence each of the two has upon the other.

Not that this third person is fixed by any means either. When two people first meet, they bring to their first meeting the selves they usually do in the particular context they're meeting. Thus, an employer and an employee might bring their "visionary leader" and "responsible employee" selves, and a man and a woman might bring their "charismatic charmer" and "fiery siren" selves, and so on. But relationships also evolve. Thus, an employer may soon find her controlling self arguing with her employee's dissatisfied self. Or a man may find his interested self pursuing a woman's demure self (or, perhaps, her equally interested self). Much later on, then, a man may bring his distant self and a woman her apathetic self.

Thus, the people we pull out of others and the people they pull out of us change over time. It only requires a subtle change in one "action-reaction" couplet—perhaps he stops telling her he loves her and she begins to think he doesn't—to initiate others. And then, months or years later, the people we pull out of others and who others pull out of us have become completely different from who they were originally, and often not who we want them to be at all.

Because the people with whom we surround ourselves have more control over what we feel than we often do ourselves and because we have more control over what they feel than they often do themselves, we have to take responsibility for whom we pull out of them if we want to enjoy whom they pull out of us. If we want to be warm toward others, for example, we should figure out what other people do to trigger us to be warm and trigger them to trigger it. And if we want to be courageous, we should figure out what other people do to make us feel brave and trigger them to trigger that. If we want to be our best selves—in other words, the selves we like the most—we should aim first to pull the best selves we can out of the people around us.

Or, I reflected as I watched Jeremy leave his mother's room, we should aim to surround ourselves with people whose mere *presence* pulls out of us our best selves. I thought suddenly of the movie *As Good as It Gets,* in which Helen Hunt's character did this for Jack Nicholson's character, who told her in response to her request for a compliment: "You make me want to be a better man."

Which made me think about how *my* presence had been triggering Rita. I was the person to whom she was supposed to present all her complaints, and from whom she expected help. Little wonder, I suddenly realized, that her interactions with me brought out her weakest, most fearful self.

"How are you doing really?" I asked her.

"I'm okay," she said.

Though I could tell she meant for me to believe it, I could also see she was struggling to suppress her fear, which, given how she'd always behaved in the past, I found nothing short of heroic. I took her hand in mine. "Rita, you really will be out of here in no time."

She gave my hand a quick squeeze. "I know."

I smiled. "Who's encouraging who here?"

She smiled back at me briefly, and then her expression clouded. "Do you think he's worried?" She glanced at the door.

I regarded her curiously. "What son wouldn't be?"

"I don't want him to worry," she said. Her chin trembled a little and her voice broke with sudden emotion. "The last thing I want for him is . . . a life like mine."

I squeezed her hand again and sat with her silently. Then I asked, "How old is he?"

"Three," she said, and we laughed.

And only at that moment did I fully understand why her anxiety had finally calmed. Other people don't pull courage and leadership out of us, I realized, by asking us to lead them courageously. They don't even do it by expecting it. They do it by *needing* it. Or, more accurately, by triggering our *perception* that they need it, as Rita's son, I finally understood, had done for her. Rita had at long last found a way to master her anxiety by doing something none of us, her doctors, would ever have thought to suggest: by finding someone for whom she felt she needed to be strong.

She hadn't just suppressed her fear when Jeremy had moved in with her. She'd actually stopped feeling it. Either that, or she was now feeling a courage that made her fear irrelevant.

And though this had been entirely unconscious on Rita's part—and undoubtedly difficult for many of us to make work for ourselves—I thought what she'd done was brilliant. The key was finding someone in our lives for whom we didn't just *want* to be strong but for whom we felt we *had* to be, and then simply keeping them around.

"You're showing him how to be brave," I told her.

She laughed again and then started coughing. I heard a small wheeze as she inhaled once sharply. And then she looked at me in surprise, as if she'd been jabbed by something—and suddenly her eyes started rolling to the right.

"Rita?" I said. She didn't answer. I shook her. "Rita?" She wasn't moving. An alarm started sounding. "Oh, you've got to be kidding me. . . ." I felt for a pulse but couldn't find one. I hit the nurse call button and started doing chest compressions.

Afterward, I came out to find Jeremy and his father. They both stood up from their chairs as they saw me approach, their expressions falling as they read mine. I told them we'd done everything we could, that we'd used all our skills to try to save her, but that they hadn't been enough. We simply hadn't been able to get her heart going again.

"She died," I said. I shook my head. "I'm so sorry."

"What happened?" Jeremy asked. "She was doing okay. We were just talking."

I told them we didn't yet know but that we suspected a massive pulmonary embolism (a subsequent autopsy would later confirm this as the cause of death). "Severe trauma can sometimes cause clots to form in the veins of the leg," I told them, "which can then travel to the lung. She was on medicine to prevent it, but sometimes it happens anyway."

"But she was doing okay," Jeremy said again, helplessly.

"I know," I nodded.

They looked at me in anguish.

"I just can't believe she's gone," Jeremy said, shaking his head as he tried to wrap his mind around what had happened. "Ever since her heart attack, she was so scared of everything," he said. "Hospitals especially. And doctors. She hated doctors—except for you, Dr. Lickerman. She loved you. But I swear when I was talking with her, she actually seemed almost calm." He shook his head again. "In the ICU of all places."

I looked at him, my throat constricting, thinking abruptly of my own son. When my time came to die, I wondered, would I be able to leverage my desire to protect him as Rita had her desire to protect Jeremy, to unshackle myself from fear as Rita had done? Would I be able to show him how to face illness with courage and grace, as Rita had shown Jeremy? What lovelier a gift, I wondered, could a child give to a parent and a parent back to a child? What lovelier a gift could *any* of us give to anyone?

No one ever demonstrated to me more convincingly than Rita that resilience can be learned. Though the upper limit of our strength is likely determined by our genes, how much strength we actually manifest in any one circumstance, in any one moment, is determined by the choices we make. In this, resilience, I'm convinced, is more like muscle size than body height: with effort it can indeed be increased.

For we can resist discouragement by articulating our life's mission; accomplish that mission by making a great determination; overcome the obstacles that naturally arise when we make such a determination by changing poison into medicine; gain the strength to change poison into medicine by accepting responsibility and standing against injustice;

endure pain by accepting it and loss by letting go of what we cannot keep; enjoy what we have by learning to appreciate it and help ourselves through trauma by helping others; conquer fear by leveraging our connections to the ones we love. And, finally, I realized, gain inspiration from others who've managed to forge an undefeated mind of their own—as I did in that moment from Rita.

"It was because of you, Jeremy," I told him finally. "She overcame her fear because of you."

Afterword

O ver the last twenty years, I've watched thousands of patients struggle with many of the same problems that confronted the patients whose stories I tell in this book. And though the majority of them eventually found relief from their suffering, the suffering of some of them left me breathless: the pilot who became so vertiginous he couldn't sit up for two years without vomiting; the mother who died of a rare cardiac tumor knowing she was leaving three small children behind with no relatives to care for them; the elderly man who donated a kidney to his son only then to watch him die of AIDS.

What I've learned from these patients is that our capacity to suffer may be immense, but so is the strength we possess to endure it. The things we may be called upon to do may not be easy; they may not be what we want to do; they may not even do much. But as long as our minds can think, our hearts can find their way to victory.

Sometimes it requires a single dramatic intervention fraught with risk; at other times, a series of multiple, small interventions whose individual effects may be minor but whose collective power is vast. Such, in fact, is what I've observed often occurs when applying the interventions I've described throughout this book. Acceptance, for example, really does make pain easier to withstand, yet sometimes only slightly. But when added to a fierce determination to accomplish an important mission, as well as to an expectation that accomplishing that mission will require the feeling of even more pain, strength often appears that makes large problems seem abruptly small. Though the effort required to maintain a high life-condition often seems great, in reality it only needs to be wise. As when Steve's crippling anxiety resolved in the moment he discovered the value he most wanted to create with his life, sometimes we only need to pull a lever a few degrees to move our lives in a radically different direction.

On the other hand, sometimes no matter how hard we pull, our lives don't seem to move at all. Some struggles, in fact, take years or even *decades* to win (one of the titles bestowed upon the Buddha was "He Who Can Forbear"). But as long as we refuse to give in to despair and resolve to continue taking concrete action, some kind of victory is always possible. So when everything seems hopeless and you want to give up, no matter how much others may doubt you or you may doubt yourself, hold that knowledge fast to your heart and fix your mind unwaveringly on this most imperative of calls to action: *never be defeated*.

Notes

Introduction

1. Ronald Kessler et al., "Lifetime and 12-Month Prevalence of DSM-III-R Psychiatric Disorders in the United States—Results from the National Comorbidity Survey," *Archives of General Psychiatry* 51 (1994): 8–19.

2. Yang Yang, "Social Inequalities in Happiness in the United States, 1972 to 2004: An Age-Period-Cohort Analysis," *American Sociological Review* 73 (2008): 204–226.

3. Judith Beck, *Cognitive Therapy: Basics and Beyond* (New York: Guilford Press, 1995), 1–2.

4. Viktor Frankl, *Man's Search for Meaning* (Boston: Beacon Press, 1959), 65–66.

5. Mark Seery, Alison Holman, and Roxane Silver, "Whatever Does Not Kill Us: Cumulative Lifetime Adversity, Vulnerability, and Resilience," *Journal of Personality and Social Psychology* 99 (2010): 1025–1041.

6. Herman Hesse, *Siddhartha* (New York: Bantam Books, 1951), 142.

Chapter 1

1. Marsha Somers, "A Comparison of Voluntarily Childfree Adults and Parents," *Journal of Marriage and Family* 55 (1993): 643–650.

2. Douglas Jordan and J. David Diltz, "Day Traders and the Disposition Effect," *Journal of Behavioral Finance* 5 (2004): 192–200.

3. Daniel Gilbert, *Stumbling on Happiness* (New York: Vintage Books, 2006), 142–143.

4. Viktor Frankl, *Man's Search for Meaning* (Boston: Beacon Press, 1959), 112.

5. George Bonanno et al., "Resilience to Loss and Chronic Grief: A Prospective Study from Pre-Loss to 18-Months Post-Loss," *Journal of Personality and Social Psychology* 83 (2002): 1150–1164.

6. Nelson Mandela, *Long Walk to Freedom* (New York: Hachette Book Group, 1994).

Chapter 2

1. David Lyyken and Auke Tellegen, "Happiness Is a Stochastic Phenomenon," *Psychology Science* 7 (1996): 186–189.

2. Ed Diener, Richard Lucas, and Christie Scollon, "Beyond the Hedonic Treadmill: Revising the Adaptation Theory of Well-Being," *American Psychologist* 61 (2006): 305–314.

3. Richard Lucas et al., "Reexamining Adaptation and the Set Point Model of Happiness: Reactions to Change in Marital Status," *Journal of Personality and Social Psychology* 84 (2004): 527–539.

4. Bruce Headey, "The Set-Point Theory of Well-Being Has Serious Flaws: On the Eve of a Scientific Revolution?" *Social Indicators Research* 97 (2010): 7–21.

5. Ibid.

6. Dianne Vella-Broderick, Nansook Park, and Christopher Peterson, "Three Ways to Be Happy: Pleasure, Engagement, and Meaning—Findings from Australian and U.S. Samples," *Social Indicators Research* 90 (2009): 165–179.

7. Bruce Headey, "The Set-Point Theory of Well-Being Has Serious Flaws: On the Eve of a Scientific Revolution?" *Social Indicators Research* 97 (2010): 7-21.

8. Sonja Lyubomirsky, Kennon Sheldon, and David Schkade, "Pursuing Happiness: The Architecture of Sustainable Change," *Review of General Psychology* 9 (2005): 111–131.

9. Galen Switzer, "The Effect of a School-Based Helper Program on Adolescent Self-Image, Attitudes, and Behavior," *Journal of Early Adolescence* 15 (1995): 429–455.

10. A. A. Sappington, John Bryant, and Connie Oden, "An Experimental Investigation of Viktor Frankl's Theory of Meaningfulness in Life," *International Forum for Logotherapy* 13 (1990): 125–130.

11. Rostyslaw Robak and Paul Griffin, "Purpose in Life: What Is Its Relationship to Happiness, Depression, and Grieving?" *North American Journal of Psychology* 2 (2000): 113–120.

12. James Fowler and Nicholas Christakis, "Dynamic Spread of Happiness in a Large Social Network: Longitudinal Analysis over 20 Years in the Framingham Heart Study," *British Medical Journal* 337 (2008): 2338–2347.

13. Ibid.

14. Mary Vachon, "Staff Stress in Hospice/Palliative Care: A Review," *Palliative Medicine* 9 (1995): 91–122.

15. Janice Ablett and R. S. P. Jones, "Resilience and Well-Being in Palliative Care Staff: A Qualitative Study of Hospice Nurses' Experience of Work," *Psycho-Oncology* 16 (2007): 733–740.

16. Philip Zombardo et al., "Control of Pain Motivation by Cognitive Dissonance," *Science* 151 (1966): 217–219.

17. Galen Switzer, "The Effect of a School-Based Helper Program on Adolescent Self-Image, Attitudes, and Behavior," *The Journal of Early Adolescence* 15 (1995): 429–455.

18. Kurt Gray, "Moral Transformation: Good and Evil Turn the Weak into the Mighty," *Social Psychology and Personality Science* 1 (2010): 253–258.

19. Shelley Fahlman et al., "Does a Lack of Life Meaning Cause Boredom? Results from Psychometric, Longitudinal, and Experimental Analyses," *Journal of Social and Clinical Psychology* 28 (2009): 307–340.

20. Daniel Kahneman and Angus Deaton, "High Income Improves Evaluation of Life but Not Emotional Well-Being," *Proceedings of the National Academy of Sciences* 107 (2010): 16489–16493.

Chapter 3

1. Helen Keller, *The Story of My Life* (New York: Signet Classics, 2010), 4–14.

2. Wendy Wood and David Neal, "The Habitual Consumer," *Journal of Consumer Psychology* 19 (2009): 579–592.

3. Rena Wing and Suzanne Phelan, "Long-Term Weight Loss Maintenance," *American Journal of Clinical Nutrition* 82 (2005): 222S–225S.

4. Ibid.

5. F. Matthew Kramer et al., "Long-Term Follow-Up of Behavioral Treatment for Obesity: Patterns of Weight Regain Among Men and Women," *International Journal of Obesity* 13 (1989): 123–136.

6. M. McGuire, Rena Wing, and James Hill, "The Prevalence of Weight Loss Maintenance Among American Adults," *International Journal of Obesity* 23 (1999): 1314–1319.

7. Ibid.

8. Daniel Wegner, "Ironic Processes of Mental Control," *Psychological Review* 1 (1994): 34–52.

9. Jouko Salminen et al., "Prevalence of Alexithymia and Its Association with Sociodemographic Variables in the General Population of Finland," *Journal of Psychosomatic Research* 46 (1999): 75–82.

10. Wayne Katon, "The Epidemiology of Depression in Medical Care," *International Journal of Psychiatry in Medicine* 17 (1987): 93–112.

11. John Bargh and Tanya Chartrand, "The Unbearable Automaticity of Being," *American Psychologist* 54 (1999): 462–479.

12. John Bargh, Mark Chen, and Lara Burrows, "Automaticity of Social Behavior: Direct Effects of Trait Construct and Stereotype Activation on Action," *Journal of Personality and Social Psychology* 71 (1996): 230–244.

13. Justin Feinstein, Melissa Duff, and Daniel Tranel, "Sustained Experience of Emotion After Loss of Memory in Patients with Amnesia," *Proceedings of the National Academy of Sciences of the United States of America* 107 (2010): 7674–7679.

14. Vivan Zamel, "Writing: The Process of Discovering Meaning," *TESOL Quarterly* 16 (1982): 195–209.

15. Sonja Lyubomirsky, Nicole Caldwell, and Susan Nolen-Hoeksema, "Effects of Ruminative and Distracting Responses to Depressed Mood on Retrieval of Autobiographical Memories," *Journal of Personality and Social Psychology* 75 (1998): 166–177.

16. Bayard Nielsen, Cynthia Pickett, and Dean Simonton, "Conceptual Versus Experimental Creativity: Which Works Best on Convergent and Divergent Thinking Tasks?" *Psychology of Aesthetics, Creativity, and the Arts* 2 (2008): 131–138.

17. Ibid.

18. Charles Neuhoff and Charles Schaefer, "Effects of Laughing, Smiling, and Howling on Mood," *Psychological Reports* 91 (2002): 1079–1080.

19. Dana Carney, Amy Cuddy, and Andy Yap, "Power Posing: Brief Nonverbal Displays Affect Neuroendocrine Levels and Risk Tolerance," *Psychological Science* 21 (2010): 1363–1368.

20. Dean Simonton, "Age and Outstanding Achievement: What Do We Know After a Century of Research?" *Psychological Bulletin* 104 (1988): 251–267.

21. Susan Fiske, "Envy Up, Scorn Down: How Comparison Divides Us," *American Psychologist* 65 (2010): 698–706.

22. Nico Van Yperen, Veerle Brenninkmeijer, and Abraham Buunk, "People's Responses to Upward and Downward Social Comparisons: The Role of the Individual's Effort-Performance Expectancy," *British Journal of Social Psychology* 45 (2006): 519–533; Neils Van de Ven, Marcel Zeelenberg, and Rik Pieters, "Leveling Up and Down: The Experiences of Benign and Malicious Envy," *Emotion* 9 (2009): 419–429.

23. Penelope Lockwood and Ziva Kunda, "Superstars and Me: Predicting the Impact of Role Models on the Self," *Journal of Personality and Social Psychology* 73 (1997): 91–103.

24. Nico Van Yperen, Veerle Brenninkmeijer, and Abraham Buunk, "People's Responses to Upward and Downward Social Comparisons: The Role of the Individual's Effort-Performance Expectancy," *British Journal of Social Psychology* 45 (2006): 519–533.

25. Ibid.

26. Justin Kruger and David Dunning, "Unskilled and Unaware of It: How Difficulties in Recognizing One's Own Incompetence Lead to Inflated Self-Assessments," *Journal of Personality and Social Psychology* 17 (1999): 1121–1134.

27. Thomas MacKenzie, Rocio Pereira, and Philip Mehler, "Smoking Abstinence After Hospitalization: Predictors of Success," *Preventive Medicine* 39 (2004): 1087–1092.

28. Janet Polivy and C. Peter Herman, "If at First You Don't Succeed: False Hopes of Self-Change," *American Psychologist* 57 (2002): 677–689.

29. Ibid.

30. Michael Wiederman, Randy Sansone, and Lori Sansone, "Obesity Among Sexually Abused Women: An Adaptive Function for Some?" *Women & Health* 29 (1999): 89–100.

31. Kristin Laurin, Aaron Kay, and Grainne Fitzsimons, "Divergent Effects of Activating Thoughts of God and Self-Regulation," *Journal of Personality and Social Psychology* 102 (2012): 4–21.

32. John Norcross, Albert Ratz, and Dorothy Payne, "Ringing in the New Year: The Change Process and Reported Outcomes of Resolutions," *Addictive Behavior* 14 (1989): 205–212.

33. Heather Kappes and Gabriele Oettingen, "Positive Fantasies About Idealized Futures Sap Energy," *Journal of Experimental Social Psychology* 47 (2011): 719–729.

34. Nichiren Daishonin, "Reply to Kyo'o," in *The Writings of Nichiren Daishonin*, vol. 1 (Japan: Soka Gakkai, 1999), 412.

35. Dasiaku Ikeda, *Faith into Action* (Los Angeles: World Tribune Press, 1999), 108.

36. Edwin Locke et al., "Goal Setting and Task Performance: 1969–1980," *Psychological Bulletin* 90 (1981): 125–152.

37. Nancy Newall et al., "Regret in Later Life: Exploring Relationships Between Regret Frequency, Secondary Interpretive Control Beliefs, and Health in Older Individuals," *The International Journal of Aging and Human Development* 68 (2009): 261–288.

38. Katherine Trottier, Janet Polivy, and C. Peter Herman, "Effects of Exposure to Unrealistic Promises About Dieting: Are Unrealistic Expectations About Dieting Inspirational?" *International Journal of Eating Disorders* 37 (2005): 142–149.

39. Ibid.

40. Edwin Locke et al., "Goal Setting and Task Performance: 1969–1980," *Psychological Bulletin* 90 (1981): 125–152.

41. Rachel Barnes and Stacey Tantleff-Dunn, "Food for Thought: Examining the Relationship Between Food Thought Suppression and Weight-Related Outcomes," *Eating Behaviors* 11 (2010): 175–179.

42. Loran Nordgren and Eileen Chou, "The Push and Pull of Temptation: The Bidirectional Influence of Temptation on Self-Control," *Psychological Science* 20 (2011): 1–5.

43. Roy Baumeister et al., "Ego Depletion: Is the Active Self a Limited Resource?" *Journal of Personality and Social Psychology* 74 (1998): 1252–1265.

44. Mathew Gailliot, "Self-Control Relies on Glucose as a Limited Energy Source: Willpower Is More Than a Metaphor," *Journal of Personality and Social Psychology* 92 (2007): 325–336.

45. Robert Kurzban, "Does the Brain Consume Additional Glucose During Self-Control Tasks?" *Evolutionary Psychology* 2 (2101): 244–259.

46. Dianne Tice et al., "Restoring the Self: Positive Affect Helps Improve Self-Regulation Following Ego Depletion," *Journal of Experimental Social Psychology* 43 (2007): 379–384; Mark Muraven and Elisaveta Slessareva, "Mechanisms of Self-Control Failure: Motivation and Limited Resources," *Personality and Social Psychology Bulletin* 29 (2003): 894–906.

47. Walter Mischel and Ebbe Ebbesen, "Attention in Delay of Gratification," *Journal of Personality and Social Psychology* 16 (1970): 329–337.

48. Walter Mischel and Nancy Baker, "Cognitive Appraisals and Transformations in

Delay Behavior," *Journal of Personality and Social Psychology* 31 (1975): 254–261.

49. Kathleen Vohs et al., "Making Choices Impairs Subsequent Self-Control: A Limited-Resource Account of Decision Making, Self-Regulation, and Active Initiative," *Journal of Personality and Social Psychology* 94 (2008): 883–898.

50. Charles Duhigg, *The Power of Habit* (New York: Random House, 2012).

51. Phillipa Lally et al., "How Are Habits Formed: Modelling Habit Formation in the Real World," *European Journal of Social Psychology* 40 (2010): 998–1009.

52. Ibid.

53. Shawn Achor, *The Happiness Advantage* (New York: Crown Business, 2010), 154–156.

54. Wendy Wood, Leona Tam, and Melissa Witt, "Changing Circumstances, Disrupting Habits," *Journal of Personality and Social Psychology* 88 (2005): 918–933.

55. Walter Mischel and Ebbe Ebbesen, "Attention in Delay of Gratification," *Journal of Personality and Social Psychology* 16 (1970): 329–337.

56. Kimberly Kirby et al., "Situations Occasioning Cocaine Use and Cocaine Abstinence Strategies," *Addiction* 90 (1995): 1241–1252.

57. Steven King, "Quitters, Inc.," in *Night Shift* (New York: Signet, 1979).

58. Nichiren Daishonin, "Reply to Kyo'o," in *The Writings of Nichiren Daishonin*, vol. 1 (Japan: Soka Gakkai, 1999), 412.

59. Marsha Pelchat, "Food Addiction in Humans," *The Journal of Nutrition* 139 (2009): 620–622.

60. Lucas Oudenhove et al., "Fatty Acid-Induced Gut-Brain Signaling Attenuates Neural and Behavioral Effects of Sad Emotion in Humans," *Journal of Clinical Investigation* 121 (2011): 3094–3099.

61. Ayelet Fishbach, Tal Eyal, and Stacey Finklestein, "How Positive and Negative Feedback Motivate Goal Pursuit," *Social and Personality Psychology Compass* 4 (2010): 517–530.

62. Raija-Leena Punamaki, "Can Ideological Commitment Protect Children's Psychosocial Well-Being in Situations of Political Violence?" *Child Development* 67 (1996): 55–69.

Chapter 4

1. Nichiren Daishonin, "The Three Obstacles and the Four Devils," in *The Writings of Nichiren Daishonin*, vol. 1 (Japan: Soka Gakkai, 1999), 637.

2. Richard Kraig et al., "TNF-alpha and Microglial Hormetic Involvement in Neurological Health and Migraine," *Dose-Response* 8 (2010): 389–413.

3. Joan Arnold et al., "Exploring Parental Grief: Combing Quantitative and Qualitative Measures," *Archives of Psychiatric Nursing* 19 (2005): 245–255.

4. Viktor Frankl, *Man's Search for Meaning* (Boston: Beacon Press, 1959), 112–113.

5. Matthew McDonald, "The Nature of Epiphanic Experience," *Journal of Humanistic Psychology* 48 (2008): 89–115.

6. Jameson Hirsch et al., "Optimistic Explanatory Style as a Moderator of the Association Between Negative Life Events and Suicidal Ideation," *Crisis* 30 (2009): 48–53.

7. Richard Bach, *Illusions* (New York: Dell Publishing, 1977), 100.

8. Samuel Ho et al., "Relationships Between Explanatory Styles, Posttraumatic Growth and Posttraumatic Stress Disorder Symptoms among Chinese Breast Cancer Patients," *Psychology and Health* 26 (2011): 269–285.

9. Jameson Hirsch et al., "Optimistic Explanatory Style as a Moderator of the Association Between Negative Life Events and Suicidal Ideation," *Crisis* 30 (2009): 48–53.

10. Martin Seligman et al., "Explanatory Style as a Mechanism of Disappointing Athletic Performance," *Psychological Science* 1 (1990): 143–146.

11. Randall Gordon, "Attributional Style and Athletic Performance: Strategic Optimism and Defensive Pessimism," *Psychology of Sport and Exercise* 9 (2008): 336–350.

12. Ibid.

13. Michael Moore and David Fresco, "The Relationship of Explanatory Flexibility to Explanatory Style," *Behavior Therapy* 38 (2007): 325–332.

14. David Fresco, Nina Rytwinski, and Linda Craighead, "Explanatory Flexibility and Negative Life Events Interact to Predict Depression Symptoms," *Journal of Social and Clinical Psychology* 26 (2007): 595–608.

15. David Fresco et al., "Self-Administered Optimism Training: Mechanisms of Change in a Minimally Supervised Psychoeducational Intervention," *Journal of Cognitive Psychotherapy* 23 (2009): 350–367.

16. Marianne Miserandino, "Attributional Retraining as a Method of Improving Athletic Performance," *Journal of Sport Behavior* 21 (1998): 286–297.

17. David Le Foll, Oliver Rascle, and N. C. Higgens, "Attributional Feedback-Induced Changes in Functional and Dysfunctional Attributions, Expectations of Success, Hopefulness, and Short-Term Persistence in a Novel Sport," *Psychology of Sport and Exercise* 9 (2008): 77–101.

18. Ibid.

19. Darleen Douglas and Hymie Anisman, "Helplessness or Expectation Incongruency: Effects of Aversive Stimulation on Subsequent Performance," *Journal of Experimental Psychology* 1 (1975): 411–417.

20. Jeffery M. Quinn et al., "Can't Control Yourself? Monitor Those Bad Habits," *Personality and Social Psychology Bulletin* 36 (2010): 499–511.

21. Charles Duhigg, *The Power of Habit* (New York: Random House, 2012), 62.

22. Ibid.

23. Dylan Smith et al., "Happily Hopeless: Adaptation to a Permanent, but Not to a Temporary, Disability," *Health Psychology* 28 (2009): 787–791.

24. Nichiren Daishonin, "Letter from Sado," in *The Writings of Nichiren Daishonin*, vol. 1 (Japan: Soka Gakkai, 1999), 302.

25. Heidi Stiegelis et al., "Cognitive Adaptation: A Comparison of Cancer Patients and Healthy References," *British Journal of Health Psychology* 8 (2003): 303–318.

26. Tali Sharot, Tamara Shiner, and Raymond Dolan, "Experience and Choice Shape Expected Aversive Outcomes," *The Journal of Neuroscience* 30 (2010): 9209–9215.

27. Timothy Wilson et al., "Preferences as Expectation-Driven Inferences: Effects of Affective Expectations on Affective Experiences," *Journal of Personality and Social Psychology* 56 (1989): 519–530.

28. Andrew Geers and G. Daniel Lassiter, "Effects of Affective Expectations on Affective Experience: The Moderating Role of Optimism-Pessimism," *Personality and Social Psychology Bulletin* 28 (2002): 1026–1039.

29. Jerry Suls and Choi Wan, "Effects of Sensory and Procedural Information on Coping with Stressful Medical Procedures and Pain: A Meta-Analysis," *Journal of Consulting and Clinical Psychology* 57 (1989): 372–379.

30. Darleen Douglas and Hymie Anisman, "Helplessness or Expectation Incongruency: Effects of Aversive Stimulation on Subsequent Performance," *Journal of Experimental Psychology* 1 (1975): 411–417.

31. Ibid.

Chapter 5

1. Nichiren Daishonin, "The Opening of the Eyes, Part I," in *The Writings of Nichiren Daishonin*, vol. 1 (Japan: Soka Gakkai, 1999), 279.

2. Robin Kowalski, "Whining, Griping, and Complaining: Positivity in the Negativity," *Journal of Clinical Psychology* 58 (2002): 1023–1035.

3. Joachim Brunstein, Gabriele Dangelmayer, and Oliver Schultheiss, "Personal Goals and Social Support in Close Relationships: Effects on Relationship Mood and Marital Satisfaction," *Journal of Personality and Social Psychology* 71 (1996): 1006–1019.

4. John Darley and Bibb Latane, "Bystander Intervention in Emergencies: Diffusion of Responsibility," *Journal of Personality and Social Psychology* 8 (1968): 377–383.

5. Grainne Fitzsimons and Eli Finkel, "Outsourcing Self-Regulation," *Psychological Science* 22 (2011): 369–375.

6. Gerald Davison and Stuart Valens, "Maintenance of Self-Attributed and Drug-Attributed Behavior Change," *Journal of Personality and Social Psychology* 11 (1969): 25–33.

7. Jennifer Lambert, JoAnn Difede, and Richard Contrada, "The Relationship of Attribution of Responsibility to Acute Stress Disorder Among Hospitalized Burn Patients," *The Journal of Nervous and Mental Disease* 192 (2004): 304–312.

8. Howard Tennen and Glenn Affleck, "Blaming Others for Threatening Events," *Psychological Bulletin* 108 (1990): 209–232.

9. Ellen Langer and Judith Rodin, "The Effects of Choice and Enhanced Personal Responsibility for the Aged: A Field Experiment in an Institutional Setting," *Journal of Personality and Social Psychology* 34 (1976): 191–198.

10. Judith Rodin and Ellen Langer, "Long-Term Effects of a Control-Relevant Intervention with the Institutionalized Aged," *Journal of Personality and Social Psychology* 35 (1977): 897–902.

11. Stanley Rachman and Padmal DeSilva, "Abnormal and Normal Obsessions," *Behaviour Research and Therapy* 16 (1978): 233–248.

12. Paul Salkovskis et al., "Responsibility Attitudes and Interpretations Are Characteristic of Obsessive Compulsive Disorder," *Behaviour Research and Therapy* 38 (2000): 347–372.

13. Marc Hauser et al., "A Dissociation Between Moral Judgments and Justifications," *Mind and Language* 22 (2007): 1–21.

14. Kurt Gray, "Moral Transformation: Good and Evil Turn the Weak into the Mighty," *Social Psychology and Personality Science* 1 (2010): 253–258.

15. Ibid.

16. Marc Hauser et al., "A Dissociation Between Moral Judgments and Justifications," *Mind and Language* 22 (2007): 1–21.

17. Jonathan Haidt, "The Emotional Dog and Its Rational Tail: A Social Intuitionist Approach to Moral Judgment," *Psychological Review* 108 (2001): 814–834.

18. Vanessa LoBue et al., "When Getting Something Good Is Bad: Even Three-Year-Olds React to Inequality," *Social Development* 20 (2011): 154–170.

19. Kurt Gray, "Moral Transformation: Good and Evil Turn the Weak into the Mighty," *Social Psychology and Personality Science* 1 (2010): 253–258.

20. Kurt Gray and D. Wegner, "Moral Typecasting: Divergent Perceptions of Moral Agents and Moral Patients," *Journal of Personality and Social Psychology* 96 (2009): 505–520.

21. Kurt Gray, "Moral Transformation: Good and Evil Turn the Weak into the Mighty," *Social Psychology and Personality Science* 1 (2010): 253–258.

22. Russell Fazio, Edwin Effrein, and Victoria Falender, "Self-Perceptions Following Social Interaction," *Journal of Personality and Social Psychology* 41 (1981): 232–242.

23. Kurt Gray, "Moral Transformation: Good and Evil Turn the Weak into the Mighty," *Social Psychology and Personality Science* 1 (2010): 253–258.

24. Stanley Milgram, "Behavioral Study of Obedience," *Journal of Abnormal Social Psychology* 67 (1963): 371–378.

25. Stanley Milgram, *Obedience to Authority: An Experimental View* (New York: Harper & Row, 1974), 145–146.

26. Ibid.

27. Thomas Blass, "The Milgram Paradigm After 35 Years: Some Things We Now Know About Obedience to Authority," *Journal of Applied Social Psychology* 29 (1999): 955–978.

28. Stanley Milgram, *Obedience to Authority: An Experimental View* (New York: Harper & Row, 1974), 145–146.

Chapter 6

1. Edmund Rolls et al., "Representations of Pleasant and Painful Touch in the Human Orbitofrontal and Cingulate Cortices," *Cerebral Cortex* 13 (2003): 308–317.

2. Jin-Yan Wang et al., "Morphine Modulation of Pain Processing in Medial and Lateral Pain Pathways," *Molecular Pain* 5 (2009): article 60.

3. Arnoud Arntz and Lily Claassens, "The Meaning of Pain Influences Its Experienced Intensity," *Pain* 109 (2004): 20–25.

4. Donald Price, Stephen Harkins, and C. Baker, "Sensory-Affective Relationships Among Different Types of Clinical and Experimental Pain," *Pain* 28 (1987): 297–307.

5. Ibid.

6. Henry Beecher, "Relationship of Significance of Wound to Pain Experienced," *Journal of the American Medical Association* 161 (1956): 1609–1613.

7. Christopher Brown et al., "Modulation of Pain Ratings by Expectation and Uncertainty: Behavioral Characteristics and Anticipatory Neural Correlates," *Pain* 135 (2008): 240–250.

8. Metin Basoglu et al., "Psychological Preparedness for Trauma as a Protective Factor in Survivors of Torture," *Psychological Medicine* 27 (1997): 1421–1433.

9. Kurt Gray and Daniel Wegner, "The Sting of Intentional Pain," *Psychological Science* 19 (2008): 1260–1262.

10. Russell Fazio, Edwin Effrein, and Victoria Falender, "Self-Perceptions Following Social Interaction," *Journal of Personality and Social Psychology* 41 (1981): 232–242.

11. Mark Litt, "Self-Efficacy and Perceived Control: Cognitive Mediators of Pain Tolerance," *Journal of Personality and Social Psychology* 54 (1988): 149–160.

12. Trevor Thompson et al., "Anxiety Sensitivity and Pain: Generalisability Across Noxious Stimuli," *Pain* 134 (2008): 187–196.

13. Jeroen Swart et al., "Exercising with Reserve: Exercise Regulation by Perceived Exertion in Relation to Duration of Exercise and Knowledge of Endpoint," *British Journal of Sports Medicine* 43 (2009): 775–781.

14. Marcia Meldrum, "A Capsule History of Pain Management," *JAMA* 290 (2003): 2470–2475.

15. Peter Croft, Fiona Blyth, and Danielle van der Windt, *The Global Occurrence of Chronic Pain: An Introduction* (New York: Oxford University Press, 2010), 9–18.

16. Douglas Henry, Anthony Chiodo, and Welbin Yang, "Central Nervous System Reorganization in a Variety of Chronic Pain States: A Review," *Physical Medicine and Rehabilitation* 3 (2011): 1116–1125.

17. Michael Von Korff et al., "Long-Term Opioid Therapy Reconsidered," *Annals of Internal Medicine* 155 (2011): 325–328.

18. Matisyohu Weisenberg, Inbal Tepper, and Joseph Schwarzwald, "Humor as a Cognitive Technique for Increasing Pain Tolerance," *Pain* 63 (1995): 207–212.

19. Ibid.

20. Ibid.

21. Marco Loggia, Jeffrey Mogil, and M. Catherine Bushnell, "Experimentally Induced Mood Changes Preferentially Affect Pain Unpleasantness," *The Journal of Pain* 9 (2008): 784–791.

22. Elna Nagasako, Anne Oaklander, and Robert Dworkin, "Congenital Insensitivity to Pain: An Update," *Pain* 101 (2003): 213–219.

23. Rikard Wicksell et al., "Can Exposure and Acceptance Strategies Improve Functioning and Life Satisfaction in People with Chronic Pain and Whiplash-Associated Disorders (WAD)? A Randomized Controlled Trial," *Cognitive Behaviour Therapy* 37 (2008): 169–182; Kevin Vowles et al., "Effects of Pain Acceptance and Pain Control Strategies on Physical Impairment in Individuals with Chronic Low Back Pain," *Behavior Therapy* 38 (2007): 412–425; Joanne Dahl, Kelly Wilson, and Annika Nilsson, "Acceptance and Commitment Therapy and the Treatment of Persons at Risk for Long-Term Disability from Stress and Pain Syndromes: A Preliminary Randomized Trial," *Behavior Therapy* 35 (2004): 785–801.

24. Michael Hsu et al., "Sustained Pain Reduction Through Affective Self-Awareness in Fibromyalgia: A Randomized Controlled Trial," *Journal of General Internal Medicine* 25 (2010): 1064–1070.

25. Fadel Zeidan et al., "Brain Mechanisms Supporting the Modulation of Pain by Mindfulness Meditation," *The Journal of Neuroscience* 31 (2011): 5540–5548.

26. James Brown et al., "Effectiveness and Safety of Morphine Sulphate Extended Release Capsules in Patients with Chronic Moderate-to-Severe Pain in a Primary Care Setting," *Journal of Pain Research* 4 (2011): 373–384.

27. Fadel Zeidan et al., "Brain Mechanisms Supporting the Modulation of Pain by Mindfulness Meditation," *The Journal of Neuroscience* 31 (2011): 5540–5548.

28. R. Christopher deCharms et al., "Control over Brain Activation and Pain Learned by Using Real-Time Functional MRI," *Proceedings of the National Academy of Sciences* 102 (2005): 18626–18631.

29. Ethan Kross et al., "Social Rejection Shares Somatosensory Representations with Physical Pain," *Proceedings of the National Academy of Sciences* 108 (2011): 6270–6275.

30. C. Nathan DeWall et al., "Acetaminophen Reduces Social Pain: Behavioral and Neural Evidence," *Psychological Science* 21 (2010): 931–937.

31. Nichiren Daishonin, "Happiness in This World," in *The Writings of Nichiren Daishonin,* vol. 1 (Japan: Soka Gakkai, 1999), 681.

32. John Blackledge and Steven Hayes, "Emotion Regulation in Acceptance and Commitment Therapy," *Psychotherapy in Practice* 57 (2001): 243–255.

33. Jessica Flynn, Tom Hollenstein, and Allison Mackey, "The Effect of Suppressing and Not Accepting Emotions on Depressive Symptoms: Is Suppression Different for Men and Women?" *Personality and Individual Differences* 49 (2010): 582–586.

34. Lizabeth Roemer, Susan Orsillo, and Kristalyn Salters-Pedneault, "Efficacy of an Acceptance-Based Behavior Therapy for Generalized Anxiety Disorder: Evaluation in a Randomized Controlled Trial," *Journal of Consulting and Clinical Psychology* 76 (2008): 1083–1089.

35. John Blackledge and Steven Hayes, "Emotion Regulation in Acceptance and Commitment Therapy," *Psychotherapy in Practice* 57 (2001): 243–255.

36. Michael Twohig, Steven Hayes, and Akihiko Masuda, "Increasing Willingness to Experience Obsessions: Acceptance and Commitment Therapy as a Treatment for Obsessive-Compulsive Disorder," *Behavior Therapy* 37 (2006): 3–13.

37. Evan Forman et al., "An Open Trial of an Acceptance-Based Behavioral Intervention for Weight Loss," *Cognitive and Behavioral Practice* 16 (2009): 223–235.

38. Elizabeth Gifford et al., "Acceptance-Based Treatment for Smoking Cessation," *Behavior Therapy* 35 (2004): 689–705.

39. Tobias Lundgren, JoAnne Dahl, and Steven Hayes, "Evaluation of Mediators of Change in the Treatment of Epilepsy with Acceptance and Commitment Therapy," *Journal of Behavioral Medicine* 31 (2008): 225–235.

Chapter 7

1. John Blackledge and Steven Hayes, "Emotion Regulation in Acceptance and Commitment Therapy," *Psychotherapy in Practice* 57 (2001): 243–255.

2. David Berkowitz, "On the Reclaiming of Denied Affects in Family Therapy," *Family Process* 16 (1977): 495–501; David Mawson et al., "Guided Mourning for Morbid Grief: A Controlled Study," *British Journal of Psychiatry* 138 (1981): 185–193.

3. John Jordan and Robert Neimeyer, "Does Grief Counseling Work?" *Death Studies* 27 (2003): 765–786.

4. Christopher Davis et al., "Searching for Meaning in Loss: Are Clinical Assumptions Correct?" *Death Studies* 24 (2000): 497–540.

5. Ibid.

6. Ibid.

7. Ibid.

8. Roxane Silver, Cheryl Boon, and Mary Stones, "Searching for Meaning in Misfortune: Making Sense of Incest," *Journal of Social Issues* 39 (1983): 81–102.

9. Christopher Davis et al., "Searching for Meaning in Loss: Are Clinical Assumptions Correct?" *Death Studies* 24 (2000): 497–540.

10. Wendy Lichtenthal and Dean Cruess, "Effects of Directed Written Disclosure on Grief and Distress Symptoms Among Bereaved Individuals," *Death Studies* 34 (2010): 475–499.

11. Susan Lowey, "Letting Go Before a Death: A Concept Analysis," *Journal of Advanced Nursing* 63 (2008): 208–215.

12. Christopher Davis et al., "Searching for Meaning in Loss: Are Clinical Assumptions Correct?" *Death Studies* 24 (2000): 497–540.

13. Ed Diener, Richard Lucas, and Christie Scollon, "Beyond the Hedonic Treadmill: Revising the Adaptation Theory of Well-Being," *American Psychologist* 61 (2006): 305–314.

14. Daniel Gilbert, *Stumbling on Happiness* (New York: Vintage Books, 2006), 112–113.

15. Christopher Davis et al., "The Undoing of Traumatic Life Events," *Personality and Social Psychology Bulletin* 21 (1995): 109–124.

16. Ibid.

17. Philip Watkins et al., "Taking Care of Business? Grateful Processing of Unpleasant Memories," *The Journal of Positive Psychology* 3 (2008): 87–99.

18. Paul Gilbert and Sue Procter, "Compassionate Mind Training for People with High Shame and Self-Criticism: Overview and Pilot Study of a Group Therapy Approach," *Clinical Psychology and Psychotherapy* 13 (2006): 353–379.

19. Ibid.

20. Andrew Akelaitis, "Studies on the Corpus Callosum: IV. Diagnostic Dyspraxia in Epileptics Following Partial and Complete Section of the Corpus Callosum," *The American Journal of Psychiatry* 101 (1945): 594–599.

21. Paul Gilbert and Sue Procter, "Compassionate Mind Training for People with High Shame and Self-Criticism: Overview and Pilot Study of a Group Therapy Approach," *Clinical Psychology and Psychotherapy* 13 (2006): 353–379.

22. David Sbarra, Hilary Smith, and Matthias Mehl, "When Leaving Your Ex, Love Yourself: Observational Ratings of Self-Compassion Predict the Course of Emotional Recovery Following Marital Separation," *Psychological Science* (2012): 261–269.

23. Kristin Neff, Kristen Kirkpatrick, and Stephanie Rude, "Self-Compassion and Adaptive Psychological Functioning," *Journal of Research in Personality* 41 (2007): 139–154.

24. Kimberly Calderwood, "Adapting the Transtheoretical Model of Change to the Bereavement Process," *Social Work* 56 (2011): 107–118.

Chapter 8

1. Barbara Fredrickson et al., "What Good Are Positive Emotions in Crises? A Prospective Study of Resilience and Emotions Following the Terrorist Attacks on the United States on September 11th, 2001," *Journal of Personality and Social Psychology* 84 (2003): 365–376.

2. Barbara Fredrickson and Robert Levenson, "Positive Emotions Speed Recovery from the Cardiovascular Sequelae of Negative Emotions," *Cognition and Emotion* 12 (1998): 191–220.

3. Barbara Fredrickson et al., "What Good Are Positive Emotions in Crises? A Prospective Study of Resilience and Emotions Following the Terrorist Attacks on the United States on September 11th, 2001," *Journal of Personality and Social Psychology* 84 (2003): 365–376.

4. Ibid.

5. Ibid.

6. Michele Tugade and Barbara Fredrickson, "Regulation of Positive Emotions: Emotion Regulation Strategies That Promote Resilience," *Journal of Happiness Studies* 8 (2007): 311–333.

7. Christopher Peterson et al., "Strengths of Character, Orientations to Happiness, and Life Satisfaction," *The Journal of Positive Psychology* 2 (2007): 149–156.

8. Ibid.

9. Alex Wood, Jeffrey Froh, and Adam Geraghty, "Gratitude and Well-Being: A Review and Theoretical Integration," *Clinical Psychology Review* 30 (2010): 890–905.

10. Ibid.

11. Alex Wood et al., "Gratitude Influences Sleep Through the Mechanism of Pre-Sleep Cognitions," *Journal of Psychosomatic Research* 66 (2009): 43–48.

12. Rosanna Lau and Sheung-Tak Cheng, "Gratitude Lessens Death Anxiety," *European Journal of Ageing* 8 (2011): 169–175.

13. Alex Wood, Jeffrey Froh, and Adam Geraghty, "Gratitude and Well-Being: A Review and Theoretical Integration," *Clinical Psychology Review* 30 (2010): 890–905.

14. Neal Roese, "The Functional Basis of Counterfactual Thinking," *Journal of Personality and Social Psychology* 66 (1994): 805–818.

15. Shelley Taylor, "Adjustment to Threatening Events: A Theory of Cognitive Adaptation," *American Psychologist* 38 (1983): 1161–1173.

16. Lizbeth Roemer and Thomas Borkovec, "Effect of Suppressing Thoughts About Emotional Material," *Journal of Abnormal Psychology* 103 (1994): 467–474.

17. Christopher Davis et al., "The Undoing of Traumatic Life Events," *Personality and Social Psychology Bulletin* 21 (1995): 109–124.

18. Daniel Kahneman, *Thinking, Fast and Slow* (New York: Farrar, Straus and Giroux, 2011), 405.

19. Minkyung Koo et al., "It's a Wonderful Life: Mentally Subtracting Positive Events Improves People's Affective States, Contrary to Their Affective Forecasts," *Journal of Personality and Social Psychology* 95 (2008): 1217–1224.

20. Alex Wood, Jeffrey Froh, and Adam Geraghty, "Gratitude and Well-Being: A Review and Theoretical Integration," *Clinical Psychology Review* 30 (2010): 890–905.

21. Minkyung Koo et al., "It's a Wonderful Life: Mentally Subtracting Positive Events Improves People's Affective States, Contrary to Their Affective Forecasts," *Journal of Personality and Social Psychology* 95 (2008): 1217–1224.

22. Ibid.

23. Shelley Taylor, "Adjustment to Threatening Events: A Theory of Cognitive Adaptation," *American Psychologist* 38 (1983): 1161–1173.

24. Araceli Frias et al., "Death and Gratitude: Death Reflection Enhances Gratitude," *The Journal of Positive Psychology* 6 (2011): 154–162.

25. Ibid.

26. Arnaud D'Argembeau and Martial van der Linden, "Individual Differences in the Phenomenology of Mental Time Travel: The Effect of Vivid Visual Imagery and Emotion Regulation Strategies," *Consciousness and Cognition* 15 (2006): 342–350.

27. Maya Schroevers, Vivian Kraaij, and Nadia Garnefski, "Cancer Patients' Experience of Positive and Negative Changes Due to the Illness: Relationships with Psychological Well-Being, Coping, and Goal Reengagement," *Psycho-Oncology* 20 (2011): 165–172.

Chapter 9

1. Christopher Peterson et al., "Strengths of Character, Orientations to Happiness, and Life Satisfaction," *The Journal of Positive Psychology* 2 (2007): 149–156.

2. Susan Sprecher and Beverly Fehr, "Enhancement of Mood and Self-Esteem as a Result of Giving and Receiving Compassionate Love," *Current Research in Social Psychology* 11 (2006): 227–242.

3. Gabriel Marcel, *Man Against Mass Society* (South Bend, IN: St. Augustine's Press, 2008), 117.

4. Stefan Hofmann, Paul Grossman, and Devon Hinton, "Loving-Kindness and Compassion Meditation: Potential for Psychological Interventions," *Clinical Psychology Review* 31 (2011): 1126–1132.

5. Carolyn Schwartz and Meir Sendor, "Helping Others Helps Oneself: Response Shift Effects in Peer Support," *Social Science and Medicine* 48 (1999): 1563–1575.

6. Ibid.

7. Stephanie Brown et al., "Coping with Spousal Loss: Potential Buffering Effects of Self-Reported Helping Behavior," *Personality and Social Psychology Bulletin* 34 (2008): 849–861.

8. Ibid.

9. Netta Weinstein and Richard Ryan, "When Helping Helps: Autonomous Motivation for Pro-Social Behavior and Its Influence on Well-Being for the Helper and Recipient," *Journal of Personality and Social Psychology* 98 (2010): 222–244.

10. Ibid.

11. Alice Isen and Paula Levin, "Effect of Feeling Good on Helping: Cookies and Kindness," *Journal of Personality and Social Psychology* 21 (1972): 384–388.

12. Ibid.

13. Ginka Toegel, N. Anand, and Martin Kilduff, "Emotion Helpers: The Role of High Positive Affectivity and High Self-Monitoring Managers," *Personnel Psychology* 60 (2007): 337–365.

14. Robert Thayer, "Energy, Tiredness, and Tension Effects of a Sugar Snack Versus Moderate Exercise," *Journal of Personality and Social Psychology* 52 (1987): 119–125.

15. Nichiren Daishonin, "On the Three Virtues of Food," in *The Writings of Nichiren Daishonin*, vol. 2 (Japan: Soka Gakkai, 2006), 1060.

16. Ervin Straub and Johanna Vollhardt, "Altruism Born of Suffering: The Roots of Caring and Helping After Victimization and Other Trauma," *American Journal of Orthopsychiatry* 78 (2008): 267–280.

17. Ibid.

Chapter 10

1. John Blackledge and Steven Hayes, "Emotion Regulation in Acceptance and Commitment Therapy," *Psychotherapy in Practice* 57 (2001): 243–255.

2. Nic Hooper, "Comparing Thought Suppression and Mindfulness as Coping Techniques for Spider Fear," *Consciousness and Cognition* 20 (2011): 1824–1830.

3. Ibid.

4. T. Reeves and J. M. Stace, "Improving Patient Access and Choice: Assisted Bibliotherapy for Mild to Moderate Stress/Anxiety in Primary Care," *Journal of Psychiatric and Mental Health Nursing* 12 (2005): 341–346.

5. Ibid.

6. Stephanie Bughi, Jennifer Semcad, and Stefan Bughi, "Effect of Brief Behavioral Intervention Program in Medical Students from Two Southern California Universities," *Medical Education Online* 11 (2006): 1–8.

7. Janice Kiecolt-Glaser et al., "Omega-3 Supplementation Lowers Inflammation and Anxiety in Medical Students: A Randomized Controlled Trial," *Brain, Behavior, and Immunity* 25 (2011): 1725–1734.

8. Ibid.

9. Ibid.

10. Bryan Hiebert and E. E. Fox, "Reactive Effects of Self-Monitoring Anxiety," *Journal of Counseling Psychology* 28 (1981): 187–193.

11. Ibid.

12. Daniel Kahneman, *Thinking, Fast and Slow* (New York: Farrar, Straus and Giroux, 2011), 129–136.

13. Lars-Goran Ost, "One-Session Group Treatment for Spider Phobia," *Behaviour Research and Therapy* 34 (1996): 707–715.

14. Richard Heimberg et al., "Treatment of Social Phobia by Exposure, Cognitive Restructuring, and Homework Assignments," *The Journal of Nervous and Mental Disease* 173 (1985): 236–245.

15. Daniel Gilbert, *Stumbling on Happiness* (New York: Vintage Books, 2006), 112–113.

16. Timothy Wilson et al., "Focalism: A Source of Durability Bias in Affective Forecasting," *Journal of Personality and Social Psychology* 78 (2000): 821–836.

17. Ibid.

18. Ibid.

19. Irvin Yalom, *Staring at the Sun* (New York: Jossey-Bass, 2008), 33.

20. Ricky Finzi-Dottan, Yael Segal Triwitz, and Pavel Golubchik, "Predictors of Stress-Related Growth in Parents of Children with ADHD," *Research in Developmental Disabilities* 32 (2011): 510–519.

21. Samuel Ho et al., "Relationships Between Explanatory Style, Posttraumatic Growth, and Posttraumatic Stress Disorder Symptoms Among Chinese Breast Cancer Patients," *Psychology and Health* 26 (2011): 269–285.

22. Irvin Yalom, *Staring at the Sun* (New York: Jossey-Bass, 2008), 83.

23. Ibid., 84.

24. Steven Pinker, *The Better Angels of Our Nature* (New York: Viking, 2011).

25. A. E. Van Vogt, "Asylum," in *Adventures in Time and Space*, ed. Raymond Healy and J. Francis McComas (New York: Del Rey, 1974), 588–640.

26. Charles Grob et al., "Pilot Study of Psilocybin Treatment for Anxiety with Advanced-Stage Cancer," *Archives of General Psychiatry* 68 (2011): 71–78.

27. Roland Griffiths et al., "Psilocybin Occasioned Mystical-Type Experiences: Immediate and Persisting Dose-Related Effects," *Psychopharmacology* 218 (2011): 649–665.

28. Mark Snyder, Elizabeth Tanke, and Ellen Berscheid, "Social Perception and Interpersonal Behavior: On the Self-Fulfilling Nature of Social Stereotypes," *Journal of Personality and Social Psychology* 35 (1977): 656–666.

29. Russell Fazio, Edwin Effrein, and Victoria Falender, "Self-Perceptions Following Social Interaction," *Journal of Personality and Social Psychology* 41 (1981): 232–242.

30. Ibid.

About the Author

Alex Lickerman, MD, is a physician, former assistant professor of medicine and director of primary care, and current assistant vice-president for Student Health and Counseling Services at one of the world's most prestigious universities, the University of Chicago. He is also a practicing Nichiren Buddhist and leader in the Nichiren Buddhist lay organization, the Soka Gakkai International, USA (SGI-USA). Dr. Lickerman is a prolific writer, having written for medical textbooks, national trade publications, and even for Hollywood with an adaptation of Milton's *Paradise Lost*. He has extensive speaking experience, having given lectures at high schools, colleges, and medical conferences, and was recently selected by the Consumers' Research Council of America as one of America's top physicians in their publication *Guide to America's Top Physicians*. Dr. Lickerman's blog "Happiness in this World" is syndicated on the website of *Psychology Today*, and receives over one hundred thousand unique visitors per month. Please visit his website at www.alexlickerman.com.

Index